404

£8.75
N

Australian Economic Policy

Australian Economic Policy

Edited by

J. P. NIEUWENHUYSEN
Reader in Economics, University of Melbourne

and

P. J. DRAKE
Professor of Economics, University of New England

MELBOURNE UNIVERSITY PRESS
1977

First published 1977

Printed in Australia by
Wilke and Company Limited, 37-49 Browns Road, Clayton, Victoria for
Melbourne University Press, Carlton, Victoria 3053
U.S.A. and Canada: International Scholarly Book Services, Inc.,
Box 555, Forest Grove, Oregon 97116
Great Britain, Europe, the Middle East, Africa and the Caribbean:
International Book Distributors Ltd (Prentice-Hall International),
66 Wood Lane End, Hemel Hempstead,
Hertfordshire HP2 4RG, England

National Library of Australia Cataloguing in Publication data
Australian economic policy.

Index.
ISBN 0 522 84123 6.

1. Economics–Addresses, essays, lectures.
I. Nieuwenhuysen, John Peter, 1937– , ed. II. Drake, Peter Joseph, 1932– , joint ed.

330.08

to Wilfred Prest, C.B.E., M.A. (Leeds),
M.A. (Com.) (Manc.), M.Com.
Truby Williams Professor of Economics
at the University of Melbourne, 1946–72

Contents

Acknowledgements

We wish to thank all contributors for their cheerful subjection to editorial whips, and Lois Payne and Colleen Thomas, of the University of Melbourne, who bore the main burden of typing.

Support from a Hallsworth Research Fellowship at the University of Manchester, which was held at the same time as Peter Drake wrote his own chapter and conducted much of his editorial work, is gratefully acknowledged.

We greatly regret that this book does not contain a contribution by the late Professor R. I. Downing, who was Wilfred Prest's colleague for so many years at Melbourne. Dick Downing had promised and planned an essay but died before he could compose it.

Finally, we wish to thank the trustees of the Wilfred Prest Portrait Fund for finance to cover the cost of preparing an index.

J.P.N. P.J.D.

February 1977

Abbreviations

ACTU	Australian Council of Trade Unions
AIDC	Australian Industry Development Corporation
ALP	Australian Labor Party
ANZAAS	Australian & New Zealand Association for the Advancement of Science
DINDEC	Department of Industries and the Economy
DLP	Democratic Labor Party
EEC	European Economic Community
GATT	General Agreement on Tariffs and Trade
GMH	General Motors-Holden
GNE	Gross National Expenditure
GNP	Gross National Product
IAC	Industries Assistance Commission
JEL	Journal of Economic Literature
MITI	Ministry of Trade and Industry
MNC	Multinational Corporation
MOA	Municipal Officers' Association
OECD	Organization for Economic Co-operation and Development
OEEC	Organization for European Economic Co-operation
OPEC	Organization of Petroleum Exporting Countries
PJT	Prices Justification Tribunal
RED	Regional Employment Development
SDR	Special Drawing Rights
UNCTAD	United Nations Conference on Trade and Development
U.S.	United States of America

Wilfred Prest: An Appreciation

The unity of this volume is assured by more than its systematic consideration of important problems of economic policy in Australia. All the contributors have enjoyed, whether as students or colleagues, an association with Wilfred Prest, so that although his name does not appear in the list of contributors, he is in a sense the most important contributor of all.

When Wilfred Prest left England in 1938 to become senior lecturer in economics at the University of Melbourne he took a decisive step in his academic career. But he probably did not contemplate transportation for life. The immediate prospects were good. For a young man of thirty, a senior lectureship, even if it were 12 000 miles from home, was a prize indeed, and experience in a large university in a developing economy would be an asset.

Born in York in 1907, he had begun his education at Archbishop Holgate's School and won a scholarship at the University of Leeds where he took a B.A. in history. During this course he became interested in economics and stayed a further two years to complete an economics degree. He then went to the University of Manchester where, in 1932, he took a master's degree in economics.

At that time, it was difficult, even for an outstanding graduate, to find an academic job, so he filled in two years in various teaching posts until, in 1934, he obtained a lectureship at the University of St Andrews. Over the next four years he taught a variety of economics courses, continued his research into the British coal industry and published two important articles, in the *Economic Journal* and in the *Quarterly Journal of Economics*. But St Andrews had a tiny department of two, opportunities were limited and, by 1937, he was ready for a change.

The faculty at Melbourne was large and diversified but there were still only four full-time staff (as there had been in the 1920s) and although several new appointments were soon to be made, it depended on part-time lecturers for many of its courses, especially in the 'commerce' subjects. Student numbers, however, were large in comparison with most British universities. Since the 1850s, economics had been taught to a handful of Arts students but, when the faculty of commerce was established under the dynamic leadership of D. B. Copland, student numbers increased dramatically to over 300 in 1925 and 650 by 1938. All were taking the economics major, and mature part-time students still predominated. The pattern of large lecture classes and small tutorial groups was well established and the perennial problems of staff/student ratios and inadequate accommodation were all too apparent. This was to be Prest's new academic environment.

While it was taken for granted that a man appointed to a senior post would be prepared to handle undergraduate courses in any area of economics, it was hoped that Prest would develop his interest in the economics of industry and contribute to the wide-ranging research into the operation of the Australian economy which distinguished the Melbourne school. He slipped easily and unobtrusively into his new role and, within a year, Copland was congratulating himself that he had chosen 'the right man for Melbourne'.

Only Prest knows whether his own early impressions were equally favourable for, when war broke out in 1939 and Copland and Giblin and others were absorbed into the wartime economic administration, he had to take over the main responsibility for all the economics subjects. This, despite the fall in enrolments, was a formidable task. Not only did he widen his own range of teaching and take his full share of administrative work, but he somehow managed to keep up a flow of publication and new research. He was deeply involved, too, in the planning which led to the post-war introduction of new course structures, a new honours degree and expanded post-graduate courses. It came to seem more and more likely that his academic future would lie in Melbourne.

In 1944 there was a major reconstruction of the faculty. The Truby Williams chair of economics was established, to which Copland was appointed. G. L. Wood replaced him as professor of commerce and a third department, economic history, was set up under Herbert Burton. Prest became acting-professor of economics until Copland's return. In the event, Copland did not return to Melbourne, the vacancy was advertized world-wide and, to the intense satisfaction of all who knew him, Prest became the Truby Williams professor.

He proved himself to be the complete professor: a scholar with the full range of skills in teaching, research and administration which professors were expected to possess; and with qualities of leadership which, in his own particular style, were to be as crucial in the growth and development of the department and the faculty over the following twenty-five years as Copland's had been in the pre-war years.

He summarized his views on the teaching of economics in a contribution to *Essays in Honour of Sir Douglas Copland.* His own practice was a nice blend of theory and empiricism: sometimes a lucid exposition of some difficult point in theory, sometimes an enlightening appraisal of the facts and figures. He was always a true disciple of Marshall, believing that 'Economics is the study of mankind in the ordinary business of life', and that established doctrine is constantly in need of reconsideration in the light of changes in social conditions and institutions. His own copy of Marshall's *Principles* was famous. Lavishly interleaved with scraps of paper covered in tiny pencil script, it was commonly referred to as 'Prest's bible', and his students at one time pretended to believe that he was preparing the 9th edition. But they read their Marshall, and they read the modern works, and learned the importance of finding out the facts of the Australian economy. As one student put it—'There's a lot of reading but his lectures are rather like a road map—you recognize the landmarks'. Not all students appreciated his approach, but they remembered his courses and he soon became used to being greeted, often in unlikely places, with 'You won't remember me but you taught me in . . .'. He took pride, too, in the achievements of his honours graduates whom he often met at academic conferences or in the corridors of power so many of them frequent.

As the department grew and the range of subjects widened even further, specialization in teaching developed, but although his own courses were mainly in micro-economics, he somehow maintained his reading even of the current periodicals and kept up-to-date in what was being taught by his colleagues. He was always aware of the gaps to be filled and the shifts of emphasis that might prove useful. He trusted his staff and they valued his wise advice and judgement. More than anything else, however, they valued his concern for their welfare and advancement. He was always accessible and, no matter how busy he was, their personal problems had top priority. He became in fact a kind and understanding father to the department, a stern father sometimes, but this was soon forgotten, or perhaps more likely, remembered with affection.

Not only was he head of the department of economics for over twenty-five years but he was also deeply involved in other administrative tasks. He was dean of the faculty on seven separate occasions, the last a five-year term before his retirement. He was chairman of the professorial board from 1962 to 1964 and a member of council. He served on the research committee and others too numerous to record. For a short time, when he was simultaneously head of the department, dean, chairman of the professorial board and acting vice-chancellor, he could have referred matters right to the top without them leaving his hands. However, he always scrupulously wore only one hat at a time. There were those who found his calm, methodical approach to each new problem too conservative but they came to see that he was simply realistic, and that he understood the system. The faculty grew and flourished; new courses were introduced, new departments were created, staff increased and new buildings were eventually completed. He was too experienced to expect miracles or to be diverted from the main issue by each short-term 'crisis'.

His was a period in university history when the skills of the economist were becoming increasingly relevant. When he arrived in 1938 the university, though large, retained much of its nineteenth century character, its Academic-Gothic buildings set in spacious grounds, and a lake where wild duck still sought sanctuary. His appointment to the chair in 1946 brought the number of professors to thirty. When he retired he was the second most senior of about 100, and quotas and Commonwealth funding and submissions to the Australian Universities Commission had become the natural order of things. The optimum use of scarce resources for competing ends was a less novel problem for an economist than for scholars in other disciplines.

Since the days of Giblin, a Melbourne economist had been a member of the Commonwealth Grants Commission, and Prest continued the tradition. He was appointed in 1953, and served for twelve years through a period of important changes in the role of the Commission. Though this was a part-time appointment, it was demanding and his daily schedules became even more like a complicated jigsaw puzzle. It was, however, a most rewarding experience, giving him new insights into the practical problems of economic policy, widening his contacts with the men in power and the men behind the scenes, and providing the opportunity to see at first hand the problems of Australian development. More importantly, it served to confirm and develop his interest in the many-sided problem of federal-state financial relationships which is still his main field of research.

He has always been active in research and in fostering research in the department. His own list of publications both in Australian and overseas journals is long and varied, ranging from theoretic analysis of income and depreciation through the economics of industry to his more widely known work in federal finance. This in itself covers a wide range of theoretic and applied problems, and he has kept up-to-date with new developments and institutional change. There is one skeleton in his research files which occasionally bothers him—a social survey of Melbourne undertaken during the early years of World War II. Some of the results were published, but pressure of events interrupted the work and, though the material has become a valuable source for the social historian, he has never had time to resume the historian's role.

Though never so much in the public eye as Copland had been, he became widely known outside the university and followed Copland's example in developing a happy and fruitful relationship with the business community and government organizations. His overseas visits also yielded many benefits to the department. A sabbatical year at Cambridge or at the Institute of Commonwealth Studies in London or as a visiting professor at Pittsburgh seemed to be almost as demanding as his normal university life, with visits to numerous universities and other research centres (often to present a paper) and conferences of economists as incidental complications to his main programme. He came back refreshed and stimulated by new developments and renewed opportunities of participating in the current debates, meeting old friends and making new ones. The department was less isolated from the main stream of economic thought, better able to judge its own courses by world standards, and distinguished overseas economists were encouraged to visit Melbourne. When his colleagues and graduate students were going overseas, his up-to-date inside knowledge and the personal approaches he made on their behalf were immensely helpful.

If applicants for chairs were judged not only on their own qualifications but, as some business executives are reported to be, on the qualifications of their wives, his appointment would have been even more certain. His wife Marjorie, like himself Yorkshire born and bred, and endowed with the same qualities of kindness and concern for others, has been a true friend of the faculty and has made her own contribution to the achievements of the Prest era. They often entertained at their Brighton home, perhaps for a distinguished visitor or to welcome a new member of staff or for no particular reason, and these occasions always created the atmosphere of a happy family party. A former colleague remembers his first experience when he arrived with no very high expectations, for, after all, professors were professors. By the end of the evening he had forgotten he was homesick and was helping Wilfred with the washing up. It must be said that this was not a usual privilege!

Those who thought the translation from Truby Williams professor to professor emeritus would mean retirement into a leisurely life were soon proved wrong. It has simply meant more freedom to choose what to do next; a year researching in Canberra, more overseas trips, another semester teaching at Pittsburgh, new committees and consultations as new problems of federalism developed, more publications and still more work in the pipeline.

Perhaps he may find time to tell his own story of the years in Melbourne, but he is a modest man and would probably not throw much light on the question his colleagues often ask—how did one man achieve so much? Meanwhile, the answer must be the simple one—because he was Wilfred Prest.

Jean Polglaze C. S. Soper

J. O. N. PERKINS

1 Lessons of Macro-economic Policy in Australia, 1951–1976

One dominant thread that appears to run through the past quarter-century of Australian macro-economic policy is a remarkable disinclination to use the market. This was true of import regulation, controls over interest rates, Statutory Reserve Deposits (or special accounts) as a means of influencing the money supply, and the official fixing of the exchange rate. Most countries of a comparable economic size and importance learned these lessons much more quickly than Australia, which consequently suffered substantial misallocation of resources and unnecessary inflation before policy-makers and advisers perceived the sheer inefficiency of relying upon non-market oriented macro-economic measures. It is worth stressing that over virtually the entire period academic advice on macro-economic policy attempted to persuade policy-makers to adopt the broader, market-oriented, approach—advice which was only eventually accepted.

At the same time, it would not give a correct impression of the period as a whole to suggest that it saw a steady progress towards macro-economic enlightenment. For in the 1970s, there were opposite excesses of policy: first, an excessive expansion of government spending, taxation and the money supply; and then an excessive faith in the questionable, as well as in the valid, aspects of the monetarist approach to economic policy-making. Australia, at least as much as other comparable countries, was in the mid-1970s still searching for a macro-economic policy that would reconcile a high rate of growth with a tolerable price inflation. The main part of this chapter discusses these issues, while the concluding section suggests some of the lessons that still need to be learned.

The Korean Boom

At the beginning of the 1950s the Korea commodity boom presented Australia with a problem of strong external surplus and the threat of domestic inflation. Australia's outstanding success in avoiding serious inflation in the later 1940s was at once prejudiced by the failure to revalue the currency upwards and to allow interest rates to rise sharply. At the outset of the period, therefore, there were policy deficiencies arising from politically inspired distortions in these two crucial prices—the exchange rate and the interest rate. The government did not lack for advice from some authoritative quarters that it should appreciate the Australian pound. There was also Copland's suggestion of a form of forced saving for those exporters benefiting from the export boom (on the lines of the New Zealand schemes); but failure to take action on the required scale gave a windfall gain to exporters that was used to justify increases in award wages. The very sharp inflation—at a rate unparalleled subsequently in Australia until the 1970s—worked its way through at about the time the Korea commodity boom collapsed. Partly because of the lagged effects of the high level of demand in Australia in 1950–1, but partly also because of the sudden increase in availability of supplies from overseas (as the world recession of 1951–2 began), there was an enormous rise in Australia's imports in 1951/2, and most of the earnings of the wool boom were quickly drained from the reserves, necessitating the import controls imposed in 1952, which persisted with varying intensity until 1960.

Furthermore, it was not until the so-called 'horror' budget of 1951 that tighter budgetary measures, and a simultaneous increase in interest rates, were used to try to check inflation. It is true that the readily available weapon of calls to the banks' special accounts (later to be transmuted into Statutory Reserve Deposits or SRDs) had already been used earlier in the boom to dampen the rise in bank advances; but with the unavoidable need to finance the rush of imports, it was essential to meet the liquidity needs of importers, and those of the holders of the stocks of goods subsequently piling up on the wharves.

The lessons that could and should have been learned from this period, and which might usefully have been applied in subsequent periods of boom, even as late as 1973, were as follows. First, if there is a world commodity boom, a speedy appreciation of the Australian dollar, or a cut in tariff rates, might usefully be permitted as a means of minimizing the upward effects on prices in Australia. Second, so far as there is inflation in Australia, a timely increase in nominal interest rates to levels that reflect (to a considerable extent—if not completely) the expectation of higher inflation needs to be undertaken early in the day, and not merely when the export-induced boom is more or less over. Similarly, if measures, such as higher tax rates, are to be introduced to eliminate excess demand, the worst possible time to do this is at the end of the boom, when excess demand has almost run its course.

It is true that the deflationary policy pursued (deflationary rather than merely anti-inflationary) in 1952 helped to eliminate the very rapid inflation of the preceding year. Some observers have, erroneously in my view, tried to draw upon this experience to justify similar policies in the very different situation of the 1970s. It should therefore be emphasized that the double-digit inflation of 1950–1 was a temporary aberration from the preceding period of relative price stability (in contrast to more recent experience), and was clearly generated by the special circumstances of the 1950/1 Korea boom. Because it had been preceded by a period of near price stability, there was no built-in expectation of regular rapid increases in prices and money incomes. In this combination of circumstances, it is not surprising that a policy of fairly mild deflation (that is, by comparison with that of the mid-1970s) quickly squeezed most of the inflation out of the Australian economy.

The correct lessons to learn from the period were, therefore, that the exchange rate and the interest rate probably need both to be used early in an export-led boom. It is wrong to suppose that, in a very different situation such as that of the 1970s, a small recession could have the speedy effect in removing inflation that resulted from the deflation of 1951–2.

After the Boom, 1952–1960

In the period 1952–4 the gradual recovery of the economy from the deflationary effects of the upsurge in stocks of imports and of the tight monetary and budgetary policy, might have been accelerated if devaluation had gradually been allowed to take the place of the import controls. Once the inflation had been squeezed out of the economy, it is unlikely that, in the depressed business conditions then prevailing, a devaluation would have sharply increased the price level (again, in marked contrast to the mid-1970s). It could have been used to avoid the wasteful import licensing machinery, which continued distorting the pattern of production and consumption during the rest of the decade. Furthermore, some devaluation at that time would incidentally have given a fillip to domestic demand.

The next boom, that of 1955, was induced partly by domestic influences, but it again coincided with a world boom. Here the deficiencies of monetary and budgetary policy were once more largely the same as those that were apparent in 1950/1. It was not until after the statement of a group of leading economists in early 1956 (by which time, in retrospect, the worst of the boom was over) that really strong monetary and budgetary measures were taken.

Once again, this did much to cause the ensuing recession or

stagnation to continue longer than necessary. The later 1950s were indeed a rather curious period; not quite real recession, but without any clear sign of recovery. (It was at about this time that the late Dick Downing complained that he was bored with having to give the same talk on the economy for two or three years.) In this state of uncertainty as to what were the real problems, it was understandably difficult for the macro-economic policy-maker to decide how weapons should be varied; an existing slight deficiency of demand might be about to be reversed even without further policy measures. It is equally difficult at any given time for the armchair macro-economic critic to say with confidence that the policy-maker is wrong to take this view. But one could also point out, as Downing did, that if the macro-economic policy-maker is being successful one would expect to be in what he called the 'twilight' zone, where it is uncertain whether the main problem of the day is to stimulate or to restrain demand.

The 1960s

The recovery of export receipts at the end of the 1950s and into 1960 at last made possible the abolition of the import controls. The upsurge in imports and the occurrence of a partial domestic boom in 1960 could usefully have been restrained by a speedy upward adjustment of those interest rates under government control, and perhaps some (earlier) tightening of the budget. Or perhaps a small devaluation would have served to keep the current account from deteriorating too sharply, and its upward effects on domestic prices and activity could have been offset (if required) by the use of some restraint in monetary and budgetary policy. In any event, the violent restraint of the measures of November 1960 was clearly a case of 'too much too late'. ('We have lit a time-bomb under the economy', one senior minister is reported to have said as he came out of the cabinet meeting, 'and we don't know what its effects will be'.) Perhaps, with the reserves ebbing away, something drastic had to be done. But there was adequate advice available from private and published comment to urge that more should have been done earlier in 1960. If even minor variations in the exchange rate had been used and rather more done by way of domestic measures of restraint earlier in 1960, the ham-fisted policies of November in that year could have been avoided; or, at any rate, the measures taken at that time could then have been of a more moderate nature. Again, the inhibition against the use of the exchange rate, and also against a timely rise in interest rates or the use of the budget (at least on a sufficient scale) made the fluctuations worse than they need have been. A steady expansion of the money supply and of the main budgetary variables, coupled with some greater element of exchange-rate flexibility, could not have done worse. In the (inevitable) ensuing recession the, by then irrelevant, lessons of the boom were applied with remarkable fidelity. That is, there was a great reluctance to stimulate recovery in case another boom was just around the corner (a fear that had some echoes in the recession of 1975–6). Interest rates (especially real interest rates) were kept unusually high. Finally, enough courage was plucked up to introduce budgetary measures of stimulation early in 1962, and the recovery did, at last, set in.

The Period of Success, 1963–1970

There then began a most remarkably successful period for macro-economic policy in Australia, and perhaps one of the most successful anywhere. A critic who has made many carping remarks over the years about macro-economic policy in Australia from 1950–62, and even harsher ones about it from 1971–6, ought to say with special emphasis how outstanding was the record of success between about 1963 and 1970. One cannot, of course, say with confidence how much of this was due to good management and how much to good fortune; just as one ought also to acknowledge that in the periods when bad mistakes were apparently made the problems facing the policy-makers were often much more difficult than those of the halcyon days (as they now seem) of the middle and later 1960s. In any event, the mistakes, and the troubles, of the years 1963–70 were (especially as seen in retrospect from the vantage point of 1976) relatively little ones. In the boom of 1964, monetary measures, including increases in official interest rates and open-market operations, were (at long last) used fairly early in the boom, and reasonably strong export receipts prevented serious troubles from arising on the external front. In contrast to earlier periods, budgetary and monetary measures were generally employed in a timely manner, though the mild recession of 1966–7 was a minor blot, which might have been handled better. In any event, there was neither serious unemployment nor rapid inflation, and no major anxieties arose on the external front.

The 1970s

In common with most other countries, the 1970s have presented Australia with new versions and combinations of old problems. The previous problems of avoiding excess demand or serious unemployment, and of maintaining a rough external balance, remain. But the new problems of 'stagflation'—an unduly rapid rate of inflation coupled with high unemployment—have arisen to plague the policy-makers here and elsewhere. This different combination of problems arose partly because of the long experience in the post-war years of a rate of inflation, which, while still low by the subsequent standards of the 1970s, had been steady and consistent. Wage demands, asset-holdings, and price expectations therefore became gradually more fully adjusted to the expectation of inflation, and these very reactions naturally made it worse. On the other hand, policy-makers did not adjust their instruments, especially tax rates and nominal interest rates, fully and speedily enough to the changed state of people's expectations and their consequent reactions. Nominal income tax rates were kept unchanged into a period where rapid inflation was sharply increasing effective rates, and thereby increasingly making wage and salary earners take account of the change in their post-tax income in making wage demands, as well as probably encouraging an unduly rapid growth of government spending. Nor were the methods of taxing companies prior to 1976 adjusted to take account of the effects of inflation on profits as assessed for tax liabilities. Nominal interest rates were allowed to lag so far behind people's expectations of the rate of inflation that real returns to the lender were often strongly negative, especially after tax. Even in a closed economy, this combination of inflexible policy formulation with changing economic attitudes would have been a serious liability.

But the problem was reinforced by certain considerations relating to Australia's situation as an open economy. There had been a progressive realization in the world outside Australia that the alteration of exchange rates at only rare intervals, and then by large kangaroo jumps (as M. G. Porter has called them), was singularly inappropriate, especially in a world where greatly varying rates of inflation (and other influences on different countries' balance of payments) made it highly inappropriate to maintain 'fixed' exchange rates (or, more accurately, the 'adjustable peg', which was adjusted only infrequently). There was, of course, always the risk that if exchange rates were readily variable politicians would use variations in them in a misguided way; but the remedy for that should have been to use them in the proper way—not to postpone any change until it was too late.

Furthermore, the much greater international mobility of capital made it especially difficult to use monetary policy as a means of affecting the domestic level of activity, so long as exchange rates were fixed. For any tendency to raise interest rates in Australia above those in the rest of the world was likely to be offset to a large extent (especially from the later 1960s) by an increased net capital inflow. In addition, the method of setting the exchange rate, by keeping it constant in terms of some other major currency—sterling or the dollar—was itself singularly inappropriate in the world of the 1971–6 period, when all the main currencies were varying in relation to one another. To let the Australian dollar vary in step with one of them was equivalent to determining the setting of this major macro-economic variable by a sort of lottery. Australia was very belated in realizing the inappropriateness of this method of fixing the rate: for example, Malaysia and New Zealand had moved to a system of setting it on the basis of a 'basket' of currencies, with weights determined by the relative importance in their trade of each of the countries concerned, long before Australia did so. At the same time a fixed-rate policy of any sort had really become inappropriate—unless one could argue, with a mixture of cynicism and realism, that by tying the rate to one major currency, the Australian policy-makers might be more likely—by pure accident—to cause the effective exchange rate for the Australian dollar to move in the proper direction.

With this combination of real problems and self-imposed rigidities it is perhaps not surprising that Australia's history of macro-economic mismanagement in the 1970s is no cause for pride. But, making all allowances for the unavoidable difficulties, one of the reasons for the blemishes was simply a straightforward failure to look facts in the face; though others arose because economists (presumably including economic advisers) had not devised a satisfactory framework for giving advice in circumstances such as these; and so far as such a framework existed it often did not penetrate the consciousness of Australian financial journalists and politicians, even when academics and economic advisers were using it.

The failure to use the exchange rate, and appropriate accompanying measures in 1971–2 was inexcusable. Comments from Australian academics (and, one hopes, from the official economic advisers) were virtually unanimous that an appreciation (or preferably a cut in the general level of tariffs) was desirable. It is true that any such measure taken alone would have had a depressing effect on demand; but it would also help to curb the rise in the price level, which was occurring at an undesirably rapid rate, partly because of external factors. Any undesirable domestic effects of an appreciation or tariff cut could and should have been offset by reflationary measures such as tax cuts.

At the end of 1972, with the change of government, the much-needed adjustment of the exchange rate was made, yet no adequate attention was apparently given to the essential matter of ensuring that it would in future be varied in a flexible and appropriate way, so as to play its full part in macro-economic policy. A conscious decision was rightly taken to refrain from devaluing the Australian dollar with the U.S. dollar in February 1973; but otherwise the rate as against other currencies was tied to altering with the fortunes of the U.S. dollar. One can imagine the outcry that would have resulted if Australia had tied some other macro-economic weapon, such as tax rates or interest rates, to being raised automatically with those of, say, Britain or Japan; but that would have been no more outrageous than the method actually adopted for setting the exchange rate during this period.

In 1973 (as in 1950/1) there was a world commodity boom, the inflationary effects of which upon Australia might have been offset by a timely appreciation or tariff cuts, coupled with appropriate monetary and budgetary measures. As it was, the tariff cuts and appreciation came far too late (not till July and September, respectively), and the budgetary policy applied was initially far too expansionary, and then subsequently insufficiently expansionary to offset the downward effects of the appreciation and the tariff cuts on domestic activity when they had their (delayed) effects on domestic industries. Indeed, instead of reflation (preferably by tax cuts—for reasons to be analysed below) the thoroughly reprehensible measure of tariff increases and even quantitative restrictions, and the equally misguided one of a depreciation (in September 1974), were adopted to deal with what was essentially a deficiency of domestic demand. A further defect of this policy was that it gave the appreciation and tariff cuts a quite unjustifiably bad name; for it was the insufficiency of domestic demand that was to blame if unemployment had become too high in 1975.

The special problem of cost-push, especially tax-push, inflation raised new issues in Australia as elsewhere. No longer was it reasonable to count on deflation alone to curb inflation reasonably quickly and without an undue creation of unemployment. The rapid expansion of government spending under the Labor government was accompanied by a very rapid growth of tax receipts; but both indirect taxes and direct taxes had an increasing tendency to be passed on by way of wage and price increases.

Stagflation and Over-devaluation in 1976

The stagnation of the economy at well below full employment during 1975–6 was in part apparently the intended result of government policy, on the basis of the hope that the unemployment would swiftly curtail the rate of inflation. But in fact the operation of the economy at a much lower level relative to trend than for most other OECD countries during that period had a significantly smaller degree of success in restraining inflation than was achieved in OECD countries as a whole. This policy may be especially inappropriate for Australia, whose manufacturing industry is so overwhelmingly dependent on the home market that a decline in domestic sales has a correspondingly larger impact on unit costs (and so on prices, so far as these are cost-determined) than in countries that export a substantial part of their manufacturing output.

But another reason for the failure of the Australian economy to revive, even though some recovery had occurred in the world economy during 1976, was the government's almost obsessive optimism about the revival of private demand. Moreover, the government seemed to have acquired the extraordinary notion that a cut in government spending could actually raise the level of activity. If the country's macro-economic policy really was based on this fallacy it is not surprising that stagnation continued. The view seems to have been a Through-the-Looking-glass distortion—' "Where I come from", said Alice, "we have hills that make your hills look like valleys" '—of the 'crowding out' thesis that a rise in government spending tends to cause offsetting falls in private spending. It is true that when an economy is near full employment competition for resources between government and the private sector is likely to mean that a rise in government spending will displace a virtually equivalent amount of private spending; though this was far from the situation that prevailed in Australia in 1975–6—especially as private investment was then being held back largely by fears that government policies were insufficiently expansionary. But even in conditions of full employment, the most that the 'crowding out' thesis could argue would be that a rise in government spending would not raise aggregate demand, and not (as the Prime Minister on several occasions suggested) that it could actually reduce activity.

The continued high rate of inflation during 1976, coupled with the failure of the economy to revive, provided the background to the devaluation of November 1976. For several months there had been widespread discussion of the possibility of a devaluation, much of it based on a rather crude purchasing-power-parity approach, the limitations of which the press did not emphasize. But the underlying state of the balance of payments was by no means dangerously weak, nor was the level of the reserves particularly low, though one should bear in mind the very high level of official overseas borrowing during 1976 that was helping to sustain the reserves. Indeed, statistics that became available after November 1976 reinforced doubts as to whether any devaluation was really required. But the main adverse factor was the large capital outflow, coupled with the delays in bringing in some of the long-term capital required for major mineral projects—a delay prompted by hopes of a devaluation. It may therefore be true that the popular discussion of the possibility of a devaluation had led to the country being talked into a situation where a basically unnecessary and harmful devaluation was actually unavoidable. But the choice of the huge figure of 17½ per cent was quite unjustifiable in terms of the national interest. The aim should have been to choose the smallest figure that would have carried the conviction that another bite at the cherry would not be necessary; for any substantial devaluation was bound to intensify the problem of dealing with what the government professed to regard as its primary concern, the reduction of the rate of inflation. One might also have hoped that a government led by primary producers would have leaned over backwards to avoid giving a basis for the criticism that, in the choice of the new parity, the national interest had been permitted to give way to considerations of sectional gain. The choice of the very high figure of 17½ per cent singularly failed to meet these desiderata.

The magnitude of this error of policy was soon implicitly acknowledged by the government by means of a series of small appreciations. These quickly brought the effective devaluation (against a weighted average of major currencies) down to about 12½ per cent (comparing early November with the end of 1976). When the devaluation was announced in November provision had been made for the rate to be changed in future by small and more frequent alterations, by a process that was alleged to be 'somewhat after the manner of a managed float', though some would question this description. This did, however, represent a very belated official recognition of what had been obvious for some time to most comparable countries; namely, that alterations of parity by large amounts at infrequent intervals is the worst possible form of adjustment, especially in a world where widely varying rates of inflation co-exist in different countries. But it was still a reluctant and begrudging admission in the sense that it made no real move in the direction of creating a genuine foreign exchange market.

One motive for the 1976 Australian devaluation may well have been the hope that it would give a stimulus to activity within the country; indeed, that it was to a large extent a 'beggar-my-neighbour' remedy for unemployment, in a world that was still suffering from recession. If so, it was a remedy from which the world had happily been remarkably free during 1975–6, thanks to the restrained policies of more enlightened governments. At any rate, this was an interpretation of Australia's action that inevitably, and not unreasonably, suggested itself to many observers in the outside world.

But, quite apart from any possible effects it might have on the outside world (especially if it should start a chain reaction of such measures), it could reasonably be questioned even from the narrowest of Australian viewpoints, as a remedy for unemployment. For the swift response of prices and incomes to devaluations in the modern world, especially in an economy as open as that of Australia, made it more likely than in the past that any considerable devaluation would have a high proportion of its effect on prices rather than on the volume of trade and the real level of activity. The likelihood that activity would not be stimulated would be reinforced so far as the government decided to pursue a still more deflationary policy in the hope of thereby avoiding the effects of the devaluation on the price level. But, still more important, even so far as devaluation might stimulate domestic activity, it would do so by one of the worst possible means, as it was bound to have a considerable upward effect on the rate of inflation. A cut in tax rates could have been better used to stimulate activity, and to reduce cost-push inflation at the same time.

The Budget Deficit as a Guide to Policy

In the mid-1970s the budget deficit attained a measure of importance in the pronouncements of ministerial and opposition spokesmen, and of some commentators, disproportionate to its real importance. This is not to deny its relevance in the total context of macro-economic policy, but simply to point out the limitations to which it is subject as a measure of the degree to which policy may or may not be inflationary. Firstly, it is not the actual budget outcome that is relevant at all. In a recession, tax receipts tend to be held down and total unemployment benefits up by the low level of activity; and so far as this causes an increased deficit, it constitutes a reason for cutting taxes or increasing government spending—or, of course, for taking alternative measures to stimulate activity. One may allow for this qualification by speaking of the 'full employment' or 'cyclically adjusted' budget deficit, defined as the budget outcome that would occur if the economy were at some stated level of activity (for example, 'full but not overfull employment'). Secondly, the budget deficit is only one element affecting the money supply. In particular, the net cash effect of government operations is influenced also by the sale of securities to the public. If one considers that the net effect of government spending and tax receipts on the money supply is too great, there is the alternative of offsetting part of this by offering securities on more attractive terms to the public. Thirdly, in a world where high tax rates certainly have some cost-push effect, the actual level of tax receipts may be as important as the budget deficit. There will then be various combinations of deficit and total tax receipts that will be considered equally tolerable (or intolerable) in the light of their probable effects on the rate of inflation.

Finally, it is not sufficient to condemn a budget deficit for being too large, merely because inflation is thought to be too rapid, at a time when unemployment is also high. For a cut in the budget deficit, taken alone, will tend to make unemployment worse. Before one could reasonably advocate cutting the deficit, one would therefore have to adduce reasons for thinking that this unfavourable effect would be less than the benefits of any check to inflation that might result. One would, moreover, have to set it against alternative ways of reducing the rate of inflation—such as higher interest rates and an appreciation or tariff cuts. If one of these were adopted the appropriate complementary budgetary policy might well be an increase in the deficit.

The Mix of Macro-economic Measures and Exchange Rate Policy

One aim of policy must be to keep the overall level of demand at a suitable level, though the high employment of earlier decades may not be normally achievable (at least not by merely varying macro-economic measures) in future. But attention needs to be devoted also to finding the most appropriate blend, or 'mix', of macro-economic measures for achieving this desired level of activity with the minimum upward effect on the price level. Firstly, a mix that keeps the cost-push effects of taxes relatively low (with the other measures correspondingly set to achieve the desired level of activity), would be preferable to one with high taxes. This implies lower government spending, higher nominal interest rates, or the exchange rate set more towards appreciation, than would otherwise have been appropriate for achieving the desired level of activity.

The degree of flexibility of the exchange rate is also relevant. If it is left free to float, a tight budgetary policy will probably tend to make it appreciate: but if the international flow of capital is very mobile the effectiveness of budgetary measures for influencing demand may be reduced by exchange rate flexibility. This suggests that monetary policy should then be varied primarily with an eye to the level of domestic activity. Within the overall setting of the budget, the lower the level of taxes can be, the better from a cost-push point of view. That is to say, if the aim is to make the exchange rate appreciate (or avoid a depreciation) it will be preferable to restrain government spending rather than raise tax rates. By the same token, if the exchange rate is flexible it will become imperative to vary monetary measures promptly to affect the desired level of activity.

It is not essential for the exchange rate to vary from day to day (without any official intervention) for the foregoing argument to be applicable. Provided that external changes are allowed to affect the rate, even if only with some lag, there will still be a case for using monetary policy mainly with an eye to the level of domestic activity or the rate of inflation. Only if the aim is to keep the exchange rate constant, or to cause it to move in a direction that will not necessarily enhance the effect of monetary policy on domestic activity, does the argument require qualification.

Overall, the exchange rate is no longer a reliable weapon for bringing about a lasting improvement in the current account of the balance of payments, and it is still less likely to be a reliable means of stimulating domestic activity. People who advocate its use for either of those purposes may therefore be following a line of policy that is no longer defensible. On the other hand, it is certainly truer than it used to be that a depreciation adds quickly and considerably to the rate of inflation. This means that the overall setting and the particular mix of the other measures available to a government need to be set in such a way as to achieve the desired level of activity with a rate of inflation as low as possible. The exchange rate should be thought of as just one price, which will adjust itself automatically to the net effect of these various measures (in Australia and in other countries), and should certainly not be thought of as an aim of policy in itself, nor as something that can be set or varied separately from the other instruments.

Interest Rate Policy

Perhaps the greatest obstacle to achieving a macro-economic mix that reduces the rate of inflation is the psychological difficulty in the way of accepting a level of nominal interest rates that appear high by past standards for as long as inflation continues.

When prices are rising at 10 per cent per annum, an interest rate in nominal terms of 10 per cent amounts to an interest-free loan, even if the lender is paying no tax. Unless the post-tax real return is high enough to make the lender willing to hold the existing stock of financial assets at their present prices, there will be an increasing inclination to try to move into real estate and other durable goods, thereby forcing up the price level of not only these goods but of other goods also, at any given level of activity.

If governments are tempted to raise tax rates in the hope of holding down nominal interest rates, they will make the cost-push inflation problem worse. If they are tempted to try to stop inflation by permitting a higher level of unemployment they will obviously reduce living standards and the level of activity. It is therefore essential that they adopt a combination of nominal interest rates and tax rates on the income of lenders that will not make them unwilling to hold financial assets yielding a return. Failure to do this will make inflation at any given level of activity worse. Willingness to allow nominal interest rates to rise to their natural level in the face of inflation—preferably by the introduction of index-linked securities–will make it possible to reduce tax rates, and eventually help to check the inflation and so ultimately to reduce nominal interest rates.

Conclusion

By the end of 1976 Australia has floundered through several years of macro-economic mismanagement towards official recognition of a number of lessons that might well have been learned from the experience of the 1950s. Firstly, it was thoroughly unsatisfactory to operate an artificially fixed exchange rate altered by fairly large amounts at infrequent intervals. A system that facilitates smaller and more frequent adjustments is greatly superior. But there was still no recognition of the role that market processes can usefully be allowed to play in the day-to-day variation of exchange rates.

Secondly, attempts to hold interest rates under official control below the levels they would reach in a free market are likely to intensify inflation, as well as prove ultimately unsuccessful. (Though there was still no recognition that this general argument applies also to the zero nominal rate paid on current accounts–which is obviously a heavily negative real rate in periods of high inflation.) The acceptance of the principle of a target rate of growth for the money supply in 1976 represented some recognition of the dangers of trying to fix interest rates, for attempts to maintain both targets simultaneously cannot be expected to succeed. Similarly, the introduction of a more flexible exchange rate system may be taken as a recognition that acceptance of a money supply target is not consistent with trying also to maintain a particular exchange rate.

The third partly learned lesson is that very high tax rates have cost-push and wage-push effects, and are to that extent undesirable and even partially ineffective weapons against inflation. So far as restraint in government spending makes it easier to reduce tax rates, this is therefore an important argument for avoiding too rapid a rate of growth of government spending. Fourthly, the gradual erosion of 'money illusion' has greatly weakened the force of monetary and exchange rate policy for influencing the level of activity or the volume of trade; and suggests that these weapons of policy (which must be considered together) are best used primarily with an eye to minimizing the rate of inflation at a given level of activity.

The final lesson–by far the most important–to which Australia and the world generally is only very tentatively feeling its way, is that the particular mix of macro-economic measures chosen to achieve a particular level of activity is at least as important as establishing the 'correct' level of demand. Merely to permit a high degree of excess capacity is not likely to have much success in solving the crucial contemporary problem of restraining inflation without foregoing potential output. The essential principle of an appropriate macro-economic mix is:

(1) expansionary budgetary measures (principally tax cuts, which help diminish cost-push inflation and improve incentives and the allocation of resources) to reduce unemployment and spare capacity.

(2) a sufficiently tight monetary policy to reduce the rate of inflation chiefly by selling sufficient attractive government bonds (preferably index-linked) to the public. Also, a prices and incomes policy which will not have the effect of greatly squeezing differentials or otherwise worsening incentive or the allocation of resources, may well have a useful complementary role to play. But whether or not incomes policy proves feasible, governments must under rapid inflation be prepared to accept seemingly high (nominal) interest rates together with restraint in the growth of government spending and much lower levels of tax.

W. E. NORTON

2 The Search for Economic Stability[1]

> ... it is easy to employ 80 to 90 per cent of the national resources ... But to employ 95 to 100 per cent of the national resources is a different task altogether. It cannot be done without care ...
>
> J. M. Keynes
>
> Times, *11 March 1937*

> ... if we inflate the currency ... to keep up employment, money must be increased again and again and prices kept rising until money has no value at all and the whole thing breaks down ...
>
> L. F. Giblin
>
> *Letter to John Smith*, Herald, *24 November 1930*

Economic stability has declined markedly in Australia in recent years. What are the causes of this instability? Are some fundamental? Why do we have both rapid inflation and high unemployment? Which is the more basic problem at present? What are the possible implications for policy? These are some of the questions to which this chapter is addressed.

International Influences

Instability in the world economy has contributed to Australia's economic difficulties. From 1971 to 1973, the world economy grew strongly in response mainly to demand management policies that were highly expansionary. Major bottle-necks appeared in the markets for goods, labour and raw materials. However, owing to various economic and social influences, unemployment rates in a number of countries did not fully reflect the intensity of the boom. With strong pressures of demand, prices and incomes rose rapidly; in particular, the prices of many commodities increased at a spectacular pace. As a result, real incomes in Australia were raised. However, powerful inflationary pressures were also received from abroad; this was at a time when the Australian dollar was already tending to be undervalued because of a large boost to exports and capital inflow from the minerals boom, and a relatively low rate of inflation in the 1960s. The inflationary pressures from overseas were reflected in Australia during 1971 and 1972 in sharp rises for export prices, import prices, and holdings of international reserves; the large rise in international reserves gave a substantial boost to the money supply. In 1973, the Australian economy was largely insulated from further world inflationary pressures due to appreciations of the exchange rate, tighter controls on capital inflow and cuts in tariffs. However, by then, major inflationary pressures from abroad had been absorbed into Australia.

By contrast, deflationary effects from overseas became important in 1974 when the world economy swung sharply into recession. In 1974 and the first part of 1975 economic activity in the major industrial countries fell quickly under the influence of a marked tightening of demand management policies and of a huge rise in oil prices. The deflationary effects on the Australian economy were transmitted in several ways: a large drop in our holdings of international reserves, which cut deeply into the money supply when domestic monetary policy was also working in that direction; a large surge of imports, which added markedly to supplies when domestic demand was faltering; and a check to the growth of export incomes which reinforced the squeeze on profits caused by a rapid rise in labour costs.

Domestic Influences

Over the past five years, international influences have clearly had a role in Australia's economic troubles. But international factors are only a part of the story. Many domestic influences have been important in creating economic instability. These factors, all of which are related, include the intense boom of 1973 and early 1974, a huge rise in labour costs, a sharp squeeze on profits, a strong rise in the expected rate of inflation, and some aspects of policy. Among these factors, the boom was vital. Economic activity expanded strongly from late in 1972 and remained very high until nearly the middle of 1974, fuelled by demand management policies that were, overall, highly expansionary for the bulk of 1972 and 1973. Demand for goods, labour and materials was strong, whereas supplies were hampered by an under-valued exchange rate, cuts in immigration, and the intense world demand for materials and goods. As in many other countries, the strength of the boom was not reflected fully in the figures for unemployment, perhaps partly because of the side-effects of a higher level of welfare benefits and a marked rise in minimum wages. However, the intensity of the boom was evident in acute shortages of raw materials, record levels of overtime, long delays in the building industry and a very low ratio of stocks to sales.

With intense pressures of demand, wages and prices surged forward in 1973; food prices (especially meat) rose quickly under the twin influences of the domestic boom and a substantial lift in overseas demand. With the slump in economic activity overseas, prices of some foodstuffs rose at a slower pace in 1974. But, overall, wages and prices grew at a faster rate. Indeed, wages bolted upwards in the middle months of 1974 under the stimulus of intense pressures of demand, the earlier large lift in food prices, and a marked rise in the expected rate of inflation. Labour costs were boosted further by measures for equal pay, longer annual leave and a rise in holiday pay. The upshot was a huge increase in labour costs; this would have given a shock to the economy even if prices had kept in step.

But price rises, although rapid, did not keep pace with the swift increase in wages. Several factors caused price movements to be slower or smaller than the rise in labour costs, including the procedures of the Prices Justification Tribunal, tougher competition from imports (stimulated by the revaluations of the exchange rate and by cuts in tariffs and also by the fall in demand overseas) and a tightening of monetary conditions. With wages rising much faster than prices, real wages increased sharply in 1974; profits and cash flows were squeezed acutely. Also, monetary conditions tightened quickly during much of 1974 under the combined pressures of the higher exchange rate, a rapid increase in tax receipts (caused mainly by the fast rise in wages), and higher interest rates. In particular, the sharp tightening in monetary conditions hastened the end of a large boom in the property market. Budgetary policy remained relatively easy but the overall setting of demand policy was tight for the bulk of 1974.

In this environment, both household and business demand faltered in the middle months of 1974 just when a sharp rise in costs was also hitting output and employment. Household savings increased sharply. That was probably partly due to the usual lag between increases in incomes and demand, but other major influences could have been the uncertainty created by the mounting signs of economic instability, especially rapid inflation and high unemployment, and the efforts by many to offset the recent falls in the real value of their financial assets. The slow-down in household demand and the resulting pile-up of stocks–which was exacerbated by the strong surge of imports and to a lesser extent by a weaker growth in exports–added further to the problems of the business sector. Business activity and prospects took a major jolt. Survival rather than growth became the watchword. Output was cut sharply. Many investment plans were postponed or abandoned. With the substantial rise in labour costs, firms made a thorough review of the size of their work-force and made large cuts. Unemployment rose quickly, particularly for groups that recently had been granted substantial rises in award wages.

In response to these developments, demand management policies, especially the budget, were swung sharply and strongly towards expansion in the second half of 1974. The budget deficit was increased substantially due mainly to a large rise in outlays but also to reductions in the growth of revenues. The substantial rise in outlays and in the deficit probably cushioned the fall in economic activity, although there may have been some cuts in private spending in response to the abnormally large increase in government outlays and to related fears of a further boost to inflation. Due mainly to the large budget deficit, monetary conditions became easy and, in particular, money supply rose again at a fast pace. Also late in 1974, a sizeable devaluation in the exchange rate worked to ease monetary conditions, to reduce supplies of imports and to increase prices of imports. Specific monetary measures, including cuts in interest rates, also contributed to an easing in monetary conditions in the later months of 1974.

For most of 1975, the overall setting of demand policies continued to be very expansive. However, the stimulus to activity was less than many expected. At the same time, the Conciliation and Arbitration Commission moved to link award wages to the consumer price index, thereby tending to maintain the relatively high level of real wages reached in 1974. Partly as a result, unemployment stayed at a high level, inflation continued at a fast pace and expectations about inflation seemed to remain strong; moreover, these tendencies appeared to be hampering a rise in private spending and employment. In these circumstances, demand policy was revised during 1975 to give more attention to the restraint of inflation, partly because that was seen as essential for a sustained reduction in unemployment.

Fundamental Factors

So much for the major proximate factors in our current bout of economic instability. But, looking over a longer horizon, are there more fundamental factors? Since World War II demand management policies in most industrial countries have tended to be pushed too far in an expansionary direction. This has led to an increasing degree of economic instability in those countries; the strong boom and deep recession of 1971 to 1975 were, in this sense, an outcome of more fundamental influences. But how do highly expansionary policies lead to economic instability? Why have these policies been pursued? Also, what has been Australia's performance?

Demand management policies that are too easy lead to economic instability by causing inflation. This can happen as follows. Beginning from a position of stability, the creation of excess demand will cause prices to rise. If policies remain highly expansionary, the community will begin to expect prices to increase, partly because of views that governments will underwrite large wage increases. Spurred by strong demand pressures and a boost to price expectations, rises in incomes and prices will tend to quicken, with prices responding more readily to increases in incomes and with the incomes of various groups tending to be geared more closely to rises in prices. Hence expectations about inflation will strengthen further, incomes and prices will rise more rapidly, and so on. But, as inflation quickens, economic activity will be disrupted, partly because of a substantial increase in uncertainty, and unemployment will probably grow. In response, demand policies could be made even more expansive in an effort to offset the rise in unemployment; that extra stimulus could moderate for a short time the growth in unemployment but would also give a further boost to inflationary pressures. The upshot would be more disruption to economic activity. For the process to persist, a continued fast growth in nominal demand, fuelled by expansionary policies, is necessary; however, over time, the stimulus to employment will tend to diminish.

A further and related way in which expansionary policies may lead to economic instability is that they may also result in greater variability in policies. Policies which cause higher inflation will usually be followed by strong deflationary action to stem the inflation. As a result, unemployment may rise quickly and, in turn, this will produce pressures for a further major reversal of policy, and so on. The upshot can be a series of sharp swings in policy. This will disrupt economic activity, not least because of the uncertainty caused by large shifts in policy.

A major reason for demand management policies being too easy has been the desire of many governments to use these measures to force unemployment below the level consistent with sustained economic stability. By such policies, unemployment can be cut below its sustainable level for a short period but inflation will increase. (The sustainable rate of unemployment is the level at which inflation will not tend to rise. The sustainable rate of unemployment will change over time, partly in response to appropriate demand policies and other policies.) Moreover, with continued efforts to maintain an unsustainable level of employment, the rate of inflation will continue rising. In turn, this will disrupt economic activity and employment. Paradoxically, highly expansionary policies to force unemployment below its sustainable level could result in severe unemployment.

A related reason for demand policy being too easy has been rapidly rising claims on governments for extra goods and services. These stem partly from the tendency for the demand for some public goods, such as education and health, to rise faster than incomes, especially when those goods are priced well below cost. But, also, many groups seek aid from governments in the hope that others will bear the cost. Moreover, extra aid to some groups will tend to produce additional demands from other groups. In these ways, extra commitments to government outlays can tend to run ahead of their willingness to levy additional taxes; as a result, demand policies may be too expansionary.

Economic stability in Australia has, in general, been good since World War II, especially when compared with the two decades up to 1939. But, even before the recent economic troubles, there were some signs of a deterioration in economic stability. In particular, prices rose moderately but persistently. Gradually, the community must have come to expect inflation to continue. As that view spread, the seeds were sown for rapid inflation and high unemployment. Those tendencies were probably forestalled for a while by the relatively major and prolonged recession of the early 1960s. However, by the end of that decade, memories of the recession nearly ten years before were dimming, and views that inflation would continue or increase were once more prevalent. The environment was therefore conducive to a strong upsurge of inflation. Of course, the experience of the 1960s does not necessarily mean that a major recession each few years is a necessary part of policies for economic stability. An alternative approach could be to avoid either highly expansionary or strongly deflationary policies in favour of demand policies that are relatively moderate and stable; although, concentrating on the role of demand policy does not mean that this is the only major influence on economic stability in Australia, or in other industrial countries. But other factors have usually been less important that the difficulties created by demand policy.

Inflation and Unemployment

Unemployment involves two main costs: economic and psychological hardship for individuals; and a loss of output for the community. These costs may seem to occur mainly at the time of unemployment but longer-term effects should not be ignored; for instance, persons out of jobs today may find themselves at a relative disadvantage on the job market of the future if their skills or aspirations are unduly hampered by being unemployed. These costs underpin the case for trying to ensure not only the maximum level of employment that is consistent with economic stability but also to provide a generous level of appropriate welfare payments.

Inflation also involves large economic and social costs. Rapid inflation causes economic instability, individual hardship and social unrest in several ways: by adding an extra and major dimension of uncertainty in economic decisions, especially those of a longer-term nature and thereby eroding the productive base of the economy; by inducing sharp shifts in the distribution of income and wealth and, partly as a result, causing more frequent disputes and negotiations over incomes and prices; by undermining the accepted systems of accounting and taxation and, partly as a consequence, making much more difficult the everyday tasks of running households, businesses and governments.

The relationships between inflation and unemployment are complex, partly because of differences between short-term and longer-run aspects. In the short term, there is usually a choice between slightly more inflation and slightly more unemployment; that is, the community can for a short period have a lower level of unemployment at the cost of some extra dose of inflation or, alternatively, can have a lower level of inflation at the cost of some increase in unemployment. However, as inflation rises, the choice or trade-off between inflation and unemployment deteriorates at a pace which can be rapid when inflation is high, especially if governments are seen to be willing to underwrite inflation.

The way that the short-term trade-off can worsen bears close scrutiny. An attempt to reduce unemployment by policies that cause excess demand will normally, in the short term, have some success, although at the cost of extra inflationary pressures. But that is not the end of the story. The higher rate of inflation will cause households and businesses to revise upwards their expectations about inflation and to respond more quickly with income claims and price rises. As a result, the growth of prices and incomes will tend to rise at a faster pace and, if demand policies remain easy, expectations about inflation will strengthen further, and so on. However, expectations about inflation are likely to differ markedly and, as inflation quickens, the range of views about future rates of inflation is likely to widen and the confidence with which those expectations are held will decline. Uncertainty will increase substantially and the speculative content of economic decisions will be magnified; this will serve to undermine the capital market, especially at the longer end, and to erode the growth of the productive base of the economy. In these ways, rapid inflation can disrupt economic activity and lead to a higher average rate of unemployment.

Policy could, of course, try for a time to keep unemployment below the level currently consistent with economic stability. This would require measures to expand demand at a pace sufficient to offset the fall in demand stemming from the uncertainty caused by inflation. But, with demand policies made even easier, the inflation spiral will tend to quicken and the eventual disruption to activity —and associated rise in unemployment—will be more severe.

From this analysis, inflation emerges as the more basic problem in the circumstances of 1976. This is not to deny that unemployment is a major problem with large costs. But, in 1976, inflation is the more basic economic problem because, if permitted to continue, it will cause severe damage to economic and social stability, including higher average unemployment over a long period. Avoiding large and prolonged unemployment depends substantially on having policies that do not cause high inflation.

Demand Management Policies

The first of the policy implications of the analysis so far is that demand management which is too expansionary will result in rapid inflation; moreover, if persisted with, it will lead to severe unemployment and general economic instability. To avoid inflation, and especially the path from low rates of inflation to high inflation, should be a vital aim of demand policy.

But what should be done if inflation has become rapid and is disrupting economic activity? The resulting unemployment could be regarded as sufficient reason for demand management policies being made still more expansionary to stimulate activity. However, if inflation is high and expectations of inflation are strong, easy demand policies could also add substantially to inflation and eventually damage further the level of activity and employment. Moreover, as inflation increases, expansionary policies are likely to give a relatively smaller short-term stimulus to activity and a relatively larger and prolonged boost to inflation. In essence, continued pursuit of demand policies that are too easy leads not only to more rapid inflation but also to large unemployment.

Adopting demand management policies that are less expansionary would avoid a slide into rapid inflation. Moreover, the average rate of unemployment is likely to be minimized by pursuing policies that expand nominal demand in line with a realistic assessment of available supplies and do so in a relatively stable manner. With such policies, the sustainable rate of unemployment could gradually be lowered. Further reductions in unemployment could be sought by policies to increase the occupational and regional mobility of the work-force and to avoid sharp increases in real wages or overly rapid changes in the wage structure; however, those policies will usually work only slowly and they will be in vain if demand policies are too easy.

Budget Deficits

Budget deficits are often a major part of easy demand policies and can undoubtedly provide a short-term cushion or stimulus to economic activity and employment. However, especially when inflation is high, a much larger deficit may give only slightly more short-term stimulus to activity but provide a relatively powerful boost to inflation that will soon erode the initial rise in activity. The problems of a large budget deficit stem mainly from the need to finance it. A large deficit can either be financed by selling more government securities, which implies relatively higher interest rates (and an associated drop in asset values, and so on), or by expanding the money supply, which will add to inflationary pressures and produce, at a later stage, strong upward pressures on interest rates and disruptions to economic activity.

Greater problems could arise if large budget deficits persist. Continued rapid growth in the money supply would result in rapid inflation and, with the resulting increase in uncertainty, financial markets would eventually wither, especially at the longer end, and economic activity would be damaged severely. But financing large deficits in a non-inflationary way by selling more government securities would also involve major problems. In particular, upward pressures on interest rates would tend to strengthen: each year it would not only be necessary to sell a new batch of government securities to finance the current deficit but also be essential to ensure that the outstanding stock of securities would continue to be held. The resulting upward pressures on interest rates could weaken markedly some sectors of the economy, especially the building and construction sectors, durable goods industries and financial markets.

Social stresses could also result from large budget deficits: if financed mainly by government securities, increasing social pressures are likely gradually to result from the mounting burden of taxation to cover the growing level of interest payments on government securities; whereas if large deficits are financed by inflation, critical social stresses are likely to build up due to the likely substantial shifts in the distribution of income, to an increase in industrial unrest stemming from more frequent disputes and negotiations over income relativities, to the hardship caused to many individuals and families by large falls in the purchasing power of their incomes or wealth and, more generally, to problems caused by a likely erosion of living standards and the productive base of the community.

Budget Outlays

Expansionary demand policies also often rely heavily on a rapid increase in government outlays. Fast rises in outlays can have desirable effects in providing extra funds for certain social objectives and in giving some support to economic activity. However, too rapid a rate of growth in government outlays can also create important problems.

These problems can include excessive expectations, higher taxes and increased sectoral difficulties. A rapid rise in outlays can satisfy some demands for extra public goods and services or transfers but can also stimulate many fresh demands and create excessive expectations about what governments can achieve, especially in the short term. These expectations are likely to be jolted when the benefits of the extra spending are assessed and the tax bill arrives. The tax effects of a rapid growth in outlays can also create stresses. The fast rise in outlays must be matched eventually by a similar big increase in taxes. Even if the immediate rise in taxes is not large, many people will perceive that taxes are going to be higher in the future. This can reduce the confidence and spending of business and households. Social stresses can also increase if those who are hardest hit by extra taxes feel deprived of benefits from the extra goods and services. Sectoral problems from a fast rise in government outlays can be important also, especially in the short term. Additional outlays may give a strong boost to particular industries or regions but, because of bottle-necks, create stronger inflationary pressures and less employment than would result from a broader rise in demand.

Overall, major problems for economic stability can result from large budget deficits or too rapid a rate of growth in government outlays. That is not to deny that budget deficits and rises in government outlays can have important benefits; however, care is required if measures that are intended, at least partly, to restore economic stability are not to generate more instability.

Money Supply and Monetary Policy

The growth in money supply can, when interpreted with care, be a useful indicator of demand policies. A fast rise in money supply will not only add to demand pressures but may also be taken by the community to indicate that high inflation is likely to continue.

Monetary policy can have an important influence on growth in the money supply. However, budgetary and external policies can also have large effects on money growth; when this is so, monetary policy can be seriously hampered. For instance, a major boost to the money supply from a large budget deficit could be offset entirely by extra sales of government securities induced by much higher interest rates on those securities. But a sharp rise in yields could be highly damaging to some industries and groups that are sensitive to falls in asset values and to large changes in financial flows. This is not to suggest that monetary policy should accommodate all inflationary pressures when budgetary policy is expansionary, but rather that there can be important limits, particularly in the short run, to the control of inflation solely by monetary policy.

Monetary measures may, therefore, be prevented in practice from maintaining control over the money supply in the absence of other compatible policies. Put differently, control of the money supply is not the be-all of monetary policy; especially in the short term, movements in asset values, interest rates and liquidity ratios may be highly important. More generally, appropriate demand policies are not likely to rest heavily on any particular arm of policy but to involve a balanced use of budgetary, monetary and external policies.

Exchange Rate

Domestic demand policies can have major implications for external policies, including the exchange rate. If inflationary pressures are strong in other countries, the pursuit of domestic demand policies that are relatively tight will serve to produce an undervalued exchange rate. In these circumstances, appreciation of the exchange rate would also be required to protect the domestic economy from major inflationary pressures in the world economy. Of course, appreciation of the exchange rate can produce short-term adjustment problems for some industries and groups, but these difficulties could be moderated by avoiding sharp appreciations or by appropriate measures for temporary assistance.

Pursuing domestic demand policies that are more expansionary than in other countries will tend to make the exchange rate overvalued. Of course, the associated drop in international reserves can be a useful signal to the community that tighter domestic policies are needed for economic stability. A lowering of the exchange rate gives a direct boost to inflation and would also (especially in a climate of fast rises in prices and wages) strengthen further the community's expectations of inflation, thereby giving an additional impetus to an inflationary spiral. However, an over-valued exchange rate can involve risks, such as a sharp tightening in financial conditions and short-term difficulties for export industries, that need to be set against the possible benefits in thwarting inflationary pressures. Overall, these considerations point to the need for harmony between external policy and domestic demand measures.

A Role for Incomes Policy?

Large rises in incomes are much more likely when demand policies are highly expansionary. By avoiding these policies, large increases in wages and salaries or in profit margins will be less likely and will be short-lived. For sustained restraint in the growth of incomes, demand policies must not therefore be too easy. This is not to deny that policies to reduce directly the growth of incomes may have a role in special circumstances, such as when real wages have risen too quickly. Also, these policies could sometimes give time for tighter demand policies to take effect. But direct policies to restrain nominal incomes are a weak reed if demand policies are too expansionary; in such circumstances, the direct restraints will soon fail under the weight of demand pressures.

Conclusions

Since World War II, demand management policies in most industrial countries have tended to be too expansionary; this has been caused partly by efforts to reduce unemployment to levels that unfortunately could not be sustained and also partly by a tendency for extra outlays of governments to run ahead of their willingness to levy higher taxes. But demand management policies that are too expansive are a basic cause of inflation; if persisted with they lead not only to high inflation but also to economic and social instability, including severe unemployment.

Australia's present bout of economic instability was the product of many domestic and international causes. However, a basic factor was the highly expansive setting of demand management policies. Of course, other influences have had a role too, including the variability of demand management policies and large shifts in the wage structure; however, these influences tend to become important when demand management policies are too easy.

In a democratic society, inflation must be avoided because it leads to economic and social instability, including large unemployment. To avoid inflation, demand management policies must be tighter than in recent years. This is not, however, a prescription for deflation but, rather, for demand management policies that try to expand nominal demand in line with supplies and do so in a relatively steady way. With these policies, inflation would be avoided and unemployment could be minimized. Reductions in unemployment and inflation may be facilitated by improvements in the mobility of the work-force and the avoidance of overly fast rises in incomes or rapid shifts in the wage structure; however, these policies will be in vain if demand management policies are too expansionary.

References

1 An earlier version of this chapter was presented as a paper in July 1976 to the Public Policy Seminar at the University of Tasmania. In addition to points raised there, helpful comments have been made earlier by V. Argy, E. A. Boehm, G. G. Firth, R. C. Gates, F. H. Gruen, A. R. Hall, G. C. Harcourt, R. F. Henderson, W.

Kasper, K. E. Schott, R. H. Snape, the editors of this volume and many persons in the Reserve Bank of Australia and government departments; however, responsibility for remaining errors lies with the author. The views expressed are not necessarily those of my employer.

Other discussions of issues raised in this chapter include:

S. Brittan, *Second Thoughts on Full Employment Policy* (Centre for Policy Studies, London, 1975).

M. S. Feldstein, 'Lowering the Permanent Rate of Unemployment', in O. Eckstein (ed.), *Parameters and Policies in the U.S. Economy* (North-Holland, Amsterdam, 1976).

W. Fellner, 'Lessons from the Failure of Demand-Management Policies: A Look at the Theoretical Foundations', *Journal of Economic Literature*, March 1976.

M. Friedman, *Unemployment Versus Inflation*?, Occasional Paper 44 (Institute of Economic Affairs, London, 1975).

B. Griffiths, *Inflation: The Price of Prosperity* (Weidenfeld and Nicolson, London, 1976).

F. H. Gruen, *What Went Wrong*?, Presidential Address to Section 24, Congress of ANZAAS, Hobart, May 1976.

J. R. Hicks, 'The Quest for Monetary Stability', *South African Journal of Economics*, December 1975.

P. Jay, *A General Hypothesis of Employment, Inflation and Politics*, Occasional Paper 46 (Institute of Economic Affairs, London, 1976).

A. King, 'Overload: Problems of Governing in the 1970s', *Political Studies* 1975.

B. Klein, 'Our New Monetary Standard: The Measurement and Effects of Price Uncertainty, 1880-1973', *Economic Enquiry*, December 1975.

D. E. W. Laidler, and J. M. Parkin, 'Inflation: A Survey', *Economic Journal*, December 1975.

A. Leijonhufvud, 'Costs and Consequences of Inflation', in G. C. Harcourt and E. A. G. Robinson (eds), *The Microeconomic Foundations of Macroeconomics* (Macmillan, London, forthcoming).

A. M. Okun, 'Inflation: Its Mechanics and Welfare Costs', *Brookings Papers on Economic Activity*, 1975:2 and the references listed in W. E. Norton, 'Inflation and Unemployment', *Economic Papers*, no. 51 (February 1976).

G. G. FIRTH

3 Second Thoughts on Disinflation

The Democratic Dilemma of Disinflation

The economics of my argument presented to ANZAAS in Brisbane in 1951 depended on a very simple theory of inflation, which was said to be due to the pressure of effective demand on available resources. Although a little might be done to increase the amount or the productivity of resources, in the short run the best hope for disinflation would be to control effective demand. This could be attempted in the private sector by increasing rates of taxation, or by raising interest rates and restricting credit. In the public sector it would be necessary to reduce government expenditure, and more particularly the expenditure of state governments and their instrumentalities. It was suggested that the Commonwealth's unpopularity as the chief tax-collector might be reduced if some of the political responsibility for disinflationary measures could be shifted in the general direction of the states. A broad strategy was proposed which would leave them with the utmost possible freedom to adjust the details of taxing and spending within limits set by the need to reduce or increase the level of effective monetary demand. This suggestion seems to have foreshadowed some of the very latest notions about the future of Australian federalism.

In the economic diagnosis, not much was said about the relationship between earnings, productivity, labour costs and prices, or about any tendency for trade unions to try to anticipate future increases in retail prices. The details of the relationship between excess demand and rising prices were not elaborated. However, a passing reference was made to Colin Clark's suggestion that inflation might have been associated with attempts to increase rates of taxation in order to divert 'too high' a proportion (for example, more than 25 per cent) of current output to government purposes. The paper tacitly assumed that the quantity of money would be adjusted to the level of incomes and prices. But it was explicitly recognized that credit policy could be used to restrict the level of private capital expenditure. In so far as these terms have any meaning, the general approach was Keynesian rather than monetarist.

Because inflation was thought to be due primarily to excessive demand, disinflationary measures could not be effective unless they limited the spending (or, less plausibly, increased the efficiency) of wage earners, primary producers, businessmen or state instrumentalities. Disinflation would, therefore, be a matter of increasing taxes, making it more expensive or difficult to borrow money, and restricting public works and other government spending. All these measures were likely to be unpopular, especially because ordinary voters had not (in 1951, whatever may be the case in 1976) understood the technical requirements for disinflation. Were a substantial minority of voters prepared to transfer its political allegiance, the government might be unwilling to adopt *any* effective combination of disinflationary measures if it believed that this would result in loss of office.

It was argued that, because politicians believed that some measures (such as increased tax rates or reduced expenditures) were bound to lose votes, they assessed the practicability of economic policies according to a scale of political valuations which bore little or no relation to economic analysis. The tendency to prefer symbolism to analysis could also have been fostered by the activities of the representatives of special interests, who are paid to exaggerate the adverse political repercussions of measures which threaten the economic status of the people they represent. It was also pointed out that, from the Commonwealth's viewpoint, state ministers resemble the officials of interest groups because they represent the interests of producers and consumers of state government services.

Official economic advisers also were also criticized because of their alleged tendency to suppress any reference to alternative measures believed to be politically unacceptable to members of the government. It was argued that an economist who pressed too hard for a measure judged 'impracticable' by his political masters would risk losing influence with them in future. In retrospect, it now seems that this line of argument may have originated in the special problems of relatively young officials confronted by strong-minded and more elderly ministers. This was an important reason why an Economic Policy Tribunal was suggested as a means of dressing up disinflationary recommendations in the solemn garb of semi-judicial authority.

The Economic Policy Tribunal

The idea of the so-called 'Tribunal' originated in the observable usefulness of certain statutory bodies which were already firmly established in Australia. At least two bodies (the Tariff Board and the Grants Commission) had been given important semi-judicial powers when originally established by the Commonwealth parliament (in the 1920s and 1930s, respectively). These powers had been so wisely used that their recommendations had usually (in the case of the Grants Commission, always) been accepted by the Commonwealth government of the day. Although the reports and recommendations of these bodies concerned extremely 'political' questions, they seemed to have been successful in reaching a level of objectivity which placed their recommendations at an appreciable distance above and beyond the petty point-scoring of party politics. This outcome, moreover, seemed to have been found helpful by governments of whatever political party.

The function of the proposed Tribunal would therefore have been to examine alternative policy proposals, to make recommendations to the government, and to publicize its findings so as to better inform voters about the realities of economic policy. The Tribunal was not intended to undertake much (if any) research on its own account, but rather to assess the significance for policy of other people's results. It was certainly not to have any administrative functions because it had to remain independent of parliament as well as of the government. The essential requirement was that the Tribunal should be completely 'free from the need to pander to the prejudices and inhibitions of ministers', so that ministers themselves could rely 'on the independent status of an advisory body' to protect them from the political consequences of implementing its recommendations. It was also intended that the Tribunal should act as an impartial critic of policy decisions in much the same way as an auditor-general may criticize the handling of public money.

The membership of the Tribunal would have to be kept as small as possible in order to minimize the risk of serious dissension among its members, because its prestige would not grow 'in an atmosphere of disagreement and minority reports'.

It was suggested that a chairman and two members (all full-time) would be sufficient, assisted by a small permanent staff 'which on no account should be allowed to assume the dimensions of a research organisation'. It was considered that not more than two of the three Tribunal members should be economists and not more than one should ever have been a permanent officer of any public service. Members should be appointed for overlapping terms of about six years. They should not be eligible for reappointment, and suitable compensation should be paid on retirement.

Criticism of the Proposal

In the two or three years before the Chifley government was defeated at the 1949 federal election, economic policy seemed to be in the doldrums. The Labor government had been weakened electorally by vigorous opposition campaigns against nationalization of trading banks and against the referendum seeking federal power to control prices and charges. The Commonwealth treasury was passing through an interregnum, between the abdication of King Mac and the accession of King Roland. Most senior officials seemed physically tired after years of effort on problems of war and reconstruction, and some were no doubt sniffing the winds of change as well. In these circumstances, bold recommendations for the control of inflation were unlikely to be made; before and after 1949 it made good sense to avoid potentially contentious issues. By 1951, however, a new pattern was beginning to emerge. In one respect the Tribunal had been designed to deal with a special situation which was already ceasing to exist at the time the paper was presented at the Brisbane Congress.

Another function of the Tribunal was to provide evidence and argument in rebuttal of representations on behalf of interest groups opposed to disinflationary measures, such as (for example) exporters who might resist an upward revaluation of the Australian currency. Underlying this part of the proposal was a failure to appreciate the possibility that interest groups, lobbyists, and even practitioners in public relations, may play a useful part in the extra-market operations of an imperfectly competitive economy. The paper was written before reading *American Capitalism*, in which J. K. Galbraith set out his concept of 'countervailing power', which lays particular stress upon the positive functions of interest groups. According to this view, countervailing power may serve a useful purpose in helping to protect individuals against the collectivist powers not only of government, but also of big business, organized farmers and trade unions federated on a nation-wide basis. The concepts of countervailing power seem to suit Australia at least as well as they do the United States.

The 1951 paper was written at a time much closer than the present to the wartime assumption of an allegedly single-valued national objective carrying unchallengeable priority. Some people may still believe that the preservation of a country's monetary system should carry the same kind of priority as did national defence under wartime conditions, but probably most would regard disinflation as having a high but not an absolute priority. In exchange for a slower rate of inflation, they would accept some postponement at the margin of the attainment of other objectives of economic policy. One of the outstanding problems is how to identify, even approximately, the marginal rate of trade-off between the costs and benefits of disinflation.

Recognizing that any reduction in the rate of inflation will have to be purchased at the price of disappointing the reasonable expectations of at least some persons or businesses, a conscientious politician may honestly believe that he has a duty to try to minimize the disadvantageous effects of disinflationary measures, without necessarily thinking in terms of 'saving votes'. However, to the extent that the politician's efforts are successful they will also have tended to reduce the disinflationary effect of the government's measures. This is exactly the kind of contradiction which the Economic Policy Tribunal was designed to prevent. In so doing, the Tribunal itself would have thereby reduced the effectiveness of parliamentary institutions in protecting the micro-economic interests of individuals against the impact of macro-economic policy. The dilemma seems to be inescapable.

Slumpflation in the Seventies

The problem of inflation has changed a good deal since 1951. Politicians, officials and ordinary voters have had a much longer experience of macro-economic policy. This experience has included two longish periods (1954–9 and 1963–70) during which a tolerable level of unemployment coincided with a tolerable rate of increase in average prices. By contrast, 1971–6 has been a period when accelerating inflation has been accompanied by increasing unemployment.

Conventional wisdom has explained the conjunction of inflation and unemployment largely in terms of the mistakes of politicians. For example, the accelerating rise of prices has been traced back to the McMahon Government's anxiety to reduce the level of unemployment in time for the elections of December, 1972, and to Clyde Cameron's support for wage increases in 1973 and 1974. Indeed, the latter afford convenient explanations for both inflation and unemployment subsequently growing worse. However, any explanation which relies wholly on Australian happenings leaves out of account similar developments, over much the same period of time, in most of the non-socialist market economies.

It is tempting to say that the broad agreement of Australian experience with experience overseas is due merely to chance--to the accident that other countries happened to be experiencing similar economic discomfort at the same period as Australia. But perhaps the coincidence may not have been due to chance alone. Three occurrences may have been sufficient, together if not separately, to affect many trading countries in much the same way if not exactly at the same time or to the same extent.

One possibility is that the inflationary effects of the war in Vietnam were transmitted indirectly to Australia as well as to other countries, perhaps because the U.S. dollar became a relatively 'weak' currency for a time. This may have allowed more scope for monetary expansion in Australia and for prices to rise, without leading immediately to noticeable difficulties with the balance of payments. A second possibility could be that the increase in oil prices in 1973 had a greater indirect effect on the Australian economy than is usually believed, perhaps because costs and prices in countries with which Australia trades were raised, although a much smaller effect within Australia was felt. This would also give greater scope for Australian prices to rise without having repercussions on our balance of payments.

Of the three possible explanations why inflation has accelerated throughout the world, the third is perhaps the most likely to be controversial, the more so because it does not appear to apply directly to Australia itself. Until about 1970, the International Monetary Fund was reasonably successful in maintaining the post-war system of stable exchange rates between national currencies. Within this system, all but the largest trading countries would normally experience considerable pressure (at least potentially) to keep their internal rates of inflation as low as possible. Any country in which costs and prices were rising appreciably faster than the average would (in the absence of capital inflow) expect to lose its international reserves and might have to approach the Fund for help. In the first two decades of its existence, the Fund probably possessed sufficient authority for most countries to be reluctant to risk having to seek special assistance on account of an above-average rate of inflation, whereas countries with a below-average rate could expect to gain some advantage in competitive trade. After 1971, however, a regime of 'floating' currencies may have weakened the incentive to minimize the rate of inflation, since the depreciation of inflators' currencies would tend also to lessen the trading advantages which would have accrued to successful disinflators under the previous regime of more stable exchange rates.

The foregoing explanation certainly does not apply to Australia. The external value of the Australian currency was twice increased, in December 1972 and in September 1973, partly as a disinflationary measure and not greatly offset by a smaller devaluation in 1974. On the other hand, it seems possible that the rise in costs and prices in other countries may have been fast enough to offset the disinflationary effects of the two revaluations of 1972 and 1973, and to permit Australia's own rate of inflation to increase as fast as it has done since 1973 without (until late 1976) seriously depleting our international reserves.

But what about the increase in unemployment? Conventional wisdom says that this has been due to business uncertainty in conditions of accelerating inflation, and that anything which reduces inflation will also reduce unemployment. This sounds plausible and could even be true. However, it is not easy to understand why, if they fear inflation, businessmen would prefer to hold depreciating money or securities rather than construct tangible assets such as new buildings. After December, 1975, it cannot any longer be due to distrust of a Labor government, and surely there must be more to it than irrational funk. Here is another suggestion.

Most of the developed countries have done their best to control inflation by restricting the growth of the stock of money. As a result of this policy, interest rates in many countries–including Australia –have risen to levels without precedent in modern times. Perhaps these very high interest rates would have been less effective in choking off private capital expenditure on new productive assets if businessmen had continued to believe that costs and prices would continue to rise about as quickly as they had been rising in the recent past. However, if they do not hold this view with enough conviction, they will feel themselves to be confronted with a 'real' rate of interest much closer to the extraordinarily high money rates being charged by lending institutions. At rates like these, only short-term or exceptionally profitable long-term projects will appear to be profitable. If this explanation of the prolonged and widespread depression is correct, it would seem that conventional wisdom is mistaken: the truth may be that unemployment remains too high, not because businessmen are afraid that inflation will become worse, but because they suspect it may actually be reduced.

Disinflation in 1976

The outstanding feature of the Canberra scene in 1976 has been the commanding position occupied by the Commonwealth treasury. No need for an Economic Policy Tribunal now! The Treasury will continue to apply its own scale of national priorities, and no doubt the disinflation objective is lying very close to the top of the official scale of preferences. At the time of writing (mid-1976), the federal government appears politically impregnable. In contrast to the situation in 1951, the political auspices for disinflation could hardly be improved. What, then, is there to worry about?

The trouble is that economic policy is a part of government policy, and not the whole of it. Not even in 1976 or 1977 should disinflation be regarded as the only objective of policy, although it may be considered a very important one. If only because disinflationary measures are bound to hurt if they are to be effective, some attempt should be made to identify and minimize their undesired and perhaps unnecessary consequences. In 1932, for example, the harmful effects of the Premiers' Plan could have been reduced if powerful people had been less dogmatic about the need to reduce state government deficits at almost any cost in terms of human suffering. The analogy may not be too far-fetched.

It has to be recognized that *any* policy to remedy inflation will have an impact on various groups in the community, which will probably be different from the impact of an alternative line of policy. This will also be true of a 'do nothing' policy which, by allowing the inflation to continue unchecked, reduces the real incomes of everyone whose disposable money income rises less rapidly than the prices of the goods and services usually purchased. On the other hand, a continuing rise in money income will benefit anyone whose commitments are fixed in money terms, as used to be the case with interest and repayments on housing loans. The faster the price inflation, however, the more difficult it will be to find anyone likely to benefit from the chaos which is hyper-inflation.

Aside from the direct possibilities, but after inflation has been continuing for some time, more and more people will have taken the likelihood of rising money income into account when making plans for the future. A case in point would be a wage-earning family which has bought a comparatively expensive house, believing that the extra costs would fairly soon be covered by higher earnings. It has to be recognized that some far-sighted people are bound to be disadvantaged by any unexpected reduction in the rate of inflation. Of course this is not an argument against attempting to reduce inflation, but it should serve as a reminder that disinflation may not be equally welcomed by everybody who is affected by it.

The adjustment of wage earnings usually lags behind the rise of consumer prices. Indexation of wages was an attempt to prevent this loss from occurring, or at least to reduce it as far as possible. Unfortunately indexation also tends to perpetuate the effects of rising wage costs on prices, and this undesired result can be reduced by narrowing the scope of indexation and by making the adjustment at less frequent intervals. It was this kind of reasoning that led to the discontinuation of the old 'automatic adjustment' of the basic wage after the 1953 judgment. Whatever may be the consequences of limiting the scope and frequency of indexation for wage bargaining and industrial relations, wage earners have suffered both coming and going—at first because of delay in introducing full indexation, and later because indexation is made less effective to reduce its repercussions on wage costs and prices. Of course, sound reasons can be given to explain why disinflationary policy is bound to have a special impact on wage-earners, if only because wage cost forms such a large part of total cost. The fact remains that, seen from a wage-earner's viewpoint, some aspects of disinflation must appear to be discriminatory and unfair.

Wage-earners and potential wage-earners temporarily in receipt of pensions and cash benefits also include a majority of the people most likely to be affected by reductions in public expenditure. Yet reduction in this kind of expenditure appears likely to play an important part in the choice of measures against inflation. This need not necessarily be so. Disinflation could in theory be achieved by imposing sufficiently high rates of taxation. This would be an appropriate policy if the marginal social product of an increment of public spending were considered to be higher than that of a decrement of private spending, *provided that* the effect of higher tax rates did not seem likely to be 'inflationary' in itself.

Whatever one may believe to be the right answer on the question of marginal changes in public as compared with private spending (and this does genuinely involve a broad political value judgement), it can also be argued that total taxation in Australia is already so high in relation to current output and income that any reduction which may be feasible will itself contribute materially to reducing the rate of inflation. However, to reduce taxation without also reducing public spending would involve recourse to 'inflationary' methods of public finance—inflationary, because in one way or another they would increase the supply of money available to finance the operation of the economy at a higher level of prices. If the 'Colin Clark' effect of taxation is admitted as even a strong possibility, the case for reducing public expenditure follows from it.

If this line of argument is accepted, the need to reduce government spending on goods and services as well as on transfer payments can easily be deduced from the need to reduce taxation. It is sometimes argued also that any transfer of labour from the public to the private sector will increase (measurable) productivity, but this argument has only 'numerical' validity on account of the 'output' of public employees being valued at cost for want of any better method. To say that transfer to the private sector necessarily increases an employee's measured productivity is either a truism or political rhetoric, but has no significance for disinflation in itself.

On the other hand, reduction of public sector employment could result in an increase in the number of people experiencing involuntary unemployment. Although it can no longer be asserted that a simple inverse relationship exists between the level of unemployment and the rate of inflation, the persistence of unemployment can probably be taken as indicating a probability that disinflationary factors are operating in the economy. Any increase in unemployment associated with a decrease in public spending on goods and services would be a somewhat stronger indication. To *increase* public spending in order to reduce unemployment would therefore appear to be simply a negation or contradiction of the disinflationary policy which gave rise to the unemployment in the first place. Perhaps this is the point at which people interested in minimizing unemployment should at least press for a substantial lowering of the general level of interest rates.

Unemployment is a social evil which should be kept to a minimum. When people willing to work are unable to find employment, they have to become economically dependent in order to survive. This dependency is just as real if they rely on relatives instead of on unemployment benefit. Even the strongest people can be weakened by dependency if they remain too long in this condition. Unfortunately, it is the weaker members of the work force who are most likely to experience long-term unemployment–the young, the elderly, the slow learners, the alcoholics, in fact anyone whose productivity may be relatively low. Some of these people may appear to be more deserving than others, but none of them is likely to be improved by experiencing unemployment.

A few economists are already suggesting that, in an economy with considerable experience of inflation, it may be necessary to accept as 'natural' a rate of unemployment a great deal higher than the 1 or 2 per cent which used to be considered tolerable before 1974. To anyone who looks on a job simply as a source of disposable income, it may seem better to compensate the jobless with generous transfer payments, rather than to risk speeding up inflation by providing them with jobs. Economists who advocate this kind of policy must have failed to realize that part of its real cost will be the further degradation of weaker members of the community, whom it will relegate to economic dependency as a semi-permanent status.

The humanitarian case against tolerating an appreciably higher level of normal unemployment can be reinforced by other arguments which may be considered even more important. It has already become clear from available statistics that the incidence of unemployment is particularly high among younger people (apart from the special problem of school-leavers). As the situation in Ireland has illustrated only too well, young men with not enough to do can become a menace to public order, personal safety and even the existence of government itself. Moreover, young women are ceasing to provide a reliable influence in favour of sanity and stability, and in a few cases have proved at least as dangerous as the men. During the last ten years, outbreaks of violence have been sufficiently frequent to suggest that this could be one way in which a modern industrial state might be destroyed from within. A low normal level of unemployment cannot by itself provide any guarantee of freedom from this kind of danger. But any permanent increase in normal unemployment is almost bound to involve a more than proportionate increase in the number of young people potentially available for public mayhem or private atrocities.

What, then, should be the objective in employment policy? Best of all, we should try to return to the state of affairs which used to be considered 'normal', with the rate of unemployment fluctuating around a small percentage generally regarded as acceptable (such as 1 per cent used to be). If we *must* have an industrial reserve army (as Karl Marx called it), let us try to make sure that its members have the chance to undertake useful work, as the Regional Employment Development (RED) Scheme once encouraged them to do. In the longer run, a much more effective effort needs to be made to fit more of the individual pegs into holes of a more appropriate shape. All these seem proper and very important tasks for an economic and social policy which looks beyond the immediate necessities of disinflation in the 1970s.

G. C. HARCOURT

4 On Theories and Policies[1]

There are at least three schools of thought which may be said to underlie current debates on policy, two of which, though they start from different theoretical premises, nevertheless largely inform our present (late 1976 but pre-devaluation) policy stances.[2] They also reflect the philosophy of the leaders of the present government, in so far as they could be said to have a coherent and consistent philosophy. The third school departs from the former two both in theoretical analysis and policy prescription. The three schools are, respectively, the monetarists (which have their greatest though by no means exclusive influence in the Reserve Bank); the Bastard Keynesians (which by and large is the stance of the treasury though there are also aspects of it in the often eclectic approach of the Reserve Bank economists, just as there are some monetarist elements in treasury thinking); and the Post-Keynesians. The Post-Keynesian school is the group of theorists who draw directly on the work of Keynes himself. The most influential members include Joan Robinson and Richard Kahn (that is to say, the people who actually worked with Keynes after he had published the *Treatise* and when he was writing the *General Theory*), and their followers and contemporaries, for example, Nicholas Kaldor. The other major influences are Michal Kalecki, and Marx and the classical political economists, especially as the latter have been interpreted through Piero Sraffa's and Maurice Dobb's edition of and writings on Ricardo, and through Sraffa's own original works, most importantly, the *Production of Commodities*.[3] These are, of course, broad judgements, which try to discern major stances and trends, and to identify dominant themes. Clearly neither Reserve Bank nor treasury officials are homogeneous or abstract labour power.

The Friedman View

Milton Friedman's monetarist philosophy, which has a great influence on aspects of the Reserve Bank's approach, has its ideological roots in Smithian liberalism. It involves a policy of non-intervention, except for the creation and/or preservation of competitive institutions and relatively simple rules for the monetary authorities to follow, together with a much more modest role for the public sector than is the case at the moment. Its theoretical basis also lies in one aspect of the Smithian vision (another aspect leads to Marx and the Post-Keynesians), that of the efficacy and efficiency of the invisible hand, as achieved through the market-clearing properties of freely fluctuating prices in individual markets. The line goes through Walrasian general equilibrium rather than through Marshall, which is more the tradition of the second school in Australia, especially Melbourne—of the Prest era anyway—though not, of course, in the United States. Friedman's life work may be seen from one aspect as a concerted effort to pick off, decade by decade, the principal props of Keynes's system—the rival consumption functions; the relative impact of money versus investment on overall activity and prices; the liquidity preference theory of interest versus Friedman's capital theory; monetary versus fiscal policy; the relative importance of balance sheets *vis-à-vis* income and expenditure accounts; and so on. He wishes to reveal the so-called Keynesian revolution as an abortive aberration in the mainstream of economic theory and, incidentally, make the world safe for free men. (Harry Johnson has been the most prolific, indeed obsessive, expositor of this view. For obvious reasons, Friedman has been more muted, not least because, as Patinkin has argued and Friedman has conceded, Friedman's 'restatement' of the Quantity Theory has Keynesian innovations and attitudes in it.)

The practical implications of Friedman's views include an attack on detailed, and often variable, government intervention on fiscal matters, especially the irresponsibility and dishonesty of taxation through inflation in order to move resources into the public sector, a commitment to simple but sustained monetary rules, and encouragement of attempts to create flexible competitive institutions so that the real world may be made to work as if it were a Walrasian system. The latter is especially true of the attitude to labour markets, where a dislike of minimum wage regulations goes hand in hand with humanitarian plus efficiency support for comprehensive retraining and relocating schemes, coupled with the advocacy of the need for great increases in information flows. Allied with these views and the monetarist's version of the quantity theory of money is the central importance that is given to the role of expectations, especially wage-earners and businessmen's expectations about the future course of prices in relation to their money wage receipts or payments. In particular, Friedman (and Hayek) believe that an economy, left to itself, could find its way to that level of employment where individual labour and product markets clear at the appropriate prices (the natural rate of unemployment), a process that is being continuously frustrated by misguided attempts to run the economy below the natural rate, so creating accelerating inflation. Consequently, practical policy implications must involve intermittent spells of unemployment. The object of this is to create a new climate of more moderate expectations about prices and wages so that the 'correct' relative wage and price structures may be perceived, undistorted by the overall inflationary veil. Furthermore, from such situations, the economy's markets may grope for the 'correct' relative price structure from above the natural rate, as it were, without perpetrating new bouts of accelerating inflation. Hence we have had Reserve Bank support for the treasury's short-sharp-shock thesis (which seems to have been maintained for rather a long time now), its opposition to 'excessive' public sector spending and deficit, its belief in the primacy of curing inflation, and its lukewarm attitudes to the wage indexation experiment. (A Friedmanite variant would be, of course, indexation of everything so that the relative price system would always be revealed, regardless of the overall absolute rate of inflation. Hayek, by contrast, wants a return to a regime of fixed exchange rates in order to impose strict monetary disciplines on governments–or, failing that, have them give up altogether issuing money unless they are shown to be responsible in their behaviour. Otherwise, more acceptable counterfeiters are to take over.) It should be noted that the theoretical underpinnings of the monetarist position–do but leave well alone and all will be well–are not supported by the findings of the modern mathematical work on general equilibrium theory, in particular, the ability of a competitive capitalist economy to grope successfully to an equilibrium, an equilibrium, moreover, which even if it exists, may not be either unique or locally or globally stable.[4] The monetarists' answer is, of course, that the proof of the pudding is in the eating and that their relatively simple, causal models *are* supported by *their* abundant empirical findings.

The Bastard Keynesians

The Bastard Keynesians share a similar micro-economic foundation to that of the monetarists–markets which behave as if they were Walrasian competitive ones–but part company with them on the ability of a capitalist economy left to itself to find its way, even sluggishly, to a full employment equilibrium. That is to say, they accept, correctly in my view, that Keynes's revolutionary contribution was to demonstrate the possibility of underemployment rest states, through the development of the theory of effective demand, as Kregel recently has reminded us.[5] Hence they see a role for government intervention of a macro-economic nature, such as treasury has long been accustomed to do. The Hicks-Hansen *IS-LM* analysis is their main tool of analysis. It is unKeynesian without quotes;[6] nevertheless Keynes himself in the *General Theory* is not entirely free of blame for the micro-economic foundations, though they are Marshallian not Walrasian.[7] Thus Joan Robinson has described Keynes's and the true Keynesian approach, as exemplified in chapter 21 of the *General Theory*, as follows:

> We [the 'British Keynesians'] started from the concept of the Marshallian short-period situation, in which fixed plant, business organisation and the training of labour are all given, and can be more or less utilised according to the level of effective demand. A short-period supply curve relating the level of money prices to the level of activity (at given money-wage rates) led straight from Marshall to the *General Theory*.[8]

Whether we use the Marshallian micro model of Keynes or the Walrasian micro model of the Bastard Keynesians, we have an underlying rationale for the control of both unemployment and inflation centrally to rest in the hands of the treasury through fiscal policy (aided, no doubt, by consultations with their junior partners at the Reserve Bank). The emphasis, though, is on control of the levels of real demands, so that as the product markets work themselves out, derived demands for labour show up in job vacancies plus relative wage movements. These imply, overall, a level of money wages which, given the (short-run) level of productivity, is consistent with reasonable price stability, especially in relation to rates of increase of prices among our trading rivals.

There is, moreover, an element of Keynes's closed economy model in the argument that a cut in real wages is the only way effectively to raise employment, i.e. that a lower real wage is needed in order that the economy may move down the aggregate marginal product of labour curve towards the intersection of the demand and supply curves for labour (which signifies full employment in the labour market). This is, of course, a position which is not achievable automatically by the unaided workings of the capitalist system when there is a failure of effective demand. (In an open economy the lower real wages will also affect imports and exports.)

The micro-economic aspects of the above analysis imply that it is the product wage (the money wage deflated by the price of the products which businessmen sell) which is—in the model—the relevant one for the real wage, marginal product comparison by the profit-maximizing, cost-minimizing businessmen. It is not, in the model, the real wage as seen by the wage-earners (i.e. their money wages deflated by an index of the prices of the commodities which they habitually consume). Yet the call in Australia in 1976 for a cut in real wages, which are said to be too high, has consistently been based on the latter, which is inappropriate even in terms of the theoretical model which props up the analysis. The appropriate calculations which are needed to see whether in fact wages are too high (we would still need to ask, relative to what) would be figures for the export sector wage, the import-competing sector wage, the non-traded goods sector wage, and so on. To my knowledge, these calculations have never been done, or at least, made public. In any event, it would be necessary also to take into account the feedback repercussions on aggregate demand of the means whereby the cuts were brought into effect, and old-fashioned maxim of Keynes which rather seems to have been forgotten in recent discussions.

Supposing such a cut in real wages to have been secured without adverse consequences on planned spending then, the argument goes, there would be the added advantages of (1) allowing the bulk of Australian exports to sell at prices which, though set abroad, nevertheless would promise profits at home, (2) reducing our demand for imported goods at any given level of activity, and (3) raising profits' share in output to a level which, at least indirectly, would encourage a rise in the level of planned investment expenditure. There is no place here for either union power or indexation—hence the unswerving hostility to the latter, and the advocacy by the treasury of the short-sharp-shock thesis (and now the sustained variant) in order to blunt the former. The above theoretical underpinnings thus have the advantage of keeping economic power firmly in the treasury's hands (despite the creation in 1976 of a separate Department of Finance), so adding weight to a natural human tendency to hold on to what has been achieved already and to ward off interlopers. The severity, indeed savagery, of its practical implications for many Australian citizens reflect in part the isolation of the decision-makers in Canberra from the human aspects of their decisions. It also reflects the contempt which practical men of affairs in the treasury (and industry) have for academic criticism and developments. These are considered to be airy-fairy stuff of no practical importance—except, of course, as Frank Davidson once remarked, for those theories of the three years or so when the decision-makers themselves were undergraduates. Then, just for once, theory magically provided the necessary structures of thought which the decision-makers have retained for ever after. (This phenomenon is not confined to decision-makers.)

Post-Keynesianism

Post-Keynesianism, as mentioned, has its roots in Keynes, Kalecki, Sraffa, Marx and the classical political economists. In recent years some have tended to take the Kaleckian rather than the road that Keynes either had taken or may have meant to take—this is especially true of Joan Robinson and her closest followers. It *is* the appropriate road for analysing the present Australian situation, for a number of reasons. First, its micro-economic foundations are to be preferred as being more relevant and realistic. In the Kaleckian framework, an explicit role is given to the administered price sector, usually identified with manufacturing. The typical firm is pictured as having a reverse L-shaped marginal (equals average variable) cost curve, implying a physical limit to production at any moment of time, with actual levels of production usually below this limit. A distinction is made between direct (factory floor) labour and indirect labour (the managing director, supervisory staff and Mrs Mops who will be there as long as the firm does not close down, and so regardless of short-run fluctuations in production).[9] This has the important implication, that as output levels are raised in the short run, overall labour productivity rises, so that it is possible to obtain a shift to profits without there being any change in prices or the size of the mark-up on average variable costs (at normal levels of output) and the costs themselves (the mode of pricing which is taken to be characteristic of this section of industry). The shift to profits has important consequences for the level of private investment expenditure. The other sectors of the economy are viewed as more conventionally competitive, with Marshallian-type demand and supply forces interacting to set prices in markets which are characterized by price-taking by the individuals in them. (Hicks has dubbed these distinctions as fixprice and flexprice respectively.) A theory of the size of the mark-up completes the story—in Kalecki's models, the degree of monopoly, in more recent developments, a link between investment expenditure plans and the resulting finance required is invoked in order to determine its size within the constraints imposed by the extent of the competitive nature of the industry, the level of activity and so on.

Secondly, within the framework, a macro theory of distribution emerges at the same time as a theory of the short-run level of activity. This is especially relevant for today's problems because it focuses directly on the inflationary consequences of inconsistent income distribution demands which are a prominent feature of the present (and past) inflationary puzzles. Thirdly, the framework is explicitly one of political economy, reflecting Kalecki's Marxist background and also Keynes's view that theory was valuable only in so far as it threw light on current problems and contributed in detail to the formation of policy. It involved, moreover, an explicit recognition of what Kalecki called the political trade cycle and the class struggle over distributive shares. He recognized very early on (as did Joan

Robinson and Richard Kahn) that sustained full employment was an open-ended invitation to inflationary pressures through rises in the (efficiency) money-wage rate so that periodic interruptions of it would be needed in order 'to discipline the workers'. (The interruptions also would need to be timed *vis-à-vis* election dates.) Stability of the money wage was the clue to the stability of the whole system. Since Kalecki—and the Post-Keynesians—regard the periodic bouts of unemployment as savage and uncivilized, they, very early on again, sought alternative ways of influencing the overall level of the money-wage and, thus, given the underlying micro foundations, the overall price level: hence Joan Robinson's remark, initially in the mid 1930s, that incomes policy was her middle name.

A further desirable property of the Kaleckian version of the central propositions of the *General Theory* is that it is set in a model of cyclical growth, a model of motion, the happenings of one short period influencing the behaviour of the next. '. . . the long-run trend is but a slowly changing component of a chain of short-period situations; it has no independent entity'.[10] Furthermore, the model is explicitly set in a class context where the producing, spending and saving behaviour of broad sociological groups are differentiated and explained. (In Australia, one immediately thinks of exporters, manufacturers and wage-earners as a preliminary broad classification.) Moreover, the process of development over time is seen as a reproducing and expanding one (not necessarily steadily, of course) in which profit-making and capital accumulation are ends in themselves, not means to the end of maximizing the satisfactions of individuals through the patterns of their lifetime consumption. Again Kalecki is to be preferred to Keynes, in that Keynes has individual psychological underpinnings to his aggregate consumption function so that saving is discussed in terms of individuals' choices between the present and the future, rather than as a function of what particular classes are meant to do and are able to do, which is a characteristic of Kalecki's approach, and which, in my view, is the more relevant and realistic model of the process of accumulation in capitalist economies.

The above views have fundamental implications for the attitudes which will be taken to economic policy in general, especially when allocation over time is no longer seen to be the necessary product of an efficient price system. (Thus it could be argued that the recent clash over the company taxation portions of the *Mathews Committee Report* may be explained in terms of two very different 'visions' of how society may be thought of as working. One view is Chicago, the other is Keynesian-Marxist in spirit.) Of course, it must be pointed out that the Post-Keynesian model as a method of theory nevertheless can encompass a wide range of political attitudes and ideologies—from Keynes plus compassion through Crosland socialism and Wedgwood Benn-ery to a Marxist restructuring of the whole society. Hence, it has also been criticized as principally a closed economy model, so that when open economy puzzles have been considered, there has tended to be a rather *ad hoc* advocacy of specific controls.

Keynes has often been criticized for making the money-wage level exogenous to his system, for examining the implications of changes in money-wages but not asking first how they came about and whether there was endogenous process involved in it all. There is some merit in the criticism, as far as Keynes himself is concerned, though it could be said in his defence that an assumption of relative constancy made more sense as a practical starting point when he was writing the *General Theory* than it would in the post-war world. Moreover, there is an endogenous story told in Book Five of the *General Theory*, though it is never spelt out very fully or far,[11] and the question of sustained full employment and the money wage was not discussed. Nevertheless, as Paul Davidson and Sidney Weintraub have documented in detail, Keynes was fundamentally correct in seeing the central importance of efficiency wage stability for the stability of the system as a whole and his immediate followers—Kahn and Joan Robinson, for example—have carried on the analysis of the implications of this fundamental insight in very great detail indeed.[12] In recent years they have been joined by Hicks[13] and Phelps Brown, who see an important part of the post-war inflationary problem as founded in sociological and historical learning patterns, allied with deeply ingrained notions of 'fair' wages (which include a notion of a 'fair' rate of increase). This implies that long-established relativities are hallowed, and any major rupturings produce havoc. Phelps Brown has also stressed even more what he believes to be the inflationary consequences of what he sees as the shift in the balance of power to unions.[14]

One advantage that Keynes had over Kalecki in the development of the Post-Keynesian tradition was that Keynes was first and foremost a monetary economist, so that the *General Theory* was a major modification of Keynes's intended *magnum opus*, the *Treatise*. Much of the latter's monetary analysis was still regarded by Keynes as relevant, to be taken as given as a background to the *General Theory*. Hyman Minsky has made this the central theme of his interpretation of the *General Theory*,[15] as has Paul Davidson in *Money and the Real World*.[16] Minsky shows that the rich balance sheet analysis of firms and households of the *Treatise*, together with the new developments of the *General Theory*, imply that the main model of the *General Theory* is a theory of the (real and monetary) cyclical development of the economy. The cycles arise from the implications of disappointed expectations concerning cash flows, the accompanying distorted balance sheet patterns relative to income and expenditure accounts, themselves the products of changing states of confidence and expectations, and the reactions of firms and households to them and to their effects on the markets for financial assets. This is not to say that Kalecki ignored monetary factors. The principle of increasing risk is still a relevant part of the story and his two-sided link between profits and investment, whereby the former are both the inducement for and the means to enable, directly and indirectly, the financing of investment, are the basic ingredients of the Post-Keynesian theory of investment. The Minsky-Davidson-Keynes-Kalecki strands together may be seen as constituting the outline of a plausible alternative story to that of the monetarists (and to that of Tobin) in trade cycle analysis and the role of monetary policy.

Finally, Kalecki's approach to the theory of investment is preferable to Keynes, for it explicitly deals with plans, construction and final implementation, explicitly taking account of the time lapses between them. As we have seen, this allows the economic process to be modelled as the happenings of one short period growing out of another. Kalecki was prepared to be more cavalier than Keynes in his treatment of time. Keynes in the end thought it best to give up trying to handle time processes in analytical detail (even though he had done this successfully in the *Treatise*). He settled instead for the theory of effective demand, the possibility of underemployment equilibria (rest states), ignoring in order to make this central point (and also because he believed it was not possible to find a 'determinate time unit'), lags, processes and feedback phenomena, especially amongst expectations.

Policy Approaches

With the above as background let us finally turn to a discussion of policy approaches, both of recent years and for the future. In general, the events of recent years, especially the behaviour of the Liberal-Country Party coalition when in opposition and its method of coming to power, culminating in the governor-general's actions of 11 November 1975, make very poor the chances of conservative governments in Australia being able successfully to implement policies which would be consistent with Post-Keynesian analysis, even if they wished to, which clearly they do not. Moreover, the experiences of the Whitlam government while in office also make for scepticism about the chances of a social democratic government implementing successfully a 'Keynes plus compassion' policy such as that attempted by Labor. This reflects not only Labor's inexperience and, at times, incompetence, silliness and lack of resolution, and the extraordinarily difficult general problems faced by the Labor administration, but, more importantly, fundamental and deep-seated power sources in the political and economic structure of Australian capitalism. These together imposed constraints which virtually ruled out the Labor government's ability to act in certain ways. The constraints are set by both domestic and overseas business interests, by the power struggles and differing ideologies within the Labor and trade union movements themselves, by what the federal and state public services themselves will tolerate, and by the privately controlled media, all of which militate against fundamental changes in the public-private sector split, or major redistributions of wealth and income.[17] The 'animal spirits' of Australian business are so susceptible to policies which it feels to be against its own interests (whether its perceptions are right or not is another matter) and its ability to act by reducing investment spending is so effective, as to make the room for manoeuvre by a Whitlam-type government extremely limited indeed. The practical alternative, therefore, may be a reversion to a Lewis-type policy[18] whereby private consumer spending leads in both recovery and in sustained growth (in the latter accompanied by private investment spending), aided by a restructured tax system, with the public sector taking an increasingly modest role in the provision of goods and services.

Another alternative approach whereby the socialist nettle, such as is outlined in Stuart Holland's *The Socialist Challenge*,[19] suitably modified for Australian conditions, is grasped, seems far from being an election winner, or at least as being perceived as such by those who make policy and political decisions in the ALP. It seems unlikely then that there is yet another alternative, that of creating in Australia consensus policies embodying genuine *money* income restraints and what Joan Robinson has called 'a real social contract which would satisfy the reasonable demands of the workers for more control over their own work, more security against redundancy, better social services and so forth'.[20]

But, if this alternative were possible, what forms would it take? As far as maintaining a high level of employment and a satisfactory rate of growth is concerned (its composition will need attention, too, but that is another story for the moment), the single most important institutional change required in Australia is the creation of effective machinery with which to ensure that, by and large, we obtain the level and rate of change of prices which is acceptable, largely independently of measures designed to affect the level of employment and the rate of economic growth and its composition. Post-Keynesian theory suggests that there is a wide range of the level of activity over which money wages and prices may be regarded as independent of the level of activity, at least for quite substantial periods of time. It is this proposition that needs to be exploited. Of course, we already have gone rather haltingly and reluctantly towards establishing such a set of institutions, with the introduction of pre-tax and now post-tax indexation procedures. These constitute in effect a form of incomes policy which is historically and sociologically suited to the Australian industrial environment. Indexation is understood and by and large trusted by our wage-earning groups, and present attempts by the government and its advisers to smash it seem tragically ill-advised. As argued elsewhere,[21] it is the major reform that can remove the overriding anxiety of each wage-earning group in a period of inflation, namely that its absolute real income may be eroded. In its absence, each group of necessity pitched its money-wage demands towards the upper limit of what was considered to be feasible, and employers individually were inclined to acquiesce, with the result that the overall outcome was to give an intolerably high level and rate of increase of overall money wages and therefore prices. This led inevitably to savage fiscal and monetary policies designed to bring the rates down, policies that proved ineffectual in their aims and disastrous and tragic in their by-products. It was a weakness of the initial arguments for indexation that, in so far as they were concerned with tackling inflation, they were coupled with egalitarian considerations. Thus flat rate adjustments other than at the bottom end of the scale were advocated in order to narrow differentials. Another major weakness, given the inflation rates that had been experienced and which were to come, was not immediately to couple pre-tax indexation with post-tax indexation.

Of course, indexation by itself is not a panacea. It needs to be coupled with a relativities *plus* productivity element, that is to say, a wage fund over and above that already spoken for by the indexation procedure proper. Its size would be determined by considerations such as whether the economy is in a transition state, as far as the creation of new institutions is concerned, or whether it has reached its new ongoing path, with the institutions securely established. The fund would allow ruptured relativities to be restored (not necessarily in one fell swoop),* for relativities to change if seemingly irresistable forces suggest that this is desirable, and for all groups to receive money wage increases which allow them to absorb their share of any general rise in prosperity that is implied by the underlying trend in national productivity, if and when the latter is resumed.† What must

* The danger is that the recent inflationary experience together with plateau and/or partial indexation procedures may have so ruptured previously long-established norms that, now, no concensus may be established as to what *is* the structure which ought to be restored. Moreover, there may no longer be that measure of good will with which to allow a new pattern either to be agreed upon or arrived at.

† Even if productivity growth *is* zero, it may well be necessary to have a fund with which to tackle the inherited stock of ruptured relativities over a transition phase. Of course, a successful attack on inflation itself should allow productivity to start growing again.

be appreciated is that the same *real* gains may be realized by employed persons through a myriad of money wage and price combinations, but only a small range of them is consistent with the other aims of high employment, reasonable growth and remaining competitive in comparison with our main overseas rivals. The quid pro quo for the *money*-wage constraint involved would be the provision of goods and services through the public sector which is beneficial in particular to the wage-earning sectors and their children. Such, of course, was the rationale of much of Labor's programme. This means that by wage-earners foregoing unduly inflationary pressures on money-wage levels and, indeed, at times being prepared to make some sacrifice in the rate of increase of their real take-home pay, the government in return would be in a position to ensure jobs and redistribute resources in a more egalitarian manner, while at the same time maintaining activity at a level which ensures that adequate investment is undertaken, and profits earned, by the private sector.

Finally, governments must put forward explicitly coherent and integrated policies, the framework and broad targets of which are fully explained to all relevant sectors. Then, they must show a determination to stick to them regardless of the inevitable flak from the various interested groups who may be adversely affected, at least in the short run and sometimes permanently. Inflexibility, of course, must not be made the only virtue. There should be minor detailed alternatives and some room for manoeuvre. Nevertheless, resolution and defined objectives, of which all are made aware, are definitely needed and have been conspicuously absent in the policies of governments of recent years.

References

1 Comments on a draft of this chapter were made by John Burbridge, Jon Cohen, Ronald Henderson, Mervyn Lewis, Ian McLean, and the editors; however, they must be completely absolved from responsibility for *any* views expressed here.

2 Mervyn Lewis has pointed out that there is a fourth school which may be dubbed 'structuralist' and which considers macro policy from an essentially orthodox micro basis. Members include F. H. Gruen, R. G. Gregory and the I.A.C. economists. Although their influence on policy may have been considerable, it is not discussed in this chapter.

3 P. Sraffa, *Production of Commodities by Means of Commodities. Prelude to a Critique of Economic Theory* (Cambridge University Press, Cambridge, 1960).

4 See, for example, F. H. Hahn, 'The winter of our discontent', *Economica*, xl, 1973, pp. 322-30.

5 See J. A. Kregel, 'Economic methodology in the face of uncertainty; the modelling methods of Keynes and the post-Keynesians', *Economic Journal*, vol. 86, 1976, pp. 209-25.

6 The best short account of why, is the Appendix to Donald Moggridge's Fontana Modern Masters biography of *Keynes* (Fontana/Collins, London, 1976). The basic reason is the non-independence of the *LM* and *IS* curves. They interrelate through

the medium of interrelated and changeable expectations, so that movements of one (or along one), unless very marginal, inevitably imply movements, not always predictable, of the other. 'If both curves shift, there is no clear prediction possible . . . as to what the final outcome will be' (p. 166).

7 Three years later, in his *Economic Journal* comment on Dunlop's and Tarshis's findings on real and money wages over the cycle, Keynes changed his position and enunciated what must be one of the earliest statements of the normal cost-pricing hypothesis that now is characteristic of the micro-economic foundations of Post-Keynesian theory: see *The Collected Writings of John Maynard Keynes. The General Theory of Employment, Interest and Money*, vol. VII (Macmillan, London, 1973), appendix 3, pp. 406-12. No doubt it was all in Marshall anyway.

8 Joan Robinson, 'Review of A. Leijonhufvud, *On Keynesian Economics and the Economics of Keynes*, 1968', *Economic Journal*, vol. 79, 1969, p. 582. Putting the two strands, Hicks–Hansen and Marshall, together, the model may be set out in terms of two simple diagrams which allow the price level to be introduced explicitly: see G. C. Harcourt, 'A Post-Keynesian development of the "Keynesian" Model', in Edward J. Nell (ed.), *Growth, Profit and Property: Essays in the Revival of Political Economics* (Cambridge University Press, New York, forthcoming), pp. 12-14.

9 Of this group, cleaners are probably the most vulnerable in situations of sustained unemployment.

10 M. Kalecki, 'Trend and business cycles reconsidered', *Economic Journal*, vol. 78, 1968, p. 263.

11 This was in keeping with Keynes's method in his book, as he wrote to Hicks (see Moggridge, *Keynes*, p. 92), of not 'pursuing anything very far, [his] object being to press home as forcibly as possible certain fundamental opinions–and no more'.

12 In particular, I would refer readers to Kahn's masterly paper, 'On re-reading Keynes' (The British Academy Keynes Lecture, 1974). Kahn's analysis of the roles of money and money-wages in Keynes's own thought and in the Post-Keynesian tradition is absolutely authoritative. Incidentally, he outlines a package deal which in essentials corresponds to the analysis and policies most favoured in this paper, see, especially, pp. 30-2.

13 John Hicks, *The Crisis in Keynesian Economics*, The 1974 Yrjö Jahnsson lectures (Basil Blackwell, Oxford), Lecture 3; 'What is wrong with Monetarism', *Lloyds Bank Review*, no. 118 (October 1975), pp. 1-13.

14 Henry Phelps Brown, *Collective Bargaining Reconsidered* (Stamp Memorial Lecture, London 1971), pp. 12-13; 'A non-monetarist view of the pay explosion', *Three Banks Review*, no. 105 (March 1975), pp. 3-24.

15 Hyman P. Minsky, *John Maynard Keynes* (Columbia University Press, New York, 1975).

16 Macmillan, London, 1972.

17 There are other ratchet-type effects which put (some) constraints on *cuts* in expenditure, e.g. the education lobby, and structural changes, e.g. the protectionist lobby.

18 M. K. Lewis, 'Why aren't taxes cut?' *Australian Financial Review*, October 19 and 20, 1976.

19 Quartet Books, London, 1975.

20 Press release of public lecture in Adelaide, April 1975. Joan Robinson was clearly pessimistic about the chances of such a policy actually coming about; nor was her heart in it anyway, for she would prefer to see society restructured on much more radical lines. However, James Meade and his happy band of intelligent radicals seem much more confident of success, as indeed we all might be, if only our worlds were exclusively inhabited by civilized, humane and enlightened James Meades, and we had as much confidence as he has in the Bastard Keynesian aspects of his analysis: see James E. Meade, *The Intelligent Radical's Guide to Economic Policy. The Mixed Economy* (Allen and Unwin, London, 1975).

21 G. C. Harcourt, 'The social consequences of inflation', *Australian Accountant*, 44, 1974, pp. 520-8.

J. P. NIEUWENHUYSEN

5 The New Inflation

... We have now not only a much more permissive society but also a permissive economy. The old inhibitions—the fear of unemployment, the fear of loss of markets—which supplied some of the rigidities which could curb inflation, are crumbling.

R. I. Downing[1]

The great economic problem of our time for the western world is inflation ... the prevention [of which] involves far more than technical economic knowledge. Monetary and fiscal policy can accomplish a good deal, but the political consequences of relying upon these instruments have proved unacceptable. Given the constraints faced by democratic governments, more drastic intervention seems inevitable, even for the most market-prone administrations.

Walter Galenson[2]

There has been a tendency in the 'hard core' of the literature in Australian economics to treat discussions of prices and incomes policy with the kindly indulgence normally reserved for the irrelevant and intellectually second rate. It is true that, to their credit, two publications, the *Journal of Industrial Relations* and the *Australian Economic Review*, have taken a regular interest in this important branch of economics. And some progress has been made in recent years in arousing public awareness of the social and institutional issues surrounding the problem of inflation. But, in broaching the issue of institutional reforms which might be necessary to bolster the tools of economic regulation in Australia, some commentators have felt the need to be circumspect. Attention to the 'uneasy triangle' of the reconciliation of free collective bargaining (or 'independent' wage fixing), full employment and price stability seemed largely, in the period up to 1970, to belong in fields less economically Elysian than Australia's. And it was only a small minority of authors who, in the 1960s, gave attention to the subject of institutional props for conceivably ineffectual monetary and fiscal policies.[3]

In the 1970s, however, the scene has changed. It is no doubt true that time-honoured remedies in the shape of monetary and budgetary controls are still believed by many policy makers to be the sole salvation against inflation. But analysis of the 'new inflation', that is of rising prices in the absence of excess aggregate demand, has produced some alterations. Traditional institutions of wage fixing have been adaptable and flexible, and substantial initiatives have been taken by the Conciliation and Arbitration Commission, inducing some heady claims about the efficacy of the wage fixing system in retarding the rate of increase of wages (and prices). Where the truth lies is open to question. But, wherever it resides, the adaptation of social institutions, and the psychology of wage, spending and saving behaviour, are now more than ever in the post-war period, at the centre of the stage of the policy maker's deliberations.

The Elements of the New Inflation

The progenitors of post World War II full employment policies, such as Beveridge and Keynes, were clearly aware that success in achieving full employment could spell a more rapid rate of increase of prices. Beveridge, for example, pointed out that 'there is no inherent mechanism in our present system, which can with certainty prevent competitive sectional bargaining for wages from setting up a vicious spiral of rising prices under full employment'.[4] And Keynes warned that

> some people argue that a capitalist country is doomed to failure (in preserving stability of internal prices) because it will be found impossible in conditions of full employment to prevent a progressive increase of wages. According to this view, severe slumps and recurrent periods of unemployment have been hitherto the only effective means of holding efficiency wages (wages per unit of output) within a reasonably stable range. Whether this is so remains to be seen. The more conscious we are of this problem, the likelier we shall be to surmount it.[5]

These comments found an echo in Australia in the White Paper on full employment, published in 1945, which noted that policy would need to 'avoid inflationary pressures on prices . . . [and] ensure . . . that undue sectional pressure for wage increases does not lead merely to a rising spiral of wages and prices without any real benefit—and perhaps with disadvantage—to the workers themselves . . .'[6] Similarly, Giblin saw the danger that '. . . organised interests (may) go their accustomed way, with all take and no give . . . productivity falls . . . (and) inflation is in full career . . .'[7]

The concern about the inflationary consequences of full employment which was adumbrated in these remarks was not, however, transposed to specific remedies or radical policy experimentations, at least in the first fifteen or so years after World War II.[8] But, after the end of the 1950s there emerged, in many industrialized market economies other than Australia, renewed interest and vigorous willingness to adapt institutions and policies to try to contain inflation. The causes of this activity naturally derived partly from the general price increases themselves, and the attendant balance of payments traumas; but also from a stronger conviction that cost factors were playing an important causatory part in inflation. For example, a study by the Organization for European Economic Co-operation, *The Problem of Rising Prices*, in 1961 stressed the importance of wage cost-push forces in causing inflation, and called for national wage policies. Nearly a decade later, in December 1970, the successor body, the Organization for Economic Co-operation and Development, issued a report entitled *Inflation: The Present Problem*, the main theme of which reiterated the need for member countries to adopt incomes policies. And during the decade of the sixties, a long list of nations had embarked upon a series of adventures in incomes policy.[9] The decision to do so, however, appeared to be based primarily on the day-to-day frustrations which governments experienced in trying to attain—in swiftly changing circumstances—traditional economic goals with familiar tools of management. The emergence of new theoretical ideas about the range of economic tools and the assignment of each to a particular end in the attainment of joint internal and external balance received little explicit recognition from policy makers.

However, even if a 'theory of incomes policy' did not emerge as a justification for excursions in the field, common themes characterized the analysis of the 'new inflation' and the policies which were thought necessary to counteract it. In particular, the traditional (allegedly unreal) marginal productivity theory of wage determination was criticized, and the scant attention paid to the role of wage bargaining and power forces pointed to. It was averred that, instead, a specially important pattern of wage behaviour—the leap-frogging sequences enclosed in wage contours—should be accorded special concern by policy makers. As the former chairman of the British National Board for Prices and Incomes, Mr Aubrey Jones, put it:

> 'An inherited body of thought retains a powerful hold over the minds of men long after the moment of utterance, and the thinking [along marginal productivity theory] lines still does. It is, however, at odds with what we observe in contemporary society, because it would be more realistic to say that the present-day phenomenon is one of "wage leadership". In other words, a "leading" sector grants wage increases which set the pace for other sectors to follow.'[10]

Furthermore, Mr Jones added, 'sometimes it is not just the pay increase accruing to someone else which is followed, but the absolute differentials in levels of pay'.[11]

The 'new inflation' analysis also viewed the psychology which employees brought to bear upon wage determination as an intimate part of a wider social and economic context. In this, there was thought to be a twentieth century struggle for economic equality which paralleled in its intensity the nineteenth century struggles for political equality. An important manifestation of this psychology was said to be that employees had become accustomed to a certain annual rate of increase in real standards of living, and that they acted in advance of foreseen events. Trade unions were viewed as political bodies, rather than the economic monopolies so cherished in economics texts. Individuals, it was said, should not be regarded as behaving in markets solely in an economic strait-jacket—'once allowance is made for social aspects, inflation can also be [properly] seen as a phenomenon with important social and political roots'.[12]

The different attitude to collective bargaining and the role of unions was eloquently epitomised by the words of E. H. Phelps Brown in 1971:

> 'We are in the presence of a transformation in the working of collective bargaining . . . today the bargaining power of a group depends much less on the state of the market than on the accident of its being placed where the withdrawal of its labour at any time can inflict damage . . . The upshot of these changes in the form and style of bargaining power has been twofold. First, there is cost inflation . . . [and] second, [as] an integral part of the first process, there is a continual disturbance of relativities, and an embittered endeavour to re-establish them. Today salaried employees and wage-earners alike are aware of the changes going on in rates of pay over a wider field of comparison than ever before, and they are more able than ever before to assert their own notions of what their relativities should be. But what comes out of this is only a leap-frogging into inflation . . . Collective bargaining has ceased to be a form of self-government in industry, or a tussle for shares in the product between capital and labour, or the negotiation of a price in a given state of the market.'[13]

The Australian View

While overseas countries were experimenting with incomes policies in the 1960s, what was happening in Australia? In discussion of economic policy in general, and in particular of the institutions of wage fixation, there was, of course, considerable reference in Australia to a large number of issues that are germane to incomes policy. But there were at least three reasons why Australian economic management in the 1960s did not emulate the prevalent international fashion for incomes policy experiments. The first reason was Australia's relatively very favourable experience in the degrees of price stability and employment that were attained: in the period of 1960–9, the average annual rate of increase in prices was only 2·5 per cent, and the level of unemployment never rose above 1·5 per cent of the work force, averaging less than 1 per cent. Compared with the anguished cries of overseas governments at this time, the Australian administration, no doubt, felt able to adopt a relatively sanguine attitude. The second reason for a comparative lack of policy action was perhaps the view that the available system of wage determination in Australia afforded one of the main ingredients of an incomes policy-making body, albeit only for one half of the problems of incomes, namely wages. As J. E. Isaac said in 1964, 'we have in Australia, if not the full substance, at least the skeleton and the potential basis of a machinery for incomes policy'.[14]

But the main cause of a lack of experimentation with incomes policies in Australia in the sixties was probably the view of the 'received' economic doctrine in Australia that the available tools of economic policy were adequate to the task which they were called upon to perform. Incomes policy, which is usually regarded as a device to bolster the operation of macro-economic management, is of course also concerned with the workings of micro-economic institutions, i.e. with the processes of wage and price determination, and with the ways in which it may be possible to influence these processes so as to minimize their impact upon inflation. Yet in the Australian economics literature of the decade of the sixties, it is very easy to show that the 'received doctrine' in highly regarded texts ignored almost entirely the issues with which incomes policy and the new inflation were concerned. Numerous examples could be cited.

It was only at the end of 1970 that discussion of a 'new' inflation was embarked upon in Australia. In the literature which began mushrooming at this time, echoes were at last heard of the overseas concern for different institutions to deal with changed social and psychological circumstances. A number of authors called for some form of prices and incomes policy. However, these proponents appeared more certain of the need for such policies than of the actual shape which they might take.[15] And the responses of the Liberal government in the period 1970–2, when calls for an incomes policy were being regularly made, were scarcely positive. The Commonwealth government, despite amendments to the Conciliation and Arbitration Act, found the prospect of political unpopularity (which might well have flowed from any attempt to establish 'norms' for wage behaviour) too great an inhibition to interventionist action. Strangely, when the Labor government came to power in

December 1972, and when the minister of labour, Clyde Cameron, subsequently seemed to encourage unbounded wage rises, the calls for restraint by incomes policy proponents were little in evidence.

Wage and Tax Indexation

Between the first quarters of 1973 and 1975, average weekly earnings per male unit in Australia rose by almost exactly 50 per cent. Between the December quarters of 1973 and 1974 alone, male earnings increased by 27·7 per cent and average female earnings by 34·8 per cent.[16] This very rapid rise in earnings over a two-year period was instrumental in producing policy alterations of an intriguing kind which, in an innovative way, reflected a changed direction of thinking and analysis on the causes of inflation. The new devices were (1) the policy of wage indexation applied by the Conciliation and Arbitration Commission, beginning with the decision in the April 1975 national wage case; and (2) the policy of personal income tax indexation, based on the recommendation of the Mathews Committee Report,[17] which was adopted by the Liberal-Country Party government from 1 July, 1976. Both forms of indexation grew from suppositions or notions about the way in which the 'new inflation' was being promoted, and depended for their efficacy upon the correctness of essentially sociological propositions. In this respect, they must be counted as conceptually important deviations from the rather mechanistic preconceptions about economic regulation to which traditional attitudes to inflation may have been more prone.

Initially, the possibility of a return to *wage indexation* had been resurrected by the Labor government in 1973 as a potential instrument of equity. But, following the dramatic rises in earnings in 1973 and 1974, the policy of indexation as actually adopted by the Conciliation and Arbitration Commission in 1975 was, in effect, a wage restraint initiative. The wage indexation decisions rested partly on the interesting supposition that, if most employees were to be assured that the real purchasing power of wages would be preserved, wage claims outside the indexation guide-lines and the arbitral system would be limited. And, in the wake of the implementation of the Commission's policy, it did appear that the guide-lines were being adhered to, and there was quite clearly a substantial reduction in the rate of increase of average earnings (which dropped from some 30 per cent in 1974 to only 12 per cent in 1975).

The debate surrounding the introduction of (income) *tax indexation* is of equal interest. Again, the adoption of the policy depended upon a sociological supposition, namely that the wage explosion of 1973 and 1974 was a function of the joint impact of inflation and the high marginal rates of tax applying in Australia. It was argued that the combined pressures of this Mephistophelean merger induced individuals to seek annual wage rises of an order of 30–40 per cent, since these were what was required to maintain real after tax purchasing power. (A particularly influential table in the Mathews Report was number III–12, which indicated that a 39 per cent increase in gross income was necessary in 1974 for a tax payer on average earnings to achieve a 5 per cent increase in real disposable income.)

The adoption by the Conciliation and Arbitration Commission of wage indexation and by the Commonwealth government of tax indexation therefore represented an important addition—based on a 'new inflation' analysis—to the range of economic policy. But the insecure, ephemeral bases on which these ventures were founded was reflected in the equally flimsy means that were available for their testing. For example, while some commentators claimed that the reduction in the rate of wage increases between 1974 and 1975 was the result of indexation, others insisted that the decline had been caused by the changed balance of labour supply and demand, i.e. the rapid growth of unemployment from mid-1974.[18] While some notions of the causes and cures for the new inflation have, therefore, reached the Australian literature of the seventies, the debates on the subject have continued to be founded in seemingly endemic polarizations.

Institutional Changes

Apart from the debate and initiatives on tax and wage indexation, the 'new inflation' might well have been expected to induce experiments in institutional adaptation. The Prices Justification Tribunal, established in 1973, fell partly into this category. In the Labor Party policy speech prior to the November 1972 general election, Gough Whitlam announced that a Labor government would exert its power over prices: 'We will establish a Prices Justification Tribunal not only because inflation will be the major economic problem facing Australia over the next three years, but because industrial co-operation and goodwill is being undermined by the conviction among employees that the price of labour alone is subject to regulation and restraint.' Despite these intentions for the Tribunal, its early years of operation coincided with high rates of general price increase and with a marked rise in the incidence of industrial unrest. In the first two years of the Labor administration, between 1973 and 1975, it seemed the positive intention of government to encourage wage rises while price surveillance was exercised. (Indeed it may have been the hope of some Labor ministers to effect, by this policy, a redistribution of income away from profits and towards wages). The Tribunal was part of a series of events and influences which served to compress the share of profits, demoralize the business community, and adversely influence the investment and employment decisions made during the recession which culminated in 1974.

The recent history of the Tribunal is discussed at length elsewhere.[19] The important point for present purposes is, however, that the 'new inflation' analysis apparently formed no effective part of the policy consciousness of those who created the Tribunal, and who were responsible for actions on fronts other than prices justification. Greater public and government awareness of the issues in overseas prices and incomes policies might well have avoided the combination of government enthusiasm for wage rises coupled with private sector price restraint. On the other hand, the usefulness of the Tribunal as a standing 'concept' of policy seemed established when the Liberal-Country Party government decided in 1976 to retain it, despite firm promises of abolition before the 1975 election. And some would say in the Tribunal's favour that the centralizing changes which it appeared (at least partly and indirectly) to have wrought on the processes of wage bargaining did in fact assist the successful implementation of wage indexation in the April 1975 national wage case.

Apart from the Prices Justification Tribunal (which, as suggested, was scarcely employed in a manner that portrayed sensitivity to the ordinary overall objects of co-ordinated price surveillance bodies) there was also the question of power over prices and incomes. The Australian constitution does not permit the Commonwealth government direct power over prices, and when the Whitlam administration sought this power by referendum in November 1973, it was denied. This absence of constitutional power over prices has naturally differentiated the prices and wages policies undertaken in Australia when compared with Britain, the United States and many other countries. In Britain and the United States, for example, efforts to contain the 'new inflation' have included full circles of policies, graduating from attempts at voluntary compliance up to statutory schemes including freezes, and returning once more to voluntarism. It has been claimed, for example, that the shock of the August 1971 price freeze in the United States (which came after very recent presidential disclaimers on the need for price control) had a very great psychological impact on the community. Would power to freeze prices in Australia not afford similarly desirable scope to the authorities? Economists are divided upon this issue. But while the need for price and wage powers are pressed by many influential voices, it needs to be remembered that—on the prices side—no firm has failed to accept the Prices Justification Tribunal's recommendations. On the other hand, it is clear that, in contending with the 'new inflation', Australian economic policy is constitutionally haltered in a way that does not apply in many industrialized market economies. Some might contend, however, that this halter is not as heavy as the manacles of the mind which impede institutional innovation.

The Machinery of Economic Policy

Overseas attempts to contain the 'new inflation' have included variations in the machinery of economic policy formulation. While weathered students of the Public Service might be sceptical about the capacity for the improvement of economic advice through altering the channels of its creation, the pressure of economic events has encouraged experimentation. In Australia, however, the new inflation has failed, up to 1976, to produce attempts at adaptation. Criticism of the old order has been incidental and resistance to change powerful. It is true that, under the Labor administration between 1972–5, the role of the prime minister's department in offering economic advice was strengthened. However, the 1976 *Report of the Royal Commission on Australian Government Administration* (para. 10.1.1) stated that:

> Submissions and other material before the Commission made it clear that there was widespread dissatisfaction with existing means for the formulation and co-ordination of government economic policy. Ministers and ex-ministers, business men and trade union leaders, academic economists, and officials of departments and agencies within the bureaucracy all voiced criticisms. While, not surprisingly, the content of the criticisms varied, one set of themes tended to recur. It was argued that the Treasury held a substantial monopoly as the source of economic and financial advice and that, partly as a consequence, it had developed an almost doctrinal attitude about the theoretical basis on which policy should be developed. This, it was suggested, had led to its being insensitive to government priorities; to a failure to present ministers with a full range of options; to an isolation of policy from the influences of other departments, of professional economists outside government, and of the community—especially those sections of it actively engaged in production and commerce. While the Commission accepted that this criticism, certainly in such a bald and over-simplified form, was at least exaggerated, it could not ignore the strength and persistence with which it emerged.

The Commission's recommendation was that a department, to be called the Department of Industries and the Economy (DINDEC), be created. Its function would be with the medium and long-term aspects of industrial structure, and to act as the prime source of advice on these issues of policy. It was envisaged that DINDEC would be the source of forward-looking economic intelligence, particularly as it related to structural developments in industry; and that its concern would be with persisting and development changes rather than with short-term macro-economic fluctuations. The Department's time horizon was seen as medium and long-term, and the policies with which it would be concerned were those designed to exercise their influence progressively and often indirectly.

The proposal for the creation of DINDEC was not, however, taken up by the Liberal-Country Party government in 1976. Instead, the treasury was split in two, one portion remaining the Department of the Treasury, and concerned with economic policy advice, the other titled the Department of Finance, and concerned with the management and surveillance of public expenditure. Moreover, the Liberal government declined to support moves for Commonwealth power over prices and incomes. It thus echoed the conservative attitude to the machinery of economic policy which a former Liberal prime minister, Sir Robert Menzies, had adumbrated in rejecting the Vernon proposals in 1965.

Informed Public Discussion

It is not only, however, that there has been a resistance to change the traditional machinery of economic policy in Australia in response to the 'new inflation'. There has also been a considerable reluctance on the part of government to encourage a full flow of information upon which open public discussion could be based. The 1976 Royal Commission Report on Administration, referred to above, emphasized (p. 305) that the government and certain agencies within the administration, such as the treasury and the Bureau of Statistics, 'have a special responsibility to provide the means for a high level of public understanding and debate on economic policy'. However, although the flow of bare statistics (but not of official forecasts of national income and economic indicators) is reasonably adequate, it cannot be claimed that there is a satisfactory flow of 'policy justification' from powerful government departments, such as the treasury. For example, although the treasury was, it seemed, advising a general economic policy in 1976 which was opposed by a large body of opinion, there was very little effort on the treasury's part to fully explain the rationale of its view. The most explicit defence available appears to be a brief reference tucked away in the 1976 budget papers (statement no. 2, p. 21). The treasurer, of course, was liable (before and after devaluation, and in other matters) to confidently uphold his own and to equally confidently denounce his opponents' views. But this does not meet what the Royal Commission referred to (p. 305) as 'an effective and informed debate within and outside the decision-making machinery on economic policy issues (and) a meaningful two-way consultation process on economic policies between government and community interests'. (Although the formation in 1976 of the Economic Consultative Group, consisting of people from both sides of industry, as a regular channel of communication with the government, is an improvement.)

Perhaps one of the major issues in informed public discussion is whether or not official short and longer term forecasts should be published. The treasury has argued (before the Royal Commission, p. 305) 'against the publication of forecasts on the grounds that they may well mislead those who lack the experience to be aware of limitations on their significance, and that if they are pessimistic, they may well be self-fulfilling'. This rather patronizing attitude fails to mention that it is also upon the mystique and secrecy of official treasury forecasts that its power partly depends.. There is much strength to be had where (unspecified) forecasts, to which outsiders have no access, can be used as the font of the policies advised. Were the 'track record' of treasury forecasting to be made public (and there is ample reason to suppose that it is not a particularly good one) the aura of divinity sought for its views could well be more fully swept away. Some might argue that this would be bad for policy, and that the treasurer should, for the sake of public confidence, be allowed to exude certitude, however insecure economics may be as a source of understanding. Others might think, however, that (as with the recent granting of public access to the British treasury model) there is not much to be lost by explicitly recognizing that no government department has a monopoly on wisdom in policy formulation. Whichever view is taken, there is no doubt that the time-worn rather 'closed shop' approach to policy advice in Australia has not succeeded in dissolving the enigma of the new inflation.

The State of Economics and the New Inflation

It is interesting that, in the new inflation analysis, latter-day techniques (especially sophisticated econometric model building), have failed to make much of an impact on the institutional literature, or indeed on the apparent consciousness of some 'institutional' or 'qualitative' authors. Indeed there have almost been two worlds of thought, separate and undefiled by one another. It is true that, beginning in 1970, the Conciliation and Arbitration Commission has heard econometric 'evidence' from the parties before it. But the Commission has exercised extreme caution, and indeed a healthy iconoclasm, about the usefulness of any conclusions which might be derived from quantitative models.[20]

In conclusion, therefore, one is reminded by the current Australian literature on inflation of the overseas debates on the state of economics. The articles of E. H. Phelps Brown,[21] W. Leontief,[22] G. D. N. Worswick,[23] and P. T. Bauer and A. A. Walters,[24] are all brought to mind. Phelps Brown, for example, mentions (p. 2) that 'the learned journals are scanned by the practitioners and laid aside. Models which though complex are built out of a small number of elements that are assumed but not known to be representative of the real world, are no help to those who have to diagnose and prescribe for the actual economy.' And Bauer and Walters (p. 16) argue that 'preoccupation with elaborate and often esoteric formal analyses not only diverts attention from the determinants of economic events, it often conduces to a neglect of observation, reflection, common sense and even elementary economic theory'.

The background to the current debates on the causes of inflation and unemployment in Australia certainly highlights these remarks. From the same events, economists have drawn completely contrasting conclusions, one example being the alternate claims on the cause of the decline in the rate of wage rises since the start of 1975. It is claimed with certainty by some observers that this decline is due to the high level of unemployment, whereas others are equally sure that it is the result of the policy of wage indexation. In order to answer this form of question with greater credibility in the future, economists will need to devote far more attention to the interrelated disciplines of sociology, psychology, and politics, and to careful, painstaking observation of human behaviour and economic history.

References

1 'Inflation in Australia Today', *Australian Economic Review*, 1 (1971), p. 37.

2 *Incomes Policy: What Can we Learn From Europe?* (Cornell University Press, Ithaca, 1973), p. ix.

3 For example, there was discussion of this issue in (a) J. E. Isaac, 'The Machinery of an Incomes Policy', at the Sixth Autumn Forum of the Economic Society in Melbourne, 1964. (Reprinted in J. E. Isaac and G. W. Ford, *Australian Labour Economics: Readings*, 1st edition (Sun Books, Melbourne, 1967), chapter 12); and (b) K. Sloane, 'Co-operation and Coercion in Wages and Incomes Policies', *Journal of Industrial Relations*, March 1966.

4 W. H. Beveridge, *Full Employment in a Free Society* (Allen and Unwin, London, 1944), p. 199.

5 J. M. Keynes, 'The Objective of International Price Stability', *Economic Journal*, September 1943, p. 187.

6 *Full Employment in Australia* (Australian Commonwealth Parliament, Canberra, 1945), p. 3. (Quoted from W. E. Norton, 'Inflation and Unemployment', *Economic Papers*, no. 51 (February 1976), p. 24.)

7 L. F. Giblin, 'Financing Full Employment', *Economic Papers*, no. 5 (1944), p. 59. (Quoted from W. E. Norton, *Economic Papers*, no. 51 (1976), op. cit. p. 24.)

[8] See D. C. Smith, *Incomes Policies* (Economic Council of Canada, Ottawa, 1966), chapter 1.

[9] The country study publications of the OECD document many of these. See also (a) W. Galenson (ed.), *Incomes Policies: What can we learn from Europe?* (Cornell University Press, Ithaca, 1973); and (b) L. Ulman and R. J. Flanagan, *Wage Restraint, A Study of Incomes Policies in Western Europe* (University of California Press, London, 1971).

[10] A. Jones, *The New Inflation* (Penguin, Harmondsworth, 1973), p. 19.

[11] Ibid, p. 21.

[12] Ibid, p. 24.

[13] E. H. Phelps Brown, *Collective Bargaining Reconsidered*, Stamp Memorial Lecture (University of London Press, London, 1971), p. 15.

[14] J. E. Isaac, 'The Machinery of an Incomes Policy', reprinted in J. E. Isaac and W. G. Ford *Australian Labour Economics: Readings*, op. cit., p. 283.

[15] The literature of this period is briefly surveyed in my article with N. R. Norman, 'Australia's Inflationary Babel', in J. R. Niland and J. E. Isaac (eds), *Australian Labour Economics: Readings*, 2nd edition (Sun Books, Melbourne, 1975), chapter 12, see especially pp. 264-8.

[16] See the *Australian Economic Review*, 1 (1975), p. 10.

[17] *Report of the Committee of Inquiry into Inflation and Taxation* (Australian Government Publishing Service, Canberra, May 1975).

[18] See, for example, the *Australian Economic Review*, 3 (1975), p. 4.

[19] J. P. Nieuwenhuysen and A. E. Daly, *The Prices Justification Tribunal* (M.U.P., Melbourne, 1977).

[20] This conclusion emerged from my review of inflation with Norman. See Niland and Isaac, *Australian Labour Economics: Readings*, op. cit., p. 264.

[21] 'The Underdevelopment of Economics', *Economic Journal*, March 1972.

[22] 'Theoretical Assumptions and Nonobserved Facts', *American Economic Review*, March 1971.

[23] 'Is Progress in Economic Science Possible?' *Economic Journal*, March 1972.

[24] 'The State of Economics', *The Journal of Law and Economics*, June 1975.

J. E. ISAAC

6 On the Neglect of Social Forces in Wage Determination

> Though economic analysis and general reasoning are of wide application, yet every age and every country has its own problems; and every change in social conditions is likely to acquire a new development of economic doctrines.
>
> Alfred Marshall[1]

> The chief fault in English economists at the beginning of the century was not that they ignored history and statistics, but that they regarded man as so to speak a constant quantity, and gave themselves little trouble to study his variations. They therefore attributed to the forces of supply and demand a much more mechanical and regular action than they actually have. Their most vital fault was that they did not see how liable to change are the habits and institutions of industry. . . . Among the bad results of the narrowness of the work of English economists early in the century, perhaps the most unfortunate was the opportunity which it gave to socialists to quote and misapply economic dogmas. Ricardo and his chief followers did not make clear to others, it was not even quite clear to themselves, that what they were building up was not universal truth, but machinery of universal application in the discovery of a certain class of truths. While attributing high and transcendent universality to the central scheme of economic reasoning, I do not assign any universality to economic dogmas. It is not a body of concrete truth, but an engine for the discovery of concrete truth.
>
> Alfred Marshall[2]

The words of warning uttered nearly a century ago by Alfred Marshall apply with the same force today. We are in urgent need of being reminded that the way 'men live and move and think in the ordinary business of life', as Marshall defined economics, has changed significantly in recent times. The 'Age of Keynes' has been with us for some thirty years, and during this time much of the western world has enjoyed almost continuous high employment and rising wages as well as increased education, social security and welfare. It would be very surprising if the 'economic dogmas' of twenty years ago are still applicable today without significant modification, especially in the matter of inflation, the most persistent and the most urgent of contemporary problems.

Although Keynes was concerned with unemployment, his analysis applied also to what he called 'true inflation', when excess demand prevailed. The means for dealing with this kind of inflation were the same, though applied in reverse, as those required for removing general unemployment; the task of economic management was to manipulate the fiscal and monetary instruments so that demand was exactly appropriate for full employment without inflation.

Experience with economic management shows the difficulty of exact manipulation. In particular, inflation has been a chronic feature of most countries in the post-war period. In more recent times, it has stood out as an intractable problem even with high unemployment. In the debate about the persistence of inflation two sets of issues may be distinguished. One relates to the application of non-directive macro measures—on the magnitude of fiscal and monetary actions, on their timing and lags, on the implication of budget deficits, and on the wisdom of using 'fine tuning' discretion in monetary management instead of leaving the money supply to grow at a fixed rate. In this connection, in a number of countries, including Australia, those who placed primary emphasis on the money supply rather than excess demand as the basic cause of inflation, appear to have gained dominance over the old-fashioned Keynesians. The current debate (in 1976) on the budget deficit, is reminiscent of the controversy between Keynes and the 'treasury' view of the 1930s. Economic doctrine has come full circle in less than two generations.

The other set of issues on inflation relates to the importance of cost or sellers' inflation which has at its source social and institutional factors rather than excess demand or excess money. Cost inflation is seen as the result of incompatible income claims between groups of wage earners and between wage earners and profit earners. This process can be sustained without short-run damaging effects on employment, only with appropriate increase in the quantity of money. Cost inflation can exist with or without excess demand. The group conflicts underlying it constitute an autonomous force which are not amenable to treatment simply by regulating demand and the money supply. But those who believe that much of the recent inflation has come from cost-push pressure and that institutions need to be devised to deal with it, have had little influence on the formulation of economic policy in Australia. The monetarists who deny the importance of non-monetary forces have held sway. Why should this be so?

The Mechanistic View of Markets

Part of the explanation is the widespread tendency among economists to take a mechanistic view of the way markets operate, and to believe that generally persons and institutions, acting as 'rational' and well informed 'economic men' in pursuit of maximum economic gains, are highly responsive to demand and supply through wage and price adjustments. Undue emphasis tends to be given to the allocation of resources and the achievement of economic efficiency, with the distribution of income as incidental to this process. Concentrations of economic power in the form of large corporations and trade unions are recognized, but their impact is depreciated by the (often implicit) assumption of income maximization which denies the possibility of continuing pressure on prices through the exercise of monopoly power.[3] For those in pursuit of precision, quantifiable entities and determinate and elegant solutions, social forces are awkward to handle. Their contribution to inflation is difficult to test by conventional econometric methods. For example, attempts to measure union militancy by union membership or strike activity are a highly dubious way of accounting for union contribution to inflation. The advice of political scientists and sociologists is spurned because it is on a judgemental and less rigorous level than is apparently required by 'the usual scientific standards'. Yet, as Keynes once remarked, may it not be better to be roughly correct than precisely wrong?

The neglect of social and institutional forces is reinforced by the common practice of distinguishing between 'economic' and 'non-economic' factors. While such a distinction is convenient and at times unexceptionable, it is folly in wage determination to try to design a wage policy on 'economic' grounds in isolation from the 'industrial relations' grounds. One must be very much part of the other, if wage policy is to work.

It is, of course, necessary to take note of Friedmanite methodology and the dangers of 'undue emphasis on the descriptive realism of "assumptions" '.[4] However, because in economics reliable empirical tests are so much more difficult than in the natural sciences, the plausibility of economic propositions can in many cases only rest on the high degree of realism of their assumptions and the logic of the deductions which are drawn from them. In any case, experience shows there are grave dangers also in the 'black-box' or the 'as-if-the-assumptions-of-the-theory-were-correct' approach to economic generalizations, despite the usual caveats relating to their tentativeness. To explain inflation, this methodology harnessed to the computer has produced countless reams of print-outs of highly correlated time series, ranging over periods of considerable economic, social and institutional changes, from which spurious causal connections and bold implications for *current* policy have been drawn.[5] What a waste of talent the numerous variations on the Phillips curve theme have been! And how misleading for the framing of economy policy!

In much policy discussion, there is an unwarranted leap from what is desirable to what is possible, from exhortation to prescription. The task of the economist is not only to propose measures which would conduce to the greatest benefit of the community, but also to state clearly the conditions which would enable such measures to operate. If those conditions do not apply or cannot be made to apply, the appropriateness and the viability of the measures must be questioned. Writing about Keynes, Professor M. V. Posner has recently remarked that he

> seldom shirked the social consequences and requirements of his policies, and tried to make explicit his assumptions and aims. Many technical economists today follow and develop Keynesian analysis and arrive at similar policy conclusions; but their value judgments are often muted, or left to politicians to defend. A tendency to philosophize is sometimes a handicap for an economic adviser, but should be far more widespread than it is at present among academic economists.[6]

Partly because of their upbringing on unreal models, economists are biased in favour of economic measures which operate through the impersonal forces of the market rather than by direction of persons and institutions. The widespread and ready appeal of Keynesian economics probably derived not only from its analytical basis but also from the practical implications of its prescriptions. In particular, the 'wages solution' to general unemployment, which had been shown by the experience of trade union resistance in the 1920s and 1930s to money wage reduction to be politically unpopular and difficult to administer, could be discarded. By contrast, the manipulation of aggregate demand through the budget, the money supply and the exchange rate, provided no serious institutional and social resistance. Although greater government activity was involved, government economic management was able to work by inducement, by affecting the macro-economic environment, rather than by direction; through the market mechanism, rather than outside it or in defiance of it; and the measures conduced more to social harmony than the opposite.

The bias in favour of the impersonal market mechanism is laudable: how better to allow individual consumers and producers to exercise their preferences and to avoid the costs of bureaucracy? But market forces operate differently in different markets. There is a world of difference in Australia between the operation, for example, of the wool market and the market for baby-sitters on the one hand,

and the 'market' for labour in the oil industry on the other. Market forces are effective in meeting consumer preferences and minimizing social costs only under conditions in which a wide dispersion of economic power prevails. If, however, for technological and other reasons, such dispersion is neither possible nor, on balance, felt to be politically or socially desirable to enforce in certain areas of economic activity, then the virtues of market-oriented solutions are surely irrelevant. Repugnance of statutory regulation and direction notwithstanding, such intervention may, however, be necessary: the choice is between the manipulation of 'market forces' by private concentrations of economic power or by government power.

Economists do a disservice to their profession if their understandable bias in favour of the atomistic market and the elegant theories which can be built on such a concept, becomes an obsession which blinds them to the powerful social and institutional forces operating within certain markets. The presence of these forces cannot be removed or assumed away, at least in the foreseeable future, but must be taken into account in the formulation of economic policy.

Wage Determination and Inflation

The aim of this Chapter is to draw attention to certain features of Australian wage determination which support the proposition that a policy for dealing with inflation is incomplete and is likely to fail, if it assumes that what mainly needs to be done is to ensure that aggregate demand (or the money supply, if one is of the Chicago persuasion), is not excessive.[7] In short, cost inflation is a force not to be ignored in Australia. The labour market institutions and wage fixing arrangements are such that, in the absence of special means for dealing with them, they will lead to persistent increases in costs and prices, even when the money supply and aggregate demand are properly adjusted to avoid excess demand and over-full employment.

While J. M. Keynes[8] and W. Beveridge[9] had been aware of the dangers of cost inflation, the groundwork for a proper understanding of the processes of cost inflation was laid as far back as 1948 in an important work by A. M. Ross[10] on collective bargaining in, of all places, the United States, where for a variety of reasons, cost inflation has been a less potent source of inflation than in many other countries. The book by Ross, *Trade Union Wage Policy*, created little interest outside the U.S., and it is worth digressing on the points he raised not only to remind ourselves of their relevance to contemporary Australia but also because discussion on economic policy often seems to ignore them. Much of the lively controversy in U.S. journals centred on the validity of the proposition put by Ross that 'a trade union is a political agency operating in an economic environment'. Objection was taken to the emphasis on the 'political' rather than the 'economic' aspect of collective bargaining. It was said,[11] for example, that United States trade unions are better described as organizations whose objectives are primarily economic and whose decisions are reached through a political process. However, nearly everything can be lumped into 'economic' by introducing the indefinite 'long run' time frame into 'economic objectives'.[12] Similarly, almost any behaviour can be designated 'political' by suitable rationalization.

This sham dispute was a distraction from what was clearly the main thrust of the book: the force of cost inflation inherent in sectional collective bargaining. The important analytical contribution of the work was that it shifted the emphasis of trade union behaviour away from the 'maximizing' equilibrium model generally favoured by economists.

> Among all the participants of economic life, the trade union is probably least suited to purely economic analyses. It may be that the particular form of rationality assumed in traditional economic theory can properly be assigned to the individual entrepreneur and even to the corporation . . . But a trade union is pre-eminently a group, a collectivity. Psychologists have been insisting for more than half a century that group behaviour is fundamentally different from individual behaviour. The trade union is not only a group, but an institution as well; it leads a life of its own, separate and distinct from the lives of its members. Its problems are not merely those of the particular individuals it happens to represent at one point of time.[13]

The monopoly model of a trade union is misleading if a maximizing objective is ascribed to it. A trade union is not governed by 'the pecuniary calculus conventionally attributed to business enterprise'.[14] Instead of the maximizing objective of the trade union, Ross advanced 'equitable comparisons' as the prime basis of wage demands and discounted the relevance of the effect of unemployment on the claims of particular unions. Ross argued that the popular notion that 'responsible' unionism should have regard to the unemployment effects of wage claims, does not give sufficient weight to the fact that the union will be influenced more by the interests of the employed rather than the unemployed members.

> The employment effect of a wage adjustment is unpredictable before the fact and undecipherable after the fact. Negotiations do have a responsibility of another kind, the maintenance of law and order in industrial life; and the importance of this responsibility is insufficiently appreciated.[15]

Ross posed a number of important questions which are still relevant in wage negotiations and which are not answered by traditional analysis: Why is it important for unions to achieve higher real wages through higher money wages? Why do unions press for uniformity of rates for all firms employing their members when by exercising discriminating monopoly power, the total income of their members would be increased? Why do unions strike for long periods for very small amounts, when the resulting loss in pay could take years to make up from the anticipated increase? Why are equalizing adjustments often as important as equalizing rates? When such behaviour persists, it is not persuasive to say that unions act irrationally.

Ross pointed out that equalizing tendencies operate not when the market is more competitive and less organized, but the contrary. The strongest equalizing tendencies emanate from two sources—the force and spread of union organization which overcome market pressures by enlarging the area of wage determination; and from the force of ideas, such as 'equity' and 'justice' to which workers, unions, employers and arbitrators widely subscribe and which 'provide the substance of equitable comparisons'. But unions are more interested in the 'process of achieving uniformity than in uniformity itself'. They are interested in creating differences as well as eliminating them.

> Once they have standardized wages within an orbit of comparison, they will focus on an unsuspecting or vulnerable employer and attempt to bring him out of line. This being achieved, they will argue that other employers should offer equal pay for equal work.[16]

It is not to be inferred from the emphasis on equitable comparisons that only relativities provide the basis for a wage increase. Increases in the cost of living also feature as a strong element in wage claims. Moreover, the force of equitable comparisons is not spread evenly over the entire system but 'runs in limited circuits'. Linkages may be weakened or broken by strong economic constraints, poor union organization, ineffective union leadership and the geographical spread of industry. Thus, although economic considerations enter into the wage determining process, they form only part of a whole set of considerations.[17] This makes the prediction of union behaviour of 'economic maximizing' grounds an unreliable approach.

The force of coercive comparison may apply internationally as, for example, between the U.S. and Canada, partly because of trans-national union organization and partly because of the influence of geographical proximity on worker aspirations despite the different economic circumstances of these two countries.[18] The importance of linkages between wage settlements as a dynamic force in general wage movements, applies also in developing countries where the generosity of 'enlightened' foreign employers in capital intensive industries has at times been a source of embarrassment to the development strategy of these countries.[19]

A general increase facilitated by the linkages is based on wage leadership which provides the initial momentum in the chain reaction. So long as the initial increase secured by an established wage leader is not much above national average productivity, no inflationary problem need arise. However, it is characteristic of a wage leader in a chain reaction that the wage increases it obtains is well above national productivity; otherwise leadership would be assumed by another group which is able to obtain an increase of greater magnitude. The generalization of such an increase would therefore be inflationary. The capacity of a wage leader to obtain a potentially inflationary wage increase depends on a variety of factors. For technological reasons, the industry concerned may enjoy productivity increases well above the national average. Or, the low elasticity of the demand for its products or tariff protection may facilitate the passing on of wage increases to prices. Or, for reasons of high capital intensity and overheads, a given wage increase has a comparatively small effect on price while a strike can have a highly adverse effect on profits.[20]

Aubrey Jones, former chairman of the British Prices and Incomes Board, in addition to placing great stress on wage leadership as a force in the spread of inflationary wage gains in Britain, has also noted certain social and political forces.

> The struggle for economic equality is to the twentieth century what the struggle for political rights was to the nineteenth century . . . it is more fruitful to view trade unions as a political movement rather than as economic monopolies . . . Trade unions are political in that they see themselves as existing to protect and promote the interests of a class . . . They can pursue their aims either on the narrowly industrial front, where they are often pushed from below; or on the broader political front, where the Welfare State and prolonged full employment are the main post-war achievements . . . It is a feature of purely economic writings that they see men behaving in markets solely as economic men, instead of seeing men as importing into economic aspects of life aspirations that are affected by their social and political thinking. It is this which has led to the belief that inflation is entirely an economic phenomenon; once allowance is made for social aspects, inflation can also be (properly) seen as a phenomenon with important social and political roots.[21]

Another British commentator, Professor Sir Henry Phelps Brown, has spoken eloquently of the 'profound and pervasive change in social attitudes'[22] which are expressed in the heightened expectations that have taken place in the post-war period marked by sustained high employment, increases in real pay, the education explosion, and the wide dissemination of ideas brought about by radio and television.

The Contemporary Setting of Wage Determination

Allowing perhaps for the weaker force of class consciousness in Australia, these observations about expectations of the British largely apply to the Australian workers. Furthermore, the force of coercive comparisons is probably stronger and more widespread in Australia than in Britain or the United States. The following combination of mutually reinforcing factors may be regarded as providing the realistic contemporary Australian setting of wage determination.

(1) The expectation of continually rising real disposable pay backed by rank and file attitude of impatience to any frustration of this objective and a belief that income redistribution should deliver what productivity cannot provide. An important corollary to this point is the sensitivity of wage and salary earners to increases in prices and income tax rates. Hence their resistance to a reduction in real disposable pay.[23] This sensitivity is expressed at the grass roots level by resolutions to their union leaders demanding pay increases and more directly by bans and strikes initiated at the shop floor level. Two important assumptions which Keynes made need to be changed in the light of recent experience, namely, that wage earners are sensitive to money rather than real wages; and, perhaps a more implicit assumption, that tax increases can be levied within wide limits to damp down excess demand without leading to pressures for wage increases. In this connection, the experiences of recent years have borne out a warning made as far back as 1945 by Dr Colin Clark on the inflationary limit of government expenditure.[24]

(2) The pursuit of economic equality has taken two courses in the labour market–one directed to narrowing vertical pay differentials and the other to increasing the share of pay in national income. The early success of the first, pressed through the basic wage concept, has been limited in more recent times by the strengthened union consciousness and organization of the upper white collar pay groups. These have been drawn into the orbit of coercive comparisons not only to protect their relative positions, but also their real pay levels. The second course is limited by the ability of employers to pass on 'excessive' wage increases to the consumer. Both courses thus have inflationary consequences.

(3) The expectations of rising real disposable pay may be moderated but not quelled by substantial unemployment. To be sure, the pressure points will not be in the depressed industries but

there are usually a number of industries which suffer little if any unemployment even when the general level of unemployment is high. These provide likely openings for wage increases, which are then pressed in other areas of employment on grounds of equity. It is perhaps important also to distinguish between the phase of rising unemployment and a time when the level of unemployment has stabilized at a high level. The uncertainty and insecurity among workers during the first phase may lead to greater restraint in wage demands than the more settled, even if depressed, circumstances of the second. In the last two years (1975 and 1976), despite a sustained high rate of unemployment, the pressure for better pay and conditions has not abated; and because the indexation guide-lines have stood in the way of these claims, strikes and bans have been well above the levels prevailing in the prosperous years of the 1960s and early 1970s. As Ross pointed out nearly thirty years ago, wage claims are not made by those who are unemployed. The force of this point is even greater when a very large proportion of the unemployed are school-leavers who have not even had an opportunity of union membership.

(4) A state of affairs prevails in which wage demands are pursued group by group, each stimulated by the wage settlements that are made in a chain reaction, and each unwilling or institutionally unable to be restrained by the self-defeating total result of these sectional wage claims.

(5) The linkages are particularly strong in Australia for a variety of reasons:

(a) The work force is highly concentrated in a few capital cities and nearby industrial centres. This facilitates the spread of information about wage settlements and provides the basis for coercive comparisons.

(b) The proportion of union membership is high over a wide area of employment. This enlarges the coverage of wage settlements. The structure of unionism is even more important in this connection. A small number of large craft and occupational unions (Amalgamated Metal Workers' Union, Electrical Trades Union, Australasian Society of Engineers, Federated Engine Drivers' and Firemen's Association, Transport Workers Union, Federated Storemen and Packers Union, Federated Clerks Union—to name a few) have members scattered through many industries and locations. Consequently, there is greater pressure for the transmission of settlements than under a system dominated by industry-based unions, as in the United States. Many activities are affected sooner or later through these multi-industry unions, whose achievements then form the basis of similar actions by other unions in the industries affected.

(c) To be viable, wage fixing tribunals must operate within the generally accepted principles of the labour market. 'Equitable comparisons' is one such principle which is firmly rooted in the

> tradition of Australian wage fixation where it is known as 'comparative wage justice'. This concept tends to be applied if not as a means of equalizing rates, at least to equalizing increases in rates of pay, a process which until recently often occurred without serious questioning of the reasons and circumstances for the initial pay increase. One tribunal is influenced by another. Case-law and informal leadership develop within the system of industrial regulation, with 'parent awards' providing the basis for corresponding adjustments in 'off-spring' awards.

Dr E. A. Boehm[25] has examined certain important federal awards between 1967 and 1974 to show the operation of wage linkages and flows. It would be a laborious but not difficult exercise to trace the operation of this process over a longer period and a more extensive range of occupations and industries. The transcripts and decisions of arbitration proceedings abound with 'equitable' comparisons of rates of pay. But as Boehm notes, this process is not taken into account in aggregate statistical and econometric studies and wrong inferences may, therefore, be drawn from them.

The pressure for a flow of pay increases does not only operate among manual workers but extends from these to white collar and professional workers. This extension is subject to time lags and variations in pay increases, but the operation of the linkage process is unmistakable. Given the strength of the equity consideration, it is difficult to sever the chain at any point: if the unskilled obtain a rise, why should not the semi-skilled and the tradesmen who generally work with them? And why not also the foremen who supervise them? And what about the clerks and lower management levels and the professionals who process and plan the work of the manual workers? How to stop the chain reaction and with what reason which would be sufficiently persuasive to those whose relative position has deteriorated? In 1962, after a very lengthy enquiry, a full bench of the Commonwealth Conciliation and Arbitration Commission decided that, on the basis of their work value, professional engineers deserved a more favourable pay relativity against other professional groups.[26] Despite the firmness of the Commission's decision in this matter, the increase awarded to professional engineers largely flowed to other professional and white collar groups; and, although the link was not formally made, manual workers also increased their pay so that by the end of the decade, the engineers' relative position to the rest of the community had largely reverted to the earlier level.

In the various state public utilities, especially in Victoria, firm pay linkages exist for a very large proportion of employees, manual and non-manual.[27] In the Commonwealth Public Service, periodical surveys are made of prevailing rates of pay of comparable groups outside the Service to establish the correct rates for those inside. To a more variable extent, because of local and economic considerations, over-award payments also form part of the linkage process. They induce increases in other over-award payments as well as in award rates. In Victorian government employment, a separate amount, dignified by the title 'State Incremental Payments System', is formally paid to match the over-award payments.

In addition to these inter-industry and inter-occupational adjustments there are, of course, national wage increases which apply generally to nearly all wage and salary earners. Between 1965 and 1974, these increases became a proportionately smaller part of total wage increases[28] as wage settlements by collective bargaining and consent awards at the industry and company levels set the lead in wage increases and were extended by arbitrated awards to the rest of employment. The position has, of course, been dramatically reversed since the indexation guide-lines came into operation in April 1975.

Thus, the orbits of comparison in Australia are much wider, more general and tighter than Ross had envisaged in relation to the U.S. Where the flow of wage increases is impaired because of the weakness or absence of union organization or because of employer resistance, Australian wage fixing tribunals, by reason of their application of the equity principle, help to generalize the larger settlements.

It will be clear that in the Australian labour market, the operation of demand and supply through impersonal processes generally assumed for the commodity market does not apply. The determination of the prices of labour is carried out by administered processes which reflect not only economic forces, but also powerful social and institutional attitudes. To say this, is not to extol the virtues of these circumstances but merely to state a fact. Nor should it be taken to imply that excess demand will not lead to competitive pressures to raise the price of labour. What *is* being suggested is that the price of labour may rise without excess demand and indeed, when demand is deficient. It is possible, of course, for the formalized administrative processes to produce results which are not very different from those which would have emerged if impersonal market forces had operated. Although Marshall recognized the influence of custom and emphasized that human agents of production are not bought and sold as machinery, he nevertheless concluded in that famous passage on trade combination and alliances and counter-alliances among employers and employed that:

> They present a succession of picturesque incidents and romantic transformations, which arrest public attention and seem to indicate a coming change of our social arrangements now in one direction and now in another; and their importance is certainly

great, and grows rapidly. But it is apt to be exaggerated; for indeed many of them are little more than eddies, such as have always fluttered over the surface of progress. And though they are on a larger and more imposing scale in this modern age than before; yet now, as ever, the main body of movements depends on the deep silent strong stream of the tendencies of normal distribution and exchange; which 'are not seen' but which control the course of those episodes which 'are seen'. For even in conciliation and arbitration, the central difficulty is to discover what is that normal level from which decisions of the court must not depart far under the penalty of destroying their own authority.[29]

The economic strictures which Marshall underlined may still apply to real income movements but they do not in the light of recent history apply to money incomes and prices. For Marshall was concerned with a very different economic environment. It is fair to say that he would have assumed as the normal order of economic life, the operation of the gold or some metallic standard with the rigours of such a system on the quantity of money and budgetary policy, unencumbered by the expectations and political imperatives of full employment and rising real pay. Further, although Marshall noted that trade unions and joint stock companies were 'on a larger and more imposing scale in this modern age than before', they were in retrospect at an infant stage of development both organizationally and conceptually.

The constraint upon economic forces by social and political pressures should occasion no surprise to anyone with a sense of history. While the analogy with medieval society should not be pressed too far, it is well to remember that in medieval times, religion and its moral precepts rather than economics, dominated life. Prices and wages were based on what was 'just' and in keeping with the person's status as a consumer and producer rather than merely on the interplay of economic forces. While admitting the gap between philosophy and practice in medieval society, Professor R. H. Tawney underlined the importance of moral prescriptions in economic activity.[30] And in his concluding chapter, Tawney made certain observations which, although in a different context, are especially pertinent to the present time.

. . . economic interests are still popularly treated as though they formed a kingdom over which the *Zeitgeist* bears no sway. In reality, though inherited dispositions may be constant from generation to generation; the system of solutions, preferences, and ideals—the social environment within which the individual functions—is in process of continuous change . . . Economic efficiency is a necessary element in the life of any sane and vigorous society, and only the incorrigible sentimentalist will depreciate its sig-

> nificance. But to convert efficiency from an instrument into a primary object is to destroy efficiency itself. For the condition of effective action in a complex civilization is co-operation. And the condition of co-operation is agreement, both as to the ends to which effort should be applied, and the criteria by which its success is to be judged ... A reasonable estimate of economic organization must allow for the fact that, unless industry is to be paralysed by recurrent revolts on the part of outraged human nature, it must satisfy criteria which are not purely economic.

The economic revolution which followed the Middle Ages resulted in the release of economic forces from the constraint of moral purposes. The operation of these forces through the processes of the market has contributed greatly to the tremendous growth in the wealth and income of western society. But this development has been accompanied by increased concentrations of economic power on the part of labour and capital. In Australia, perhaps more than many other countries, the impersonal forces in the labour market have largely been displaced by well established and powerful institutions. This displacement has brought the need to fix pay in ways and on principles which do not offend the sense of 'fairness' of those whose services are being sought. This sense of fairness is not easily stilled or stemmed by monetary and fiscal measures which produce a substantial margin of unemployment. Nor would such measures encourage greater productivity. The economic order of the nineteenth century no longer prevails. In framing economic policy it is necessary to assume that the present structure of the labour market and the political requirements of high employment are here to stay for some time. It should also be clear that the cost inflationary bias of the labour market arises not from the propensity of employers, unions or their members for inflation but from the system of sectional wage determination linked together by the pressure of equitable comparisons and infused by the expectation of continuous improvement in real disposable pay. These are the sources of the problem and they cannot be ignored in any effective policy against inflation.

It is characteristic of inter-related but autonomous sectional actions, that each section, acting rationally in pursuit of its sectional interest, cannot be expected to refrain from pursuing such a course even if the overall consequences of these separate actions are not desired by any of them. The 'invisible hand' which Adam Smith postulated would guide the multitude of individual actions in pursuit of self-interest towards the advancement of the common good, cannot be relied on in an institutionalized labour market of the Australian type. The actions of a few to improve their positions, emulated by the rest, ultimately defeat and damage the interests of all. As Professor D. H. Whitehead has pointed out,[32] in these circumstances price stability is a public good which can only be enjoyed if separate groups act in concert or if their actions are regulated to bring about a concerted and co-ordinated approach to wage determination. This is at the heart of the case for an incomes policy.

In the Australian labour market, the regulation of sectional actions, in the interests of the sections and the whole economy, is inescapable if chronic inflation is to be avoided or mitigated. The question is how this regulation is to be carried out. The difficulties and lack of sustained success of incomes policies in various parts of the world provide a discouraging prospect; but this fact merely underlines the need for greater effort. The rules of pay determination and their complementary economic and social measures are still to be worked out and adapted to the appropriate institutional arrangements for carrying out an incomes policy. Experience will provide the lessons for improvement and general acceptability. The concept to be promoted is relatively new and is still widely viewed with suspicion and hostility. Certainly, its intellectual standing among influential economists is not high at present.

In his reflection on the proceedings of an international conference on wage determination, E. H. Phelps Brown put the problem this way.

> In effect we have found our way to treat our problem as one of political philosophy. Our problem is, at a time of the dissolution of the old economic order, how shall we construct a new one? The basic problem of political philosophy is, what is the foundation of social order? How do we escape from the anarchy of a world without accepted authority, without acceptance of rules in common? It is the problem of escape from the miseries of the state of nature, the 'bellum omnium contra omnes', the war of all against all, to a society which is orderly because it is regulated by accepted authority. For it is with something like a war of all against all that we are confronted in the matter of Wage Determination at the present time.
>
> One way of establishing order, the imposition of an arbitrary authority ruling by force, is denied us in a democratic society. The other way is the establishment of order through the social contract, the voluntary abandonment of one's own autonomy in exchange for the like limitation of the power of others. It is this analogy that best fits the design of policy for Wage Determination. And I would suggest, in conclusion, that the most general finding, or the finding on which perhaps the greatest degree of consensus may emerge from our discussion, is that the problems of Wage Determination have today become essentially political problems, and that it is in the philosophy and science of politics that we must find the paradigm for the developments of our own policy.[33]

In the fight against inflation, economists will need to adapt their thinking and their technical apparatus to the changed social and political environment of the times if they are to remain relevant and avoid what Marshall referred to as 'their most vital fault' in not seeing 'how liable to change are the habits and institutions of industry'.

References

1 A. Marshall, *Principles of Economics*, 8th edition (Macmillan, London, 1938), p. 37.
2 A. Marshall's Inaugural Lecture at Cambridge, 1885, quoted in J. M. Keynes, *Essays in Biography* (Macmillan, London, 1933), pp. 207-8.
3 See, for example, M. Parkin, 'Inflation: The Policy Options', *Search*, vol. 4, no. 10 (October 1973), p. 421.
4 M. Friedman, *Essays in Positive Economics* (University of Chicago Press, Chicago, 1953), p. 42.
5 The need for modesty on the achievements of economics is well argued in E. H. Phelps Brown, 'The Underdevelopment of Economics', *Economic Journal*, vol. 82, no. 325 (March 1972), pp. 1-10. For a provocative criticism of the deficiencies of current theories of inflation see P. Wiles, 'Cost Inflation and the State of Economic Theory', *Economic Journal*, vol. 83, no. 330 (June 1973), pp. 377-98.
6 'Making Economic Policy', *Economic Journal*, vol. 83, no. 329 (March 1973), p. 114.
7 Other measures which normally form part of this approach relate to improvements in manpower training and use, and anti-restrictive trade practices legislation.
8 E. A. G. Robinson, 'John Maynard Keynes: Economist, Author, Statesman', *Economic Journal*, vol. 82, no. 326 (June 1972), p. 540.
9 *Full Employment in a Free Society* (Allen & Unwin, London, 1944), pp. 198-201.
10 *Trade Union Wage Policy* (University of California Press, Berkeley & Los Angeles, 1948). Various members of the 'Berkeley School', especially Clark Kerr and Lloyd Fisher, were associated with the development of the ideas in this book.
11 Albert Rees, 'Union Wage Policies', in Industrial Relations Research Association, *Interpreting the Labor Movement*, December 1952.
12 M. Reder, 'Theory of Union Wage Policy', *Review of Economics and Statistics*, February 1952. It has been pointed out that Ross' description of a trade union applies also to large firms and to business, professional and farmers' organizations which are 'not simply institutional versions of hagglers in a market place where behaviour is dominated by every shift of local demand and supply, but also social organizations whose policy has to reconcile ambitions of leaders with the conflicting interests of diverse internal groups'. D. Jackson, H. A. Turner and F. Wilkinson, *Do Trade Unions Cause Inflation?* (Cambridge University Press, Cambridge, 1972), p. 60.
13 Op. cit., p. 7.
14 Op. cit., p. 74.
15 Op. cit., p. 19.
16 Op. cit., p. 70.
17 There is much common ground between Ross' 'orbits of coercive comparisons' and Dunlop's analysis of wage relationship in terms of 'clusters' and 'contours'. See J. T. Dunlop, *The Theory of Wage Determination* (Macmillan, London, 1957), p. 17.
18 D. A. Smith, 'Wage Linkages Between Canada and the United States', *Industrial and Labor Relations Review*, vol. 29, no. 2 (January 1976), pp. 258-68.
19 A. Smith (ed.), *Wage Policy Issues in Economic Development* (Macmillan, London, 1969), pp. 186-9.
20 The relative importance of high productivity in the leadership pattern is emphasized by Jackson & Turner in chapter 2 of D. Jackson, H. A. Turner and F. Wilkinson, *Do Trade Unions Cause Inflation?* op. cit., and J. Eatwell, J. Llewellyn and R. Tarling, 'Money Wage Inflation in Industrial Countries', *Review of Economic Studies*, vol. 61 (4), no. 128, pp. 515-23.

[21] Aubrey Jones, *The New Inflation* (Penguin, London, 1973), pp. 22-4.
[22] In 'Organisation for Economic Co-operation and Development', *Wage Determination* (Paris, 1974), p. 356.
[23] Report of Committee of Inquiry into Taxation and Inflation, *Inflation & Taxation* (Australian Government Publishing Service, Canberra, 1975), chapter 3, pp. 91-107.
[24] *Economic Journal*, vol. 55, no. 220 (December 1945).
[25] E. A. Boehm, 'Distortions in Relative Wages: The Inflationary Consequences and Policy Implications', *Australian Economic Review*, 4/74, pp. 39-50.
[26] P. C. Molhuysen, 'The Professional Engineers' Case', *Australian Economic Papers*, vol. 1, no. 1 (September 1962).
[27] The decision of Mr Justice Aird relating to a claim by the Municipal Officers' Association of Australia on a Victorian statutory authority, the Harbour Trust, contains an interesting account of the linkages within Victorian government employment. See 141 Commonwealth Arbitration Reports (1971), 1307-17. His decision in this matter should be compared with his decision affecting MOA members employed in the State Electricity Commission of Victoria in 1970, when he said that 'he could see no warrant whatever for any literal application or flow of this decision to another industry in the public utility field'. 134 Commonwealth Arbitration Reports (1970) at p. 289. The course of events within a year of this decision proved otherwise.
[28] Boehm, op. cit., p. 44.
[29] *Principles*, p. 628.
[30] *Religion and the Rise of Capitalism* (Pelican, London, 1938), pp. 44-5, 247.
[31] Op. cit., pp. 245, 250, 251.
[32] D. H. Whitehead, *Stagflation & Wages Policy in Australia* (Longman, Melbourne, 1973) chapter 13.
[33] 'Organisation for Economic Co-operation in Development', op. cit., p. 360.

E. H. PHELPS BROWN

7 A Social Contract in Australia?[1]

The experience of a number of western economies during the 1960s had made clear the requirements of an effective incomes policy. These, it seemed in 1969, were requirements that Australian institutions and attitudes were specially fitted to meet.[2]

One of them was simultaneity in the presentation and settlement of claims. When particular groups entered their claims and reached their settlements separately, no one rise could be shown to be inflationary in itself. The estimate from which the guide-lines for non-inflationary pay movements were derived showed only the limit that the rise of pay in the aggregate must not exceed. The guide-lines themselves did not show that any one group helping itself to a bigger rise would necessarily be inflicting inflation on the economy and a rise in the cost of living on its own members. Those groups that initially abided by the guide-lines had no assurance that others would not steal a march on them. There were usually good reasons, moreover, why some particular group should receive a larger rise than the average; but experience showed that others would then follow, even though their own claims had no such justification: rises in the general level of pay were often brought about by a chain reaction, in which most of the participants saw themselves as on the defensive, and as pushing on only in order to catch up. By the end of the 1960s it had become apparent that if these evasions and reactions were to be avoided, claims must be dealt with simultaneously. Only when all were tabled together would their inflationary potential in the aggregate be plain to see. Only when all were settled at the same time would each group have an assurance that in abiding by the guide-lines it was not letting itself fall behind.

Now the procedures of the Australian Arbitration Commission, as these had been developed under Sir Richard Kirby, did seem to meet this need for simultaneity. In a national wage case the Commission and the parties before it were concerned with the consequences of raising most rates of pay throughout the Commonwealth: the claims of all groups, in so far as they rested on the capacity of the economy to provide a higher standard of living for all, were thus before the Commission together. The decision was made after weighing the rise in outlay it would entail against the recent course and current prospects of the real national product. The requirement that the total effect of all claims be made apparent to the claimants, and that their permitted rises in the aggregate should not exceed the total available for distribution, were met from the outset by the Commission's procedure.

But much more was required for an effective incomes policy than this ordering of the common movement after public consideration of its aggregate effects: there had also to be an assurance that the movement was in fact ordered, and that particular groups did not break the line. There was always the possibility of some group using its own bargaining strength or militancy to do this. It might even happen that the very publication of guide-lines created the expectation that the rise they allowed would be obtained by everyone almost automatically, so that the leaders of any one group could show their mettle only by getting more for their own followers. Some sanction was needed for the guide-lines; or else those who promulgated them must be assured of the willingness of workers to abide by them. Here it seemed that Australia had an unique advantage. In earlier years, at a time when independent trade-unionism and direct negotiation were extending in many western countries, in which prevailing presumptions made all attempts to order the movements of wages appear mischievous in so far as they were not ineffective, the course of events in Australia had been very different: for here a convergence of traditions, events and personalities had not only led the legislature to establish a system of arbitration, but also led the workers to accept and rely on it.

At the end of the nineteenth century, the traditions were those of colonies whose affairs had in some respects been subject from the first to authoritative regulation. But this regulation might not have been extended to wages and industrial relations, had not the strife of the 1890s, in a depression of exceptional severity, alarmed the public and prostrated the unions. Once arbitration was established, the personality and policy of Henry Bournes Higgins gave the workers reason to believe that they could get more from the Arbitration Court than they could hope to gain by direct negotiation. Nearly seventy years later the tradition of resort to what was now the Commission, and acceptance of its awards, seemed still to characterize and distinguish the attitudes of Australian employees generally. So at least it appeared to an external observer. Over-award rates, it is true, existed and had been growing, but they were still of relatively small extent. That the Australian economy had suffered less inflation than most other economies that had sustained full employment since the war seemed evidently due in great part to the voluntary adherence of its trade unions to the arbitration system.

But this adherence was not only a matter of tradition: two further reasons for it appeared in the way that the Commission worked. The first of these was that trust in the Commission was not blind. The Commission arrived at its major decisions after public hearings in which cases for the unions and management had been stated and examined exhaustively, and in which the government's view of the prospects and needs of the economy had also been presented. When the Commission published its award, it gave an account of the considerations it had reviewed; and if its utterances were sometimes Delphic, and its judgement at the last could only be intuitive, none the less it showed that in an always complex situation it had endeavoured to take all the relevant factors into account fully and fairly. What is more, the awards were seen not to express the personal decisions of the members of the bench, so much as experienced mediators' sense of what would be not unacceptable to the parties in a negotiation over which they had presided. This was so, even though the Commissioners increasingly had regard to the probable consequences of their award for the whole economy, as well as to what being immediately acceptable would meet their statutory obligation to bring about a settlement of disputes. The trade unions had reason to believe that they had obtained as much as it was within the ability of the economy to afford them, and as much, taking one award with another, as they could have obtained by direct negotiation—or perhaps more. So they continued to resort to the Commission, and for the most part to abide by its decisions.

The other reason for their doing this was one that again marked out the Australian system as especially well adapted to the effective administration of incomes policy. Experience had shown that disputes over relativities between groups of workers as a whole, and differentials between grades within any group, were a major cause of disturbance. The application of guide-lines at any one time was always likely to be obstructed by those who, having found themselves left behind the advance of some other group when the guide-lines were promulgated, resented the lowering of their relative standing intensely, and felt themselves wholly justified in pressing for a greater rise than the guide-lines allowed. When the times called for a restraint that would involve a reduction of some real earnings, the question inevitably arose of how that reduction should be allocated between employees at different levels of earnings. Even had these difficulties not arisen, and the guide-lines had proved acceptable initially to all concerned, pressures for changes in relativities and differentials would still have made themselves felt as circumstances changed in the course of time. When one group, moreover, did obtain an outstanding rise, though this was justified solely by considerations of relativity peculiar to itself, it was apt to be viewed by others as setting a norm for themselves. Even, then, if the aim were only to regulate the rise of pay in the aggregate, some way had still to be found by which to bring about the agreed adjustment of relativities and differentials. But here again it appeared that the Australian system was especially adapted to the task. The procedures it had developed for making awards to particular groups on the basis of work value made for a reasoned adjustment of relativities, on criteria that should be acceptable to others because they were applicable to the pay structure as a whole. Its hearings on margins provided a similarly reasoned procedure for the orderly adjustment of differentials; the same purpose was served even when the margin came to be regulated only implicitly, within the total wage.

In these various ways the Australian system appeared to be capable, inherently or by adaptation, of meeting the requirements of incomes policy, and avoiding or overcoming difficulties that had frustrated successive attempts to administer such policy in economies that relied on direct negotiation. So it seemed to me at least as I looked back in 1969 over the record of the preceding twenty years, and compared the experiences of Australia and the United Kingdom. But from that standpoint I should have been aware of how the ground was shifting underneath my feet.

It was shifting because of the growth of direct negotiation, a growth to be signalized two years later by the decision of management in the Metal Trades Industrial Association to negotiate directly with the unions. So far had the movement away from the Commission gone that one Australian economist with special knowledge of this field was able to write in 1971, in a paper significantly entitled 'The demise of Australian Wage Policy?':

> Although the market and the wage-fixing institutions have always been to some degree rival forces in the determination of pay levels and relativities, and the domination of either has never been absolute, the shift towards the market over the past two years has been so pronounced as to transform the relation. Control of wage movements has not been more slender at any time since before World War I.[3]

The immediate occasion of this 'shift towards the market' lay in the train of events set in motion by the Metal Trades Work Value decision of 1967, but these events may only have made evident powers that were already latent in the unions. The success of the unions in resisting attempts to merge the rises consequent upon that decision with existing over-award rates made them conscious both of the importance they attached to their ability to negotiate directly, and of their power to maintain their independence against the wish of the Commission to keep them within its jurisdiction. Though most of the fines imposed on unions for striking in that way were collected, the imprisonment of Clarry O'Shea dramatized the difficulty, indeed the near-impossibility of imposing legal sanctions on the actions of trade-unionists in a contemporary democracy, when those actions are not reprehensible in the eyes of an electorate most of whose members are employees or the wives of employees. In both these ways the trade unions became conscious of their power to advance their members' interests as they saw them, independently of the Commission—a power which they had possessed for some time but which traditional attitudes had prevented them from realizing.

But in the last two years economic recession has made direct negotiation far less attractive, while the adoption of indexation has given the Commission more to offer. At the present time (October 1976) very little direct negotiation is going on. The question is whether this marks a reversion to the ways of the 1950s and 1960s, the events of 1967–71 being no more than one of the upsurges that occur in social history from time to time, only to subside; or whether those events manifested the coming about of a persistent change, it being the subsequent withdrawal from direct negotiation under the impact of recession that will prove episodic.

Few observers can answer this question with confidence, and by the time any reading of the present outlook appears in print, it is liable to be traversed by the course of events. But that the events of 1967–71 in Australia do mark a turning point in attitudes and procedures is indicated by their close resemblance to what was going on in the industrial relations of other western countries at just that time. The general strike in France that followed the students' revolt of 1968 proved to be the beginning of an upsurge of '*la base*', and a pressing of claims by direct and often unofficial action, that swept through a number of European economies in the two ensuing years, even disturbing the orderly industrial relations of Sweden. This cannot have been a matter only of following the French example, though probably this counted for something. That the trade-unionists of so many countries, including Australia, underwent or displayed this change at much the same time may probably be ascribed to the attitudes of those who had experienced employment only since World War II, attaining at that time a critical mass. Through the earlier years of full employment and rapidly rising standard of living after the war, the older men had continued to enter claims of a moderation, and support them with a circumspection, that had been tempered in the harsher world they had experienced before the war. But the experience of those who had entered employment only after the war had encouraged them to set their claims higher, and to believe that by striking to enforce them they had little to lose and much to gain. As the years went by the proportion of those among union members who perceived their position and powers in this way had risen, until only an incident, an example, was needed for that perception to issue henceforward in action. This change of attitude seems likely to persist. Possibly it will carry some economies into an inflation so catastrophic that a revulsion of outlook and policy occurs among trade-unionists themselves; but short of that it is hardly to be supposed that from this time any industrialized democracy will ever deliberately maintain conditions that will return the employee to his old vulnerability, and restore the apprehensions instilled by the experience of earlier hardships.

When the changes that have come about in Australian industrial relations through the last nine years are seen in that setting, their significance for the working of Australian institutions is unmistakable. A British observer is apt to evaluate that significance in the light of the basically similar but even more dramatic developments during the same period in the United Kingdom. These developments have demonstrated the power of trade unions to exercise a veto not only over the executive authority of the government in its endeavour to maintain guide-lines, but also over the legislative authority of the crown in parliament. Twice the coal-miners broke through the guide-lines. Determined to restore a position in the league table of relativities that had slipped downwards in the years of the reduction of their numbers, the miners put forward a claim in the later months of 1971 that the Conservative government of the day felt obliged to resist; but the miners' ability to stop a substantial part of the power stations obliged the government to refer the dispute to a committee of inquiry, which substantially found for the miners. Two years later the miners returned to the charge, and now they had on their side the great rise in the imputable value of their labour consequent upon the rise in the cost of oil. But this same rise in fuel costs, with its drastic effect on the British balance of payments, made the government all the more anxious to restrain the rise of pay within the guide-lines of the policy that by this time it had adopted. It made its stand, took on a strike, put manufacturing industry on a three-day week, and finally went to the country, effectively on the issue of 'Who governs Britain?' It lost the election. It had not been willing to treat the miners as a special case: evidently a substantial part of the electorate were so willing. This did not mean that they disapproved of pay restraint in general, and the margin of defeat for the government was in any case a narrow one; yet it could be said that for the first time in British history a Government had been turned out because it had opposed the demands of a trade union.

No less unmistakably, the power of the British trade unions to impose a veto on government policy in their field of interests was shown by their obliging a Labour government to withdraw its proposals for legislation on strikes, and frustrating the code of labour law that a Conservative government did enact. Concerned about the growth of unofficial strikes that a Royal Commission had seized on as a major problem of contemporary industrial relations, in 1969 the Labour government published proposals that would give the minister statutory authority to order the suspension of industrial action during a period within which the dispute could be dealt with through official procedures; persons who failed to comply with the order would be subject to statutory penalties. The Trades Union Congress would have none of this, and in what has been called 'the battle of Downing Street', in June 1969, forced the prime minister to drop it. The Conservative government that took officethe next year did introduce and enact a code of legislation for trade unionism and industrial relations, which like the Taft-Hartley Act in the U.S.A. conferred rights on the trade unions by laying obligations on the employer, but which resembled that Act also in rendering certain union practices actionable as 'unfair industrial practices'. The trade unions objected vehemently, not so much to this or that clause as to the fact that any Act had been passed at all, when it was their traditional doctrine that they must be able to operate flexibly, voluntarily and informally, outside the law. They refused to register under the Act, despite the legal disabilities that they would suffer thereby. They refused also to recognize the court that the Act had set up, despite the imposition of fines for contempt. Thereby they stultified the Act. When a Labour government returned to office it was repealed.

It is not easy for us to seize on those features of our own times that will distinguish them as a period in the eyes of the future historian, or fix on a contemporary event as marking the transition from one period to another. But it seems to me that the events just narrated mark the transition between two phases of economic organization and governance. In matters of pay and employment, in the first phase the trade unions filled an adversary role and exerted a countervailing power over against the power of governments and employers; in the second phase they begin to take up the responsibilities of policy formation, and be vested with authority within their sphere. So at least it seems to be in the United Kingdom, and the direction of change seems similar in some other western countries.

However uncongenial this is to traditional casts of thought, it is a fact. From it flow certain consequences. Those who can impose a veto on decisions are bound to be brought into the taking of those decisions, and–since they can reject any proposal of which they disapprove–they must bear the responsibility for the course adopted. But they will bear it only if it is seen to rest upon them, so that the consequences of their decisions will be brought home to them. In the matter of incomes policy this means that the final responsibility for the formulation of guide-lines and for ensuring their observance must rest upon the trade unions. Government and management clearly have their contributions to make to the discussion, and governments at least can support their arguments by some measure of bargaining power; but ultimately, in the sphere of pay and employment, the trade unions enjoy an autonomy that has not been delegated to them by government but has been conferred on them by the course of economic and social development.

Hence the 'social contract' of the last two years in the United Kingdom. The significance of this lies not in its particular terms but in the fact that it has been negotiated between the government and the Trades Union Congress in the same way as a treaty is negotiated between sovereign powers. The Conservative government in 1972 made genuine and great endeavours to reach a tripartite agreement on incomes policy with management and the Trades Union Congress, but it did so on the assumption that the ultimate authority in this as in other spheres resided with itself: it sought discussion, and was ready to make any changes in its proposals of whose desirability the discussion convinced it, but in the last resort it would do what it itself felt was right and necessary. The Labour government, on the other hand, has negotiated a contract with the Trades Union Congress: it has brought its own bargaining power to bear upon the negotiations, but has proceeded on the assumption that an incomes policy could be formulated only with a consent that Congress was free to withhold, and could be made good up and down the country only if Congress were determined to make it good. This meant that the terms of the policy would have to be in the main those proposed by Congress; and that the responsibility for the effects on the economy would largely rest with Congress.

That some part of the authority hitherto ascribed to government has been transferred to the trade unions has been assailed as unconstitutional, as an infringement of the sovereignty of the crown in parliament. But especially in the administration of economic affairs, a pluralist view of government seems to fit the facts more closely than the attribution of all ultimate authority to one centre. The institutions, moreover, by which administration is carried on, and through which authority is diffused, must in any case change as society changes. It is a major function of institutions to canalize the exercise of power. Thereby they convert coercive force into constituted authority; but as the sources of power shift, the institutional channels must be changed to accommodate them, The social contract is an institution developed to accommodate the shift of power to the trade unions.

If indeed such a shift of power has also come about in Australia, will this lead to a social contract here too?

It may be said that a social contract has already appeared, at least in embryo, for there was much talk of one following the reduction of income tax in the mini-budget of November 1974, and the successful argument before the Commission that this reduction should compensate the rise in the cost of living in the last quarter of that year. The mini-budget, moreover, contained measures designed to stimulate demand and employment, which also should have benefited employees. But it does not appear that these actions by government were taken in pursuance of an agreement negotiated with the ACTU, which thereby accepted on behalf of its members an obligation to observe particular guide-lines in pay claims.

Again it may well be said that to raise the possibility of such a negotiation is to call attention to the limited coverage of the ACTU, particularly among white collar employees, and the limited control that it can exert from the centre even over its own members. But this is the situation that obtains, in greater or less degree, in most western countries. The example of Sweden indicates that the extent of discipline among the unions depends on that among the employers. Whether an agreement negotiated with the national trade union centre or centres is vitiated by the intent of particular groups to 'go it alone' depends on the determination of employers and government to stand on the agreed line.

What is distinctive about Australia is rather the jurisdiction of its arbitral bodies, and in particular the delegation of major decisions on the level and structure of pay to the Commonwealth Commission. If the social contract is essentially negotiated between the government and the trade unions, would any function remain to the Commission other than to make a consent award? A case can be made out to that effect. The proceedings before the Commission, it may be said, do not lend themselves to a negotiation in which various possibilities are raised on both sides of the table, and the issues are stated with a frankness that is possible only behind closed doors. That the outcome must take the form of a decision by the bench makes it less possible for the responsibility to rest and be seen to rest on the parties to the negotiation. The Commission itself, it may be held further, has few bargaining counters: most of what concerns the unions outside the immediate issue of pay is in the hands not of the Commission but of the government to provide or withhold. With economic recovery the relative attractiveness of indexation will decline. On this view there would remain a wide field of usefulness to the Commission in administering changes in particular terms of employment, within the guide-lines adopted in the social contract. It would provide an essential supplement and support to the contract, by continuing to adjust the relativities of particular groups. But the provisions of the contract itself would have to be negotiated elsewhere.

As against this, it may be claimed that the Commission has already shown its ability to provide the forum in which at least a rudimentary contract can be worked out. Certainly indexation can be regarded as having been provided in return for an assurance by the unions that they would not engage in direct action for over-award rates. The *Reasons for Decision* published by the Commission in the national wage case of April 1975 made it clear that it was only on this condition that the Commission decided to adopt a provisional measure of indexation. 'We are of the view', it said (pp. 21–2), 'that some form of indexation would contribute to a more rational system of wage fixation, to more orderly, more equitable and less inflationary wage increases and to better industrial relations, *provided* that indexation was part of a package which included appropriate wage fixing principles and the necessary "supporting mechanisms" to ensure their viability'. The use of the term 'package' is noteworthy. The Commission saw the contribution of the ACTU to that package as provided by its implied acceptance of the Commission's requirement 'that wage increases other than those by way of quarterly indexation and national productivity would need to be small' (p. 22). This conception of the package was brought out by the misgivings expressed by the Commission in its *Reasons for Decision* in the national wage case of August 1976.

> We wonder, [it said on p. 5] whether the trade union movement in its totality really wants the indexation package, or if it does, whether there is sufficient realization of the behaviour necessary to make it work effectively. On each occasion since April 1975 in which the Commission has granted an indexation increase, it has emphasised the fragility of the package and we now repeat and underline that warning. The Commission's attempt to provide an equitable, rational and orderly method of wage fixation must fail if significant industrial disputation continues.

And again (p. 9), '. . . in recent quarters the incidence of stoppages, bans and limitations in support of campaigns to "beat" the indexation guide-lines has acted as a factor supporting the economic arguments for less than full indexation'.

Furthermore, it may be urged, the Commission is not limited to open hearings: it can and does call conferences behind closed doors, in quest of a consensus on principles. This is a field in which no spontaneous consensus is to be expected, and agreement can be reached only by what is in effect a negotiation: how effective a conference will be therefore depends on the willingness of the parties to make proposals. It is necessary also that government be represented at the highest level. In such a conference, moreover, the Commission does not merely act as host. For it retains its independence: neither government nor unions can tell what it will award, and each may prefer the certainty of terms that it can in effect negotiate directly with the other, to the risk that in the event the Commission will award terms that from its own point of view are less satisfactory. The Commission as a third party in the negotiation may thus be somewhat in the position of a conciliator who is empowered, should conciliation fail, to proceed to arbitrate: the reserve power conferred by its independence may act as a catalyst for the reaching of an agreement.

What developments in fact come about are likely to be shaped by the immediate pressure of events rather than designed on a long view of policy. But that there will be substantial developments in this field seems highly probable. It seems also that any government that is powerfully concerned to restrain the rise of labour costs will find in the conferences convened by the Commission the procedure best suited to its purpose.

References

[1] I am very much indebted to a number of colleagues who read this chapter in draft, and whose comments have enabled me to improve it greatly, though they are in no wise to be identified with its speculative theses. They include Keith Hancock, John Nieuwenhuysen and Donald Whitehead.

[2] This view was expressed in my Joseph Fisher Lecture at the University of Adelaide, 'Balancing external payments by adjusting domestic income', *Australian Economic Papers*, December 1969, and in my paper on 'Industrial Relations and the Law: lessons of Australian Experience', *Three Banks Review*, March 1971, reprinted in H. W. Arndt and A. H. Boxer (eds), *The Australian Economy* (Cheshire Publishing Pty. Ltd., Melbourne, 1972). The importance I attach to attitudes is further developed in my 'Non-monetarist view of the pay explosion', *Three Banks Review*, March 1975.

[3] K. J. Hancock, 'The Demise of Australian Wage Policy?' Reprinted in J. R. Niland and J. E. Isaac (eds), *Australian Labour Economics Readings*, new edn. (Sun Books Pty. Ltd., Melbourne, 1975), pp. 424-5.

A. H. BOXER

8 Personal Income Tax: The Changing Scene[1]

During the 1950s and 1960s, Australian personal income tax underwent virtually no restructuring which could fairly be described as basic reform. A glance at the tax scene as it was at the beginning of the present decade reveals that in most essential respects–the boundary line between what is income for tax purposes and what is not, the definition of the taxpaying unit, the form and coverage of concessional allowances, the degree of involvement of the states, and indeed the rate scale itself–the picture had hardly changed at all over the previous fifteen to twenty years. Nor had there been much serious public discussion of tax reform over those years, either in relation to personal income tax or in a wider context. There were, it is true, three Commonwealth committees during the 1950s (Spooner,[2] Hulme,[3] Ligertwood[4]) which inquired into aspects of income tax; but the terms of reference, especially of the second and third, were narrow and technical, and concerned more with business income than with personal income as it bears on the general run of wage and salary earners. Certainly, none of these inquiries anywhere near matched in depth or coverage the British Royal Commission of the mid-1950s, the Canadian Carter Commission, or New Zealand's Taxation Review Committee which reported some ten years later.

Indeed, it was the extreme narrowness of the Ligertwood Committee's terms of reference, with their emphasis on 'anomalies, inconsistencies and complexities in the law of income tax', which led the Social Science Research Council of Australia, in the early 1960s, to commission a group of university economists headed by Dick Downing to prepare its own report on Australian taxation.[5] This group did address itself to basic issues and did propose some quite radical changes in the structure of personal income tax, involving (among other things) a switch in concessional allowances from deductions from taxable income to tax rebates, and the adoption of a supportive wealth tax to perform the role customarily assigned to capital gains tax. It is nevertheless some indication of just how *démodé* serious discussion of tax reform was in the mid-1960s that the publication of the economists' findings produced hardly a ripple in academic, government or business circles.

In the last few years, however, the picture has altered substantially. Not merely has tax reform become a much more lively issue in public debate, but the tax system itself–specifically personal income tax–has been modified in a variety of ways. These changes include:

(1) a series of adjustments to personal tax rates, beginning in 1970, and culminating in a fairly drastic restructuring of the rate scale in 1975 and the introduction of full tax indexation a year later;
(2) adoption in 1975 of tax rebates in place of the former system on dependant allowances, followed in 1976 by the abolition of rebates for dependent children and students in conjunction with substantial increases in child endowment;
(3) as an integral part of the 1975 reforms, effective abolition of most other concessional allowances for the vast majority of taxpayers and their replacement with a general concessional rebate unrelated to manner of spending;
(4) inclusion in 1974 of a new concessional allowance involving a deduction for home loan interest payments;
(5) adoption of a property income surcharge in 1974 (discontinued after one year);
(6) imposition as from October 1976 of a special health insurance contribution distinct from personal income tax but raised through the income tax system;
(7) introduction in 1976 of tax sharing arrangements between the Commonwealth and the states, with every possibility that within a year or two each state will have the right to impose a surcharge or grant a rebate on personal income tax in its own territory.

Why has so much activity occurred? This chapter seeks briefly to supply some of the answers and to help suggest possible directions of tax changes.

Two Major Inquiries

In recent years two major tax inquiries have been undertaken under the auspices of the Commonwealth government. The Asprey Committee appointed in 1972 'to examine and inquire into the structure and operation of the present Commonwealth taxation system', and to formulate proposals for its improvement, submitted a preliminary report in mid-1974 and a final one early in 1975.[6] In the meanwhile the Mathews Committee had been asked to examine the effects of rapid inflation on the taxation paid by persons and businesses, and to recommend changes in tax arrangements to take account of these effects. Its findings were published in May 1975.[7]

The Asprey Committee's terms of reference were wide-ranging, and in its two reports--the second in effect incorporating the first--suggestions were made for a series of major tax changes touching on such matters as company income tax, capital gains tax, estate and gift duty, international aspects of income tax, and the taxation of goods and services (including the possibility of a value-added tax). None of its recommendations in these particular areas has to date (1976) been implemented. But two of its other recommendations have been adopted. One concerns the proposal that concessional allowances take the form of tax rebates (and greater reliance on child endowment) in place of deductions from taxable income. The other has to do with restructuring the personal rate scale along the lines of reducing marginal rates of tax over a middle range of income and increasing marginal rates of tax lower down the income scale. The budgets of 1975 and 1976 embodied these changes.

Although the terms of reference of the Mathews Committee were narrow, the issues it had to resolve were quite fundamental and its recommendations far-reaching. Full personal tax indexation was proposed, in conjunction with the indexation of business income through revaluation procedures involving both trading stock and depreciable assets. In the event, full personal tax indexation and a scheme for adjusting business income for stock value changes based on, though not precisely identical with, the scheme proposed by the Mathews Committee were adopted in 1976.

Just how far the findings of the Asprey and Mathews Committees induced the government to proceed with these changes will of course never be known. It seems that, even without the Asprey Committee, enough pressure had built up for tax rebates and restructuring of tax rates to ensure that these subjects were attended to when they were. Tax indexation is, however, another issue. Some degree of indexation of personal and business income would probably have occurred eventually; but the actual timing could well have been brought forward by several years or more in response to the forthright advocacy of the Mathews Committee, and the effect this had in bringing the issue to a head and mobilizing popular support.

It is of some interest that the Asprey proposals on rebates and rate restructuring, while emanating from a body appointed by the McMahon government, were implemented in the main by the Whitlam government; on the other hand, it was the Whitlam government which established the Mathews Committee but the subsequent Fraser government which took the decisive step in adopting tax indexation. This leads one to wonder whether the political swings since 1972, following a period of more than twenty years when the coalition parties held sway, may not have been responsible in some fair measure for the greater amount of activity on the tax front in recent years?

The property income surcharge introduced by the Whitlam administration in 1974 was obviously due to a change in government: it is inconceivable that the previous coalition government would have adopted a penalty levy of this kind. Other tax changes, which it is difficult to imagine would have been implemented had it not been for a change in government, were Labor's home loan interest concession; Labor's cutting back on the concessional treatment accorded education expenses, life insurance premiums and so on; and the Fraser government's tax-sharing arrangements with the states. On the other hand, irrespective of which party held office, there can be little doubt that major changes would have had to be made to the rate scale by about 1975 to take account of the effects of inflation, and that moves would have been made to substitute tax rebates and more generous family allowances for the former system of deductions from taxable income.

The Medibank levy is perhaps more debatable. While it is unlikely that there would as yet have been such a levy had Labor still been in office, the idea of imposing a separate levy to finance Medibank did after all originate with the Whitlam government; and it certainly cannot be ruled out that an earmarked health contribution raised through the tax system would eventually have been adopted even by a Labor government pressed to tap new sources of revenue in the face of further rises in public sector spending.

Reference to revenue points to a further factor which may reasonably be assumed to have played some part in governing the extent and character of tax changes in the last few years—namely overall budgetary considerations. It is apparent, for example, that the government felt able in 1976 to proceed with full personal tax indexation only because substantial pruning of public spending had reduced pressure on the tax system. Similarly, the introduction in 1976 of a health insurance levy may be accounted for—though only in part—as the budgetary response of the new government to the escalating growth in the cost of the original Medibank health scheme.

In Labor's period of office between 1972 and 1975, government spending rose dramatically as a proportion of national product. This led at the time to a degree of soul-searching as to how best the tax system might be adapted to cope with the extra calls being put on it—and the still heavier calls which could well arise in the future if the government continued to pursue ambitious spending programmes. The submissions by the treasury and the taxation office to the Asprey Committee, and the Asprey reports themselves, reflected this concern. It is especially evident in the references in these documents to the possibility of widening the commodity tax base to secure more revenue from indirect taxes and, in the process, provide scope for lightening the very heavy burden on the personal income taxpayer.

Cuts in public spending following the December 1975 change in government diffused the issue somewhat. Policy-makers will continue to be under pressure to accommodate the tax system more effectively to levels of government spending which remain high by the standards of the 1950s and 1960s. This is particularly since indexation of personal income tax has effectively stopped automatic revenue increases which were formerly generated by the combination of progressive income tax rates and high levels of inflation.

During the 1950s and 1960s, with an unchanged rate scale and a modest but persistent upward movement in prices and money incomes, taxpayers found themselves moving into successively higher marginal tax brackets more quickly than rises in real income warranted. By the early 1970s, there was much public dissatisfaction on this score, particularly on the part of so-called middle-income taxpayers who, because of the shape of the tax scale, regarded themselves as having been hit hardest.

The first expressions of dissatisfaction were mainly couched in terms of arbitrary and unintended effects on income distribution and of damage done to economic incentives. But in time two other complaints were increasingly heard. One was that the pace of inflation itself was being accentuated, since increasingly the reaction of employees seemed to be stronger demands for higher gross money wages to protect the real value of take-home pay. The second complaint was that the tendency for overall tax receipts to increase at a faster rate than costs and prices generally encouraged wasteful public spending and undermined the government's fiscal judgement.

There was also complaint about inflation eroding the real value of concessional allowances. This, however, was not wholly justified. For while it is true that dependant allowances were eroded during the 1950s and 1960s by not being adjusted upwards as fast as the rate of inflation, this was not generally the case with other concessional allowances, a number of which (for example, life insurance premiums) had their ceilings lifted somewhat faster than the rate of inflation while others (for example, gifts to charity) were not constrained by the existence of ceilings. Also, to the extent that taxpayers moved into higher marginal brackets, the real value of concessional allowances improved, since the tax saving associated with allowances in the form in which they were then given was based on the size of marginal tax.

Largely in response to these various complaints, a series of cuts in marginal tax rates was set in train—the first in 1970, with further adjustments in 1972 and 1974. A distinguishing feature of these cuts was their fairly heavy concentration towards the bottom of the income scale. For example, the 1970 changes involved a reduction of 10 per cent of tax payable on incomes up to $10 000, the reductions in tax payable above that level progressively declining to 4·4 per cent at $20 000 and zero at $32 000.

One unavoidable consequence of concentrating tax cuts towards the bottom of the income scale was to accentuate the sharpness of the rise in marginal rates further up the scale. By 1975 this sharpness had reached such worrying proportions that fairly drastic action was required. One solution would have been only to scale down marginal rates in the troublesome middle income range. But only taxpayers in the middle or upper income ranges would have stood to gain; and even though such a gain might reasonably have been regarded as an offset to the particular burden imposed on those incomes in consequence of inflation and the character of previous tax changes, there would clearly have been difficulties in a Labor government pursuing this approach. Moreover, it would have meant a very considerable loss in revenue which the government, then just beginning to accept the importance of budgetary restraint, was simply not in a position to contemplate.

The Asprey Option

The Asprey Committee had already suggested a way out, which involved matching the marginal tax cuts over a middle income band with marginal tax increases lower down the scale, the latter to be accompanied by provisions aimed at protecting the disposable incomes of those who, for want of a better term, may perhaps be described as the 'genuine poor'—meaning, in the main, persons wholly dependent on low taxable incomes. This was known as the Asprey option, and became in effect a basic ingredient in the substantial restructuring of the personal tax scale that occurred in 1975. However, the Asprey option had one quite serious defect: it turned out to be administratively impossible to devise a scheme that would effectively cushion the 'genuine poor', but *only* the 'genuine poor', from the impact of the proposed higher marginal rates at the bottom end of the income scale. All taxpayers would have to receive a rebate, but this in turn threw up two other problems.

First, if all persons on low incomes were to qualify for the general rebate, then one of the primary objects of the Asprey option—to ensure that the 'non-genuine poor' (school leavers, working wives, income splitters, and so on) contributed rather more tax than in the past—would not be achieved. As it happened, this problem was overcome in some measure by combining the general rebate with more generous dependant allowances which multi-income families—from which a significant proportion of the 'non-genuine poor' derives—were not in a position to utilize. Moreover, new tax instalment arrangements, involving tax deductions at the rate of 35 per cent at source on 'second' earnings, have served to close off an important avenue for tax evasion affecting the 'non-genuine poor'. The second, and more important, problem was that any extension of the general rebate to all taxpayers would in itself have meant a sizeable loss to revenue, more or less cancelling out the gain from introducing higher marginal rates at the bottom end of the scale and leaving the cut in marginal rates on middle incomes as a net addition to the budget deficit.

In the event, the solution adopted to minimize the loss in revenue was to proceed with the idea of a general rebate but to link it with the effective abolition (for the bulk of taxpayers) of concessional allowances for such items of expenditure as insurance payments and education expenses. With certain exceptions (for example, gifts to charity), expenditure of this type was in future to attract a rebate at the rate of 40 cents in the dollar, but only on itemized concessional allowances in excess of $1350 a year—well above the expenditure potential of the average taxpayer. The revenue thus saved was expected to go most of the way towards meeting the additional call on revenue from the general rebate. Of course, the cutting back of itemized concessional allowances was not purely and simply a revenue measure. It was certainly favoured by the Labor government on other grounds as well—notably because it went a long way towards closing what was regarded as a tax loophole mainly available to persons on higher incomes.

It was fairly apparent from the outset, however, that the new personal tax structure would have to be modified before very long if inflation remained high. In particular, the 1975 rate scale contained a very large marginal step at $10 000—a jump in fact from 35 cents to 45 cents in the dollar—which was clearly going to create difficulties within a reasonably short time as large numbers of taxpayers approached the relevant income bracket. It was hardly surprising, therefore, that the Mathews Report, which appeared at the time strongly in favour of full personal tax indexation, should have been widely seized upon as offering a neater solution than having yet another restructuring of the rate scale in a year or two. Nor was it surprising that, with the change in government at the end of 1975, the pressure for tax indexation gathered momentum; the new government was, after all, firmly set on shifting spending power back into the pockets of the private individual and, while in opposition, had strongly supported the implementing of the Mathews Committee's findings—albeit not necessarily at one fell swoop.

Personal Income Tax Indexation

As from 1 July 1976, therefore, Australia joined a small band of countries whose personal tax scale was fully indexed for inflation. In future the taxpayer whose money income rose between two years by the same percentage as the consumer price index (after correcting for any part of the price increases reflecting higher indirect taxes imposed by the Commonwealth) would not have his effective tax rate increased. Similarly, in future the real value of the dependent spouse rebate, the real value of the $540 general rebate and the real value of the $1350 floor for the concessional rebate on itemized expenditure would to be maintained by means of indexation.

The introduction of full personal tax indexation ought not, however, to be interpreted as necessarily signalling the end of the period of active tax change. Public statements by government ministers in 1976 have suggested fairly clearly that there are features of the indexed personal rate structure which are not to their liking. Most conspicuous is the inability of most taxpayers to claim itemized concessional allowances, and one can reasonably assume that the government would like to return to the pre-1975 situation in this regard. Nevertheless, to do so would be extremely costly in revenue terms unless the move were accompanied by a reduction in the general rebate (which in a sense is intended to serve as a substitute for itemized concessions). To reduce the standard rebate, however, would in turn raise awkward problems as to how to safeguard the position of the 'genuine poor' who today face much higher marginal tax rates than was the case until 1975. In effect, the new rate structure adopted in 1975 is very much an integrated whole: it is going to be difficult to replace parts of it without remodelling the whole edifice.

It is likely, too, that as long as inflation remains a serious threat, government will be under pressure from various quarters to use the tax system deliberately to help contain price increases. From time to time in recent years, suggestions have been made for tax penalties of one kind or another on individuals or firms whose behaviour appears to be reinforcing the rate of inflation. It has, for example, been contended that, with the object of stiffening the resistance of firms to excessive wage increases, employers should be disqualified from claiming tax deductions on account of wage increases to the extent that such increases are in excess of some accepted benchmark. While an inquiry by the Labor government in 1974 reported unfavourably on schemes of this kind—as did the Asprey Committee in its final report—they will no doubt continue to resurface from time to time.

There is of course a more general question which remains very much at the forefront of public debate, and that concerns whether tax cuts, over and above those already implied by tax indexation, might not be an appropriate device for beating inflation and assisting in the economic recovery. The issues are complex and controversial, going to the heart of overall economic strategy, and involving a range of budget considerations which bear only tangentially on tax matters. The argument remains lively, and one can fairly anticipate that pressure will continue to be placed on the government in future to cut income tax or commodity tax, or both, in the interest of economic management.

Conclusion

In conclusion, it must be stressed that the introduction of tax indexation still leaves unresolved a wide range of major issues pertaining to broader aspects of the Australian tax system. These include the question of the appropriate balance between direct and indirect taxes (which featured so prominently in the Asprey Committee findings), and the further question of whether social security operations can be more fully integrated into the tax system (as proposed by Professor Henderson and others in their discussion of a negative income tax). Indeed, by placing a considerable brake on further growth in tax revenue as a side-effect of inflation, the introduction of tax indexation may be expected to place pressure on the government in the years ahead to examine with very special care the whole question of the prospect of further tax changes.

References

[1] The opinions expressed are the author's and do not necessarily reflect the views of the Australian treasury.

[2] Spooner Committee, *Commonwealth Committee on Taxation*. Tabled reports on a wide range of taxation issues between 1950-4 (Government Printer, Canberra, 1950-4).

[3] Hulme Committee, *Report of the Commonwealth Committee on Rates of Depreciation* (Government Printer, Canberra, 1955).

[4] Ligertwood Committee, *Report of the Commonwealth Committee on Taxation* (Government Printer, Canberra, 1961).

[5] R. I. Downing, H. W. Arndt, A. H. Boxer, R. L. Mathews *Taxation in Australia: Agenda for Reform* (Melbourne University Press, Melbourne, 1964).

[6] Asprey Committee, *Taxation Review Committee Full Report 31 January 1975* (Australian Government Publishing Service, Canberra, 1975).

[7] Mathews Committee, *Inflation and Taxation*. Report of Committee of Inquiry into Inflation and Taxation, May 1975 (Government Printer, Canberra, 1975).

RUSSELL MATHEWS

9 Innovations in Fiscal Federalism

Introduction

The constitution of the Commonwealth of Australia was very much a product of the political philosophies and the economic conventions of the eighteenth and nineteenth centuries, and Australian electors have since been reluctant to approve constitutional amendments submitted to referendum. Nevertheless, it has proved possible for the constitution, as interpreted by the High Court, and as amended, to give effect to the Financial Agreement of 1927, and to accommodate a number of important innovations in fiscal federalism. All of these have played a significant role in the development of the federal principle, while some remain unique among federal institutions.

Among the most important of these innovations, which have all been modified or adapted during recent years with important consequences for the working of the Australian federal system, are: the statutory provision of intergovernmental tax-sharing arrangements; the systematic correction of fiscal inequalities; the co-ordination of governmental borrowing; and the systematic evaluation of needs in a wide range of public expenditure functions. These innovative ideas have been associated with constitutional or institutional developments which have themselves broken new ground in fiscal federalism. Thus the notion of revenue sharing was originally embodied in the Australian constitution itself. Fiscal equalization arrangements and the co-ordination of borrowing have been associated with the Commonwealth Grants Commission and the Australian Loan Council respectively. The evaluation of expenditure needs (which has been undertaken primarily to provide a basis for specific purpose payments from the Commonwealth to the states) has been associated with the establishment of a growing number of advisory bodies, such as the Universities Commission and the Commonwealth Bureau of Roads.

It is the purpose of this chapter to discuss two of these innovations–revenue sharing and fiscal equalization–with special reference to recent developments.

Revenue Sharing and Tax Sharing

The term revenue sharing has come to be applied to all kinds of loose arrangements whereby grants paid by one level of government to another are financed from a designated tax source. Strictly, the term tax sharing should be differentiated from revenue sharing and reserved for arrangements whereby different levels of government agree, without coercion on either side, to share a particular tax source in designated fixed or variable proportions in accordance with decisions taken jointly. Tax sharing thereby implies inter-governmental co-ordination of tax decisions, as opposed to either: (a) tax competition by governments which have concurrent powers in relation to a particular revenue source; or (b) a tax monopoly by one level of government with respect to a revenue source, whether or not that monopoly is accompanied by unilateral decisions by that level of government to share the revenues obtained from that source with other levels of government.

Whether the arrangements adopted by Australian governments in 1976 are considered to represent revenue sharing or tax sharing will therefore depend on whether or not they are viewed as resulting from an agreement reached freely and jointly. The Commonwealth-state arrangements meet some of the tests, because they have resulted from an agreement under which the states are able, within certain limits at least, to make decisions about rates of tax which will have the effect of determining the amounts of revenue that will flow to them individually and in the aggregate. Whether the agreement was reached freely and jointly is another question, which is further considered below. But the Commonwealth allocation of income tax revenue to local governments is not a form of tax sharing as defined above, because all the relevant decisions have been taken by the Commonwealth government, and local governments cannot make independent decisions which will affect their revenue yields.

Because the distinction between revenue sharing and tax sharing is not always clear cut, it will nevertheless be convenient for present purposes to regard tax sharing as a particular form of revenue sharing, without always attempting to categorize particular kinds of arrangements.

The immediate inspiration for the Australian revenue-sharing arrangements adopted in 1976, whereby specified proportions of Commonwealth income tax collections are to be paid to the states and local authorities, has been variously attributed to the U.S. (where revenue-sharing legislation was enacted in 1972); Canada (where arrangements for the sharing of income taxes have operated since World War II); or West Germany (where the distribution of tax revenues is constitutionally defined by the basic law that was adopted after World War II). It is sometimes forgotten that it was the

Australian constitution which first made formal provision for the sharing of taxes between two levels of government in a federal system.

Constitutional Provisions for Sharing Customs and Excise Duties

Several sections in the Constitution provided for the distribution of surplus Commonwealth revenues to the states, while one important section stipulated that, for a minimum period of ten years after federation, at least three-quarters of net customs and excise revenue collected by the Commonwealth must be paid to the states. This was the Braddon clause (section 87) which had proved to be one of the most contentious issues during the convention debates and which, because of strong opposition from New South Wales, at one time even threatened the achievement of federation itself.

The first constitutional referendum in 1898 had failed in New South Wales, where among other things the anti-federalists had speciously argued that the Braddon clause would unnecessarily increase taxation by requiring the Commonwealth to raise four times as much taxation as was really necessary. At a subsequent premiers' conference, the premiers were unable to agree on alternative arrangements which would provide the states with sufficient revenues during the difficult period of transition which was expected to follow their loss of customs and excise revenue. But they agreed to limit the operation of the Braddon clause to a minimum period of ten years, and they also decided to add a new clause, which (as section 96) was to empower the Commonwealth parliament to grant financial assistance to any state on such terms and conditions as it thought fit. It is ironical that this attempt to guarantee the financial safety of the states should have given the Commonwealth such far-reaching powers ultimately to erode their fiscal position. It is also ironical that New South Wales should have been the state which initiated the action to extend the Commonwealth's powers so dramatically, when its industries seemingly had most to gain from federation and its taxpayers have been required to make the largest sacrifices as a result of the Commonwealth's use of the section 96 grants power.

The Braddon clause operated only for the minimum period of ten years provided under the consititution. In 1910, the arrangements for sharing customs and excise duties were replaced by a system of fixed per capita grants to the states ($2·50 per head of population), which in turn gave way in 1927 to grants by way of debt charges assistance under the Financial Agreement. But although the 1920s were marked by attempts by conservative Commonwealth governments to obtain the agreement of the states to a separation of tax sources, and thus to revert to a system of co-ordinate federalism, there was a curious development in 1926 and 1927 when a form of revenue sharing was associated with the Commonwealth's first major incursion into the field of specific purpose payments, namely federal aid for roads.

Petrol Taxes

Road grants had been made since 1923, but in 1926 the amounts allocated to the states were financed from a customs duty on imported petrol and, in 1927, from an excise duty on locally refined petrol. The new taxes were widely criticized, not least by the states who complained that they did not receive the whole of the proceeds, that they were required to make matching contributions, and that they were not free to dispose of the funds in accordance with their own assessment of road priorities. With some modifications, including an explicit link with customs and excise collections after 1930, this tax-sharing arrangement continued until 1959 (when a new system of road grants was introduced, based on a quinquennial review of road programmes). However, both the financing and spending arrangements were the result of Commonwealth decisions rather than agreement between the Commonwealth and states.

From Co-operative to Coercive Federalism

There was a strong movement towards co-operative federalism in the 1920s and 1930s, associated with the establishment of the Australian Loan Council, the creation of ministerial councils such as the Australian Agricultural Council, the formation of the Commonwealth Grants Commission, and the elevation of the premiers' conference to a joint economic decision-making body in the early years of the depression. This movement came to an abrupt end in 1942, with the imposition of a system of uniform income taxation accompanied by tax reimbursement grants (later financial assistance grants) from the Commonwealth to the states. This marked the beginning of a sustained period of Commonwealth financial domination. Under what amounted to a system of coercive federalism, the Commonwealth was able to use its superior fiscal strength to control the main sources of state revenues, to determine the level of state borrowing and works programmes and, by means of specific purpose grants programmes and Commonwealth bodies created to advise on expenditure needs in the areas concerned, eventually to take over much of the responsibility for determining the level and pattern of expenditure in the main fields in which the states were supposed to exercise jurisdiction.

The centralizing tendencies were accentuated during the Labor government's period of office from 1972 to 1975. They were not checked until the states found a counter to the Commonwealth's financial domination in the form of political action designed to swing public opinion and withdraw electoral support for the Commonwealth's policies.

The Liberal-National Country Party Government's New Federalism Policy

It was against this background that the Liberal-National Country Party federal opposition announced that, if returned to government, it would adopt a new federalism policy; and it did so when it gained office in December 1975.

By 1975, the Labor government had itself begun to emphasize the need for policy co-ordination, and one of the main features of the new federalism policy of the Liberal and National Country Parties was a similar emphasis on co-ordination: 'we must restructure our forms and institutions of government and our attitudes of mind to achieve co-operation not conflict, partnership and not domination'.[1] But there were important philosophical differences between the two sides, marked especially by opposing ideas as to how powers and functions should be shared among the various levels of government.

The Liberal-National Country Party government's federalism policy, as modified in the course of three premiers' conferences during 1976 when general agreement was reached with the states about the implementation of the policy, contained the following elements:

(a) A system of income tax sharing with the states was to be introduced in two stages from 1976–7. Under stage 1 the states were to receive, instead of financial assistance grants, a designated share of personal income tax collected by the Commonwealth. Under stage 2, which was expected to apply from 1977–8, any state was to be free to impose a percentage surcharge or to allow a rebate of tax, and thereby vary the personal income tax paid by its citizens to its own benefit or cost.

(b) Local governments were to receive a fixed proportion (to be determined by the Commonwealth) of personal income tax collections.

(c) Specific purpose payments to the states were to be scaled down and, where appropriate, absorbed into tax-sharing or other general purpose funds.

(d) An advisory council for inter-government relations was to be established, comprising representatives of Commonwealth and state parliaments, local government representatives and private citizens, to consider matters referred to it for investigation and advice by the premiers' conference.

(e) Machinery for intergovernmental co-operation was to be strengthened, for example by making the premiers' conference a forum for debate on broad economic issues and on matters developed by the council for inter-government relations, by strengthening the role of intergovernmental ministerial councils and consultative bodies, and by reviewing Commonwealth and state functions with a view to eliminating unnecessary overlapping, waste and interference.

Income Tax Sharing

Under the new income tax sharing arrangements, which relate only to personal income tax, the Commonwealth will continue to be the sole collecting and administrative agency, and there will continue to be uniform assessment provisions and a uniform basic rate structure. Only state surcharges and rebates may vary in accordance with decisions taken by individual states, and states have agreed to consult with the Commonwealth about their actions and not to negate the latter's economic management policies.

Surcharges or rebates applied by the Commonwealth for economic management purposes are to be excluded from the base used to calculate the states' entitlement, which subject to this exception is net income tax collected in the current year in the states and, initially at least, the territories. The percentage to be applied to this base was calculated by reference to the relationship between financial assistance grants and personal income tax collections in 1975–6; it was finally fixed at the estimated figure of 33·6 per cent (although the actual percentage proved to be 33·3 per cent).

Provisions to protect state revenue yields include: Commonwealth assurances regarding advice and consultation about tax changes and possible adjustments in state entitlements in response to those changes; a guarantee that stage 1 entitlements in any year will not be less than those for the previous year; and a Commonwealth undertaking that, for the first four years, entitlements will not be less than the amounts that would have been received under the financial assistance grants arrangements.

Although the initial distribution of the states' share of income tax will be in accordance with the relativities of the financial assistance grants in 1975–6, a number of fiscal equalization provisions will apply which may eventually change the distribution. The absorption of specific purpose payments in the states' share of income taxes will also no doubt affect the relativities. There will be a periodic review of relativities between states on the advice of an independent body; whether this body will be the Grants Commission still has to be determined. The first review, which will coincide with a review of the tax-sharing arrangements generally, will be before the end of

1980–1. The four less populous states will continue to be eligible for special grants on the recommendation of the Grants Commission. Surcharges made by the states under stage 2 will also be subject to equalization on the basis of assessments made by the Grants Commission, but the equalization criterion will differ from that normally used by the Commission (see below).

Evaluation of the Tax-Sharing Arrangements

The tax-sharing element of the new federalism policy represents a significant retreat from the Commonwealth's income tax monopoly and a corresponding movement towards a system of tax co-ordination. To the extent that it restores financial balance within a co-ordinated system of responsibility sharing, it must therefore be regarded as an improvement over the situation which had existed since 1942. This is because, under the uniform tax arrangements, the link between taxing and spending decisions had been destroyed at both the Commonwealth and state levels. The consequential loss of financial responsibility had been associated with recurring budgetary imbalance, destructive political conflict and confrontation, inefficient and inequitable state taxes, the effective diminution of state access to borrowing through the Loan Council, the distortion of state expenditure priorities and, more generally, Australia's inability to reap the advantages either of decentralized decision-making within a federal system or of fully integrated planning within a unitary system.

The new arrangements also retain many of the advantages of the uniform tax system, especially: Commonwealth control over economic management policies, which must necessarily be formulated and executed at the national level; the use of income taxes as a major instrument in income distribution policy; the convenience to taxpayers of a single system of assessment and collection; and the minimization of interstate tax competition, with its wasteful effects on resource allocation and the possibility of undesirable distribution effects resulting, for example, from the creation of comparative tax havens. Despite the weaknesses in the equalization arrangements discussed below, also, the new system seems likely to result in a more rational pattern of distribution of general revenue funds among the six states.

However, it should be noted that the new arrangements do not meet unequivocally the tests of a pure tax-sharing scheme which were described above. Although they have formed the basis of an agreement between the Commonwealth and the six states (described as 'points of understanding' but not embodied in a formal agreement), decisions were not taken jointly from positions of equal bargaining strength. The states were effectively presented with a choice between uniform income tax and the Commonwealth's proposals for tax sharing, which the state premiers were able to modify only within narrow limits during the course of the bargaining.

Although the states will be free to impose surcharges during stage 2, and will thereby regain a measure of tax flexibility which has been absent since 1942, there is no indication that the Commonwealth will make tax room for the states by reducing its own rates and thus facilitating the introduction of the surcharges. Indeed, because this would merely substitute state-imposed taxes for the states' share of Commonwealth-imposed taxes, the states themselves would probably oppose such action. There has been only a limited movement towards financial responsibility and most of the effective taxing decisions will still be taken by the Commonwealth.

So long as the Commonwealth retains the power to determine the total amount of revenue which is to flow to the states, the new arrangements represent only a modest change from the system of financial assistance grants. It is therefore likely that arguments about the tax share will replace the arguments about the financial assistance grants formula which were a distinguishing feature of the old system, with the Commonwealth continuing to hold the ultimate power of decision.

For their part, the states have shown themselves to be mainly interested in possible short-term benefits—in particular in the prospect of immediate increases in revenues relative to the amounts which they would have obtained under the financial assistance grants formula. They appear to have shown little concern for increasing their long-term independence, for example by negotiating a reduction in Commonwealth rates so as to permit state surcharges to be imposed at a significant level without evoking hostility from taxpayers. It is difficult to avoid the conclusion that the states prefer to remain dependent on Commonwealth revenue raising rather than to accept political responsibility for their own taxing decisions.

In sacrificing the possibility of greater financial independence for short-term political expedience, the states have almost certainly failed to protect their own long-term interests. This is because they have gained access to a fixed share of income tax too late to benefit from future automatic growth in tax yields to the extent that would have been possible even a few years ago. The share of 33·6 per cent, which was based on the 1975–6 relationship between financial assistance grants and personal income tax collections, was thus much lower than the percentage which applied throughout the 1960s and early 1970s. This was always above 40 per cent and in the early years was above 50 per cent. Moreover, as a result of the introduction of personal tax indexation in 1976–7, the revenue base will not grow nearly so rapidly in future years. Except to the extent that they are protected by the guarantee or consultation provisions and by their ability to impose surcharges, the states will also be subject to the risk of much greater fluctuations in revenue yields than in the past. Finally, it seems likely that it will not be easy to obtain agreement on the arrangements for absorbing specific purpose grants into the states' share of income taxes, especially where the grants are at present unequally distributed among the states.

Against these limitations of the new scheme from the viewpoint of the states must be balanced the short-term financial gains which they will obtain, the prospect of a partial substitution of general revenue funds or block grants for specific purpose grants, the opportunity to impose surcharges, the prospect of greater participation in Commonwealth tax decisions and, for some of the states at least, the possibility of a more equitable distribution of revenues among the six states.

The specious argument that the new arrangements involve some form of double taxation has received some credence in political debate. It is doubly ironical that this has been especially true in New South Wales, which along with Victoria is the state most likely to benefit from the imposition of its own income tax surcharge and from a more equitable distribution of general revenue funds distributed by the Commonwealth. History seems to be repeating itself, with threats of higher taxation being used—as in the debate about the Braddon clause—to mislead taxpayers who may be expected to benefit from the new arrangements.

Fiscal Equalization: Early Grants Commission Methodology

Following pioneering work on the concept and measurement of fiscal capacity by Professor L. F. Giblin during the 1920s, systematic procedures for the evaluation of the fiscal needs of financially weaker states in a federal system were first evolved by the Commonwealth Grants Commission in the 1930s. Although equalization grants in the form of so-called special grants had been paid to Western Australia from 1910–11, Tasmania from 1912–13 and South Australia from 1929–30, it was not until the Grants Commission was established in 1933 that the financial needs of the so-called claimant states were assessed independently in accordance with explicit and consistent equalization principles.

In its early reports, the Commission rejected the arguments that special grants should be based on a principle of compensation for disabilities resulting from federation, for poverty of resources or for inequalities among individual citizens, and adopted the following criterion as the basis for special financial assistance to a state:

> Special grants are justified when a State through financial stress from any cause is unable efficiently to discharge its functions as a member of the federation and should be determined by the amount of help found necessary to make it possible for that State by reasonable effort to function at a standard not appreciably below that of other States.

The original methodology of the Grants Commission provided for a comparison of the budget results of a claimant and the average of the standard states, the differential budget results first being corrected or modified to make them comparable and then adjusted for differences between the claimant and the standard states in severity of taxation and in the standard of services.

The recommended special grant, which took the form of unconditional general revenue assistance, was intended to meet the so-called financial needs of the claimant state. Initially financial needs were interpreted as minimum needs rather than as the amounts necessary to achieve budget equality with the standard states. Thus for some years the Commission imposed a so-called penalty for claimancy, and until quite recently it would not recommend a grant which would do more than achieve a balanced budget for a claimant state, even if the standard states on average had budget surpluses.

Over the years the nature of special grants has changed in two important respects. The first involved a gradual shift from minimum needs to full budget equalization as the purpose of the grant. The second involved new methods of calculation, whereby the claimant state's financial needs have come to be assessed directly, by reference to differences in revenue-raising capacity and costs of providing services, instead of indirectly by reference to differential budget results. The special grants finally became full equalization grants in 1975, and in changing to direct assessment in 1974 the Commission described the new approach as follows:

> In making this direct calculation, the claimant State's financial needs have been assessed as the sum of:
>
> (a) its revenue needs, defined as the difference between
>
> (i) the revenue it would have raised if it had applied the average revenue effort of the standard States (the standard revenue effort) to its own revenue base, and
>
> (ii) the revenue it would have raised, on the basis of the standard revenue effort, if its per capita revenue base (or its revenue-raising capacity) had been the same as the average revenue base of the standard States; and
>
> (b) its expenditure needs, defined as the additional costs to the claimant State of providing its population with State services of the same average range and quality as those provided for their populations by the standard States.

Achievements and Limitations of the Grants Commission's Approach

The Grants Commission's procedures almost certainly represent the most sophisticated and systematic application of equalization principles in any country, federal or unitary. No other country has made provision for such detailed assessment of financial needs by an independent, quasi-judicial body. Central governments in many other countries make equalization grants to provinces, states or local governments, but the grants are usually based on *ad hoc* or political assessments, on comparisons of broad economic indicators or on some kind of formula approach. Where systematic evaluation of relative financial needs is undertaken, as in Canada or in the Federal Republic of Germany, the equalization is usually partial in the sense that it is restricted to revenue-raising disabilities and possibly to one or two expenditure disabilities. In some federal countries, notably the U.S.A., systematic equalization is not even attempted.

Despite the refinements which have been made by the Grants Commission to its equalization procedures, there remain problems and issues in existing arrangements which limit or otherwise affect the extent to which the principles of equalization can be fully achieved in Australia. Some of these will now be discussed.

(a) Although the choice of equalization standard is essentially a political decision, in practice the decision has been left to the Grants Commission. Although equalization in many other countries has been based on the average fiscal capacity of the units subject to equalization, in Australia the Commission has for many years adopted as its standard the fiscal capacity of the two states with the highest fiscal capacity, New South Wales and Victoria. This approach has both advantages and disadvantages. On the one hand, it ensures that the policies of units subject to equalization cannot influence the size of the grants. On the other, it raises the possibility that the standard may not be wholly relevant to the needs of a claimant state. Such a situation is likely to arise if the economic activities or budget structures (revenue sources or expenditure patterns) of the claimant and the standard states significantly diverge.

Consider, for example, a standard state which is highly urbanized and industrialized and a claimant state which is mainly rural and whose main economic activity is tourism. The budget structures of the two states will be quite different; for example, the standard state will tend to tax business activity while the claimant state will tend to tax tourism. But the adoption of the standard state's revenue-raising capacity as the equalization criterion will tend to understate the claimant state's capacity and thus lead to a higher grant than is really justified. This is because the claimant state's relatively low capacity for business taxation will be taken into account but, if the standard state does not tax tourism, the claimant state's relatively high capacity for tourist taxes may be ignored.

This problem has arisen in relation to royalties on minerals produced by a claimant state but not by the standard states. The Commission has dealt with it by determining notional royalty rates in order to assess the negative needs of the claimant state for that revenue source; but this involves a departure from objective assessment by reference to the standard state's revenue-raising performance.

The same kind of problem may arise in relation to expenditure needs. It has thus sometimes been argued that the Commission's procedures overstate the relative expenditure needs of claimant states by failing to take full account of the disabilities which the standard states suffer as a result of their larger and more congested cities. (It should be noted, however, that many of these disabilities relate to needs for capital outlays which are not reviewed by the Commission, although it does attempt to bring debt charges into its comparisons as far as data permit.)

A general issue in relation to this problem is whether equalization might more appropriately be based on broad economic indicators than on the detailed budgetary performance of the standard states.

(b) Equalization payments in Australia have always been financed by the Commonwealth government and not, as in West Germany, by the states with above-average fiscal capacity. It has been a fortunate accident that the highest capacity states have also been the states with the largest populations, so that equalization payments have tended to be small relative to the financial resources of the Commonwealth. But this has meant that the two standard states have shown relatively little interest in the equalization arrangements, thereby making it more difficult for the Grants Commission to assess relativities and possibly resulting in more favourable treatment for the claimant states than would occur if the standard states intervened in Grants Commission hearings in an adversary role.

Difficulties could arise, in any case, if the revenue base of one or more of the less populous states increased dramatically, to the point where equalization payments to one of the larger states became justified. This is essentially what happened recently in Canada, when the oil and gas producing provinces received very large increases in mineral royalties as a result of the world energy crisis.

It is an advantage of the West German system that it can adapt to shocks of this kind without imposing impossible burdens on the budget of the federal government. The possibility of adjusting the relativities of financial assistance grants has previously provided an insurance against such a development in Australia. The original tax-sharing proposals which the Liberal-National Country Party coalition made in 1975 would have brought the Australian system closer to that of West Germany, by integrating the equalization and the tax-sharing arrangements. But under the system finally agreed with the state premiers in 1976, the supplementary equalization arrangements have been separated from the tax-sharing arrangements and it seems that overall relativities among all six states will now only be adjusted at the time of periodic reviews.

(c) One of the major limitations of the Grants Commission's approach results from data problems, which have the effect of making it difficult to assess needs in some areas objectively on the basis of interstate comparisons. A consequence of the budget result approach originally employed by the Commission was that budget differentials due to differences in policy or differences in efficiency, as opposed to differences in need, might be reflected in special grants. To avoid this result, the Commission needed to be able to identify differences in policy or efficiency, and for some expenditure items data for this purpose were not available.

This problem has continued to exist under the Commission's new direct assessment procedures, because a claimant state's implied needs for the items in question are taken to be equal to the differences in per capita revenue or expenditure multiplied by the claimant state's population. This admits of the possibility that the size of the recommended grant will reflect not only real needs but also differences in policy or efficiency as between the claimant state and the standard states.

The Commission attempts to deal with this problem by keeping trends under review and by making appropriate modifications to exclude the effects of policy differences from the measure of needs. But it continues to be inhibited by data problems. Perhaps it is not surprising that implied disabilities for the items concerned tend to be proportionately much higher than for the items which are subject to direct measurement. In addition to general administration and debt charges, particular areas of difficulty include land revenues (due to problems of measuring the revenue base); transport undertakings (where modifications are made for differences in fares, freight charges, wage costs, depreciation and debt charges, but where residual deficits may reflect other policy differences); and expenditure on agriculture (where differences in the pattern of production, in climate and terrain, and in methods of financing research and other activities make comparisons especially difficult).

(d) Technical problems may arise when the Grants Commission is only one of several agencies capable of making equalization payments of one form or another. To the extent that the distribution of financial assistance grants or the states' share of income taxes diverges from an equal per capita distribution, it implicitly contains an equalization element. The Grants Commission allows for this by making an appropriate deduction from a claimant state's assessed needs before arriving at the recommended assessed grant.

The problem arises in a more acute form when another agency assesses needs in relation to a particular item, by reference to a criterion which may conflict with the criterion used by the Grants Commission. This has happened in the case of grants for primary and secondary schools recommended by the Schools Commission. These are based on the principle of equalizing the performance of schools as opposed to the Grants Commission's objective of equalizing state fiscal capacity. The Grants Commission has indicated that it proposes to deal with this problem by including the Schools Commission's assessment of expenditure need in its own assessment of needs, and by bringing differential schools grants received by a claimant state into its calculations as an offset against the state's expenditure need. So far as the revenue offset is concerned, the proposed procedure will be similar to that adopted for financial assistance grants or other general revenue funds. But again, data limitations make it difficult to apply the procedure.

(e) A related problem, which is of major importance in any evaluation of Australia's equalization arrangements, results from the fact that, between 1959 and 1976 at least, there has been no systematic examination by the Grants Commission or any other body of the relative financial positions of all six states. This is because, following the withdrawal of South Australia as a claimant state in 1959 and the subsequent adoption by the Commission of a two-state standard (New South Wales and Victoria), there have never been more than two standard states and three claimant states. By 1976, there was only one claimant state (Queensland) whose needs were being assessed in relation to the financial position of the standard states.

This position has arisen because of numerous *ad hoc* decisions which have been made unilaterally by the Commonwealth or which have resulted from bilateral or multilateral political bargaining with the states. These have resulted in a distribution of financial assistance and other general revenue grants which neither reflects relative financial needs as measured by the Grants Commission nor follows any other systematic assessment of relative needs. On four occasions between 1959 and 1975, bilateral arrangements between the Commonwealth government and a state government of similar political persuasion have involved substantial increases in financial assistance grants to the state concerned and its consequent withdrawal as a claimant state before the Grants Commission. The inference is that the states concerned have improved their financial position relative to that of the states which remain subject to Grants Commission comparisons (remaining claimant states and standard states), and that the overall distribution of general revenue funds no longer reflects relative financial needs.

It has now been agreed that, as one aspect of the new tax-sharing arrangements, there will be a periodic review of the relativities of the tax shares received by the six states. The new equalization arrangements are examined in the next section of the Chapter.

Equalization Aspects of the New Tax-Sharing Arrangements

One of the principal achievements of the new federalism policy was the agreement reached with state premiers regarding equalization arrangements. Because of differences in taxable capacity which were implicitly (if haphazardly) recognized under the financial assistance grants arrangements, the states did not all have the same interest in a return of taxing powers. Most previous attempts to present a common front to the Commonwealth on the question of state income taxes had failed primarily because of disagreements among the states about sharing or equalization arrangements.

The interstate equalization arrangements agreed to by the Commonwealth and states contained three elements:

(a) Although the initial distribution of the states' share of income taxes was to be based on the distribution of financial assistance grants in 1975–6, provision was made for periodic reviews of relativities between all states, in the first instance before 1980–1, in the light of advice from an independent body. There was disagreement among the states as to whether the review body should be the Grants Commission and this question was not resolved at the 1976 premiers' conference.

(b) The four less populous states were to remain free to apply for grants on the recommendation of the Grants Commission, in addition to their basic entitlements. The relationship between Queensland's special grant and the tax-sharing arrangements was to be regarded as a matter for consideration by the Queensland and Commonwealth governments.

(c) The surcharges which individual states might levy under the stage 2 arrangements were to be subject to equalization on the basis of assessments made by the Grants Commission, so that each of the less populous states would obtain the same relative advantage from a surcharge as New South Wales and Victoria. The basis for the assessment of equalization in relation to a surcharge was spelt out in some detail as follows: '. . . supplementary assistance will be provided to a less populous state levying a surcharge up to the average per capita amount which would be yielded if New South

Wales and Victoria levied a surcharge on the same basis'. The surcharge equalization was to be independent of any more general examination of relative financial positions.

In addition to the provisions for state equalization, local government revenue-sharing arrangements changed the procedures for distributing Commonwealth general revenue assistance (which from 1977–8 was to be determined as a percentage of personal income tax collections) among local governments. In particular, as from 1976–7 at least 30 per cent of the total amount within each state was to be distributed on a population basis (possibly adjusted for area, population density or other factors agreed with the Commonwealth), while the remaining assistance was to be distributed on a needs basis in accordance with recommendations made by state Grants Commissions established for the purpose. The role of the Commonwealth Grants Commission in relation to local government would then be restricted to periodic recommendations about the interstate distribution. It seems possible that a state Grants Commission could actually ignore fiscal equalization principles and allocate the whole of a state's grant to local governments on a per capita basis.

Weaknesses of the Interstate Equalization Arrangements

The new system provides a basis for a more rational and equitable distribution of general revenue funds among the six states, in particular by providing for a regular review of relativities by an independent body and thereby making it possible for equalization arrangements to be brought within a more general framework of vertical and horizontal fiscal settlement. Nevertheless, there are several respects in which the equalization aspects of the new arrangements are vague or unsatisfactory.

In the first place, the relationship between the periodic review of relative tax shares and the traditional Grants Commission equalization arrangements is not fully spelt out. Presumably, any special grants paid on the recommendation of the Grants Commission will be absorbed into the states' share of income tax at the time of the periodic reviews. Because the Commonwealth will have been financing the special grants, also, there is a question whether the amounts involved will be added to the states' entitlements generally when the new relativities come into effect.

Secondly, if the supplementary Grants Commission equalization arrangements are to operate independently of the tax-sharing arrangements between reviews, then a formal link needs to be maintained between the procedures for determining state relativities at the time of the reviews and the procedures for assessing equalization grants. If state relativities were to be determined by political bargaining or assessed by a body other than the Grants Commission, as some states have suggested, there could be a conflict between the two approaches to equalization. If left to the states, in an extreme situation the states collectively could manipulate the system to their mutual advantage. Thus all six states could agree to give New South Wales and Victoria higher than warranted proportions of the states' income tax shares, and then use Grants Commission procedures to achieve additional equalization payments for the other four states.

Thirdly, it was unwise to relate equalization on surcharges to rates imposed by states receiving equalization, instead of to rates imposed by the standard states. Not only does this conflict with the traditional Grants Commission approach, but it makes it possible for a state seeking equalization to influence the amount it receives by means of its own policies. All six states will have an incentive to substitute income tax surcharges for other forms of state taxation so long as equalization in respect of the other taxes continues to be assessed by reference to rates imposed by standard states. This is because the other four states will not receive equalization payments in respect of income taxes imposed by New South Wales and Victoria. Because equalization on surcharges will not affect relativities in relation to tax sharing generally, these two states will be able to improve their position relative to claimant states by substituting income taxes for other taxes. The other four states will also be able to maximize equalization payments by substituting income taxes for other taxes.

Although the surcharge equalization arrangements will make it worth while for the states to substitute state income taxes for their existing taxes, it is by no means certain that they will do so. To the extent that the Commonwealth does not reduce its rates to make room for the states, the imposition of surcharges will result in an increase in both marginal and average rates of income tax. Many people believe that the burden of income taxation is already too high in Australia, and the states may see political disadvantages in substituting income taxes for existing state taxes, despite the revenue advantages which will result from such action. At least one state government has indicated that it does not intend to enter the income tax field under existing arrangements.

Conclusion

It is too soon to say whether the new tax-sharing arrangements will restore vertical and horizontal financial balance in the Australian federal system, reduce the centralizing tendencies of recent years and devolve significant taxing powers on the states. Nevertheless, the new scheme provides a framework within which individual governments will have greater responsibility for their actions, and in which greater policy co-ordination among Commonwealth and state governments will be possible, than under uniform taxation. The potential scope for improving intergovernmental financial balance has undoubtedly been improved, although the opportunities for continuing conflict also remain.

Reference

1 Compare the statement made by Mr E. G. Whitlam in 1971, while in opposition: 'Each of our three levels of government has functions which it is best able to perform. The key to effective performance is not domination but consultation, not centralization but co-ordination.' Note also the statement made by Mr Whitlam as prime minister at the premiers' conference of May 1975: 'The Australian Government will be seeking in the longer term a more rational and co-ordinated system of assessing needs, setting priorites and allocating resources in the public sector—one based on co-operation between governments . . . '

FRANK CREAN

10 Patterns of International Trade

Where and What

Australia's overseas trade has shown considerable changes over the last twenty years both as to products traded and the areas with which trade has taken place. This pattern is likely to change significantly over the next twenty years.

It is doubtful if many in the 1940s, when exports and imports were each below $1000 million, would have predicted the level or direction of trade by the 1960s. In 1959/60 Australian exports were $1875 million, 51 per cent of which went to Europe; while imports were $1854 million, of which 52 per cent came from Europe. Ten years later, exports were $4137 million, only 27 per cent of which went to Europe and 42 per cent to Asia; while imports were $3881 million, of which 40 per cent came from Europe, 29 per cent from the Americas and 24 per cent from Asia. By 1974/75 Australian exports were $8687 million, of which only 21·5 per cent went to Europe, and 49 per cent to Asia. Imports were $8079 million, only 36 per cent coming from Europe, 34 per cent from Asia and 24 per cent from the Americas.

There have also been considerable changes in the nature of products traded, as Table 1 shows.

The first Annual Report (1975/76) produced by the Department of Overseas Trade mentioned (p. 5) that:

> Trade makes an important contribution to Australia's fundamental national economic goals—economic growth, full employment and higher per caput real income. Overseas trade is essential to the efficient use of Australia's resources and to the maintenance of a dynamic economy.
> Overseas trade represents approximately 28 per cent of the country's gross domestic product. It has played a significant part in improving the well-being of primary and secondary industry and of community welfare. Exports have enabled producers to take advantage of their competitive ability on overseas markets; imports of capital equipment, technology and finished goods have benefited both the Australian producer and consumer.

The level of exports and imports necessarily has an effect on the level of domestic economic activity. Generally, an increase in the level of exports stimulates economic growth and provides a higher per caput income in real terms, thus contributing to Australia's national economic objectives.

At the time of writing (in December 1976), unemployment is at higher levels in Australia than has customarily been thought to be tolerable in the era of full employment, and there is considerable unused industrial capacity. Further, manufacturing as a source of total employment has fallen from over 30 per cent to 25 per cent in less than five years.

TABLE 1

The Nature of Australian Traded Produce

	Manufacturers	*Minerals*	*Farm Products Other*		*Re-exports*	*Total Exports*
			$ million	*(f.o.b.)*		
1959–60	198	116	1451	74	36	1875
1964–65	323	249	1910	100	69	2651
1969–70	727	953	2088	198	171	4137
1974–75 (p)	1876	2358	3841	344	269	8688
			Percentage of total exports			
1959–60	10·7	6·2	77·4	3·8	1·9	100·0
1964–65	12·2	9·4	72·0	3·8	2·6	100·0
1969–70	17·6	23·0	50·5	4·8	4·1	100·0
1974–75 (p)	21·6	27·1	44·2	4·0	3·1	100·0
	Producers' materials	*Capital Equipment*	*Finished Consumer Goods*		*Non-merchandise*	*Total Imports*
			$ million	*(f.o.b.)*		
1959–60	973	417	324	135	5	1854
1964–65	1455	748	446	192	63	2905
1969–70	1729	1087	766	239	59	3881
1974–75 (p)	3279	2347	1898	437	118	8079
			Percentage of total imports			
1959–60	52·5	22·5	17·5	7·2	0·3	100·0
1964–65	50·1	25·7	15·4	6·6	2·2	100·0
1969–70	44·6	28·0	19·7	6·2	1·5	100·0
1974–75 (p)	40·6	29·0	23·5	5·4	1·5	100·0

Sources: Department of Overseas Trade and Australian Bureau of Statistics.

The recent report on the future of manufacturing industry in Australia (the Jackson Report),[1] has suggested that if manufacturing is to maintain its relative role in the economy in the future it will be necessary to expand the export of manufactures. But it is hard to imagine areas of manufacturing activity that are likely to be successful in expanding exports, although the devaluation of the Australian dollar announced on 29 November 1976 may make some new export trade in manufactures feasible. On the other hand, many would see any further expansion in manufacturing, if it is attainable, as occurring only slowly in Australia. (It is also likely that social attitudes will not make it easy in the future to site large scale manufacturing indiscriminately.)

International trade arises out of differences among nations in the availability of natural and human resources, and also out of differences in the levels of economic development between areas. Theoretically, a particular country exports those goods of which it has an abundance, or in which it enjoys a comparative advantage, in exchange for goods which it does not produce or can only produce with comparative disadvantage. In practice, however, barriers are unfortunately erected between countries to impede the 'logical' flow of trade. Australia has been both offender and victim in erecting and facing tariff and non-tariff barriers, a position by no means unique among nations. Also, exports and imports are both necessary, and conflicts of interest often arise because of incomplete co-ordination of economic activity. Friction can occur in such delicate areas as the exchange rate and capital flow.

As already indicated, for the year ended 30 June 1975 total Australian exports were $8687 million and imports $8079 million. Exports to Japan were $2401 million, the United States $832 million, United Kingdom $475 million, the European Economic Community $1336 million, New Zealand $529 million, centrally planned economies $591 million, and developing countries $2367 million. Imports were $1420 million from Japan, $1668 million from United States, $1215 million from United Kingdom, $2387 million from European Economic Community, $184 million from New Zealand, $128 million from centrally planned economies and $1448 million from developing countries.

In rounded terms, Australia's overall favourable trade balance of some $600 million was made up of $1000 million favourable with Japan, $350 million favourable with New Zealand, $450 million favourable with centrally planned economies and $900 million favourable with developing countries. Unfavourable trade balances existed to the extent of $800 million with United States, $1050 million with the European Economic Community, and $750 million with the United Kingdom. In 1974/75, farm products accounted for

46 per cent of the total value of exports from Australia, minerals for 28 per cent and manufactures for 22 per cent. And Australia's import bill for 1974/75 was 41 per cent producers' materials, 29 per cent capital equipment and 23 per cent consumer goods.

Why and How

Australia's overseas trade has grown out of a colonial background with major exports originally being primary products to the 'home country', and imports derived principally from Britain; first, then, essential stores, and more latterly capital equipment which was added after the economic growth in Australia following the gold-rush period.

Historically, there have been changes in the dependence of the Australian economy on imported manufactures, with resort in the 1930s to quite heavy protection of Australian industry. More recently, there have been changes in the direction of more sophisticated manufactured products and the motor vehicle in particular. As indicated earlier, there have been shifts both in the directions of trade and in the products traded, and it is probably true that Australia has 'arrived' where it is by travelling hopefully rather than out of any very careful planning of the journey.

In more recent years Australia has been fortunate in the favourable prices received for items such as sugar and wheat and in having potential abundance of iron ore and coal. Using the year 1966/67 as a base of 100, Australia's terms of trade showed a steady decline–that is, import prices rose faster than export prices –from 1966/67 through to 1971/72, reaching 86 in that year; but showed very sudden increases to 112 in 1972/73 and 115 in 1973/74. To a large degree, the improvements in the latter two years were because of better prices obtained from iron ore and coal sales to Japan in which the new Labor government assisted by pushing the local sellers to negotiate better terms of sale. However, 1974/75 showed a substantial upsurge in import prices which rose from 132 to 189 in a single year, and ended in the index of terms of trade dropping to 91.[2]

That there have been such variations in terms of trade over a relatively short period illustrates the still volatile nature of international trade, and Australia has in some respects been fortunate, relative to other countries, in simultaneously being (1) an exporter of raw materials and primary products with rising world prices, (2) less dependent on oil imports at rising prices than most other western economies, and (3) more able to be 'choosy' about other imports.

The situation is unlikely to be so easy in the foreseeable future when regard is had to the composition of Australian exports for 1974/75, to the principal customers for the major items, and to the makeup of Australian imports by items and origin. In fact, as at December 1976, the scenario is changing so rapidly that one hesitates to try to predict anything. But a start may be made by examining the major items and customers for Australia's exports for 1974/75. The ten principal categories of export were:

	$ million
Wheat, barley, oats	1145
Wool and sheep products	770
Iron ore	707
Coal	665
Sugar	645
Chemicals	471
Other metals	420
Beef and other meats	420
Iron and steel	377
Machinery and electrical equipment	343

These items aggregate nearly $6000 million, or almost three-quarters of Australia's total exports for 1974/75, and there may well be variations in the relative importance of any one from year to year. These variations can be caused by seasonal changes, by changes in world demand or by trade barriers (tariff and non-tariff), and sometimes the existence of trade in particular items is occasioned by sheer geographical propinquity (as with manufacturing exports to New Zealand) or by particular commodity arrangements which can terminate suddenly.

Of these ten items of exports, the major buying countries were as follows:

(1) Wheat, Barley and Oats

	$ million
Japan	229
China	161
Arab Republic	116
U.S.S.R.	100
Indonesia	80
Pakistan	72
Iran	54
Iraq	41
Korean Republic	36

The buyers here tend to fall into four groups—Japan as a regular buyer, China and U.S.S.R. both asserting their intent to ultimately become self-sufficient but at present buying out of shortfall between internal demand and local supply; Pakistan (as sometimes with India) tends to be a famine buyer, and there is a set of relatively new buyers in Iraq, Iran and Korea.

(2) Wool and Sheep Products

	$ million
Japan	216
France	108
U.S.S.R.	92
Germany (F.R.)	59
Italy	50

Here the largest customers are fairly regular buyers who still see virtue in wool as a fibre.

(3) Iron Ore

	$ million
Japan	544
Germany	42
Other European countries	70

Coal

Japan	505
Europe	68
U.K.	29

Currently, both for iron ore and coal, there is one preponderant customer, Japan, which is also a heavy direct investor in these industries.

(4) Sugar

	$ million
Canada	165
U.S.	159
Japan	106
Malaysia	50
U.S.S.R.	42
U.K.	34
Korea	34
New Zealand	14
China	14
Singapore	13

At the moment, a new international sugar agreement is in process of evolution and the final form will not be determined until mid-1977. There may well be more reliance on stocks and more flexibility in pricing. Apart from the competition between cane and beet sugar the situation in the immediate years is likely to be volatile.

(5) Chemicals

	$ million
U.S.	144
Japan	85
New Zealand	48
Canada	41

This area ranks as manufactures in which Australia seems to have been reasonably successful in recent years. But the largest single item is alumina, which local producing companies, foreign owned, sell to one or two particular firms in the U.S. and Japan.

(6) Beef and Other Meats

	$ million
U.S.	219
Japan	40
Canada	30
U.K.	19

Here the importance of the American market for beef is evident, but in almost every country Australian access is subject to quota arrangements. Australia is beginning to be successful in lamb and mutton sales to the Middle East.

(7) Iron and Steel

	$ million
Japan	57
New Zealand	53
Argentina	32
Germany	27
U.S.	22
China	18
Philippines	17

This is an area in which Australia has been successful in tailoring particular types of products to particular markets.

As regards 'other metals' and 'machinery and electrical equipment' the countries and the products are too diversified to display any particular trends. The United Kingdom is still important for the sale of lead, the U.S. for titanium and Japan for zinc. Again, while it is difficult now to see why Australia's trade patterns, both export and import, have developed as they have, very great concern should be shown as to how our trade is to be maintained and developed in the future.

As long as wool is still demanded as a fibre, Australia is in a strong position with this product. Japan is the principal customer and is important as the price setter. In fact there is a feeling that other countries who still prefer wool do not bid competitively with Japan but wait until Japan has set the price pace.

With wheat and other grains Australia has the potential to substantially increase its acreage but it cannot do this on the basis of holding supplies when other areas are in short supply. Australia has to have forward guarantees that the potential customers will buy commercially or that other international arrangements will be made for purchase on a 'famine' basis.

Australia also has tremendous potential on a long-term basis to be both a supplier of beef—still a 'rich world' product—or mutton and lamb, the 'poor world's' meat. But again Australia cannot be a producer of beef for potential export unless there is some firm arrangement with the principal customer, the U.S., about defined quantities at reasonable prices. In a sense, every American and every Australian is a regular beef-eater. This is not so with Japan. J. W. Longworth[3] has indicated some of the potential difficulties. He observed that 'beef is essentially a luxury good in Japan' and that the government appears to have decided to force beef consumers to pay for the development of a viable domestic beef industry'. Longworth concluded:

> It is futile to imagine that the Japanese Government (now or in the foreseeable future) will introduce free trade in beef. However, it is in the interests of both the Japanese Government and the overseas suppliers of beef to reduce the uncertainty which currently surrounds the Japanese beef trade.
> From the Japanese viewpoint, imports represent a source of funds with which to finance domestic subsidies (this is only true of course, wherever world beef prices remain below domestic Japanese prices). In addition, though it may seem extraordinary given the current margin between world and Japanese prices, influential people in Japan expect world prices to rise dramatically within a decade as the world enters a period of severe animal protein shortage. It would seem, therefore, that Japan may be prepared to sign a long-term bilateral agreement guaranteeing itself a source of beef. Unfortunately, from the viewpoint of the Australian beef industry, trade between Australia and Japan is not restricted to beef. It would be most unwise to expect MITI to overlook such a valuable opportunity for a little 'horse-trading'.

Australia has, at least since the introduction of GATT in 1947, been a theoretical supporter of the liberalization of world trade, and as recently as the Tokyo Round in 1973, Australia's minister for overseas trade confirmed this attitude and indicated that Australia was prepared to operate over the whole area of trade—'but he emphasised [Australia's] special interests in agricultural trade and indicated that the degree to which we could grant concessions to other countries would be conditioned by the willingness of our trading partners to negotiate on primary products and the nature of the commitments they were prepared to undertake'.[4]

The department's report indicated some degree of scepticism as to the public awareness of the issues involved. As a way of reducing the vulnerability of the economy and individual industries to the problems of access and price, Australia has long been a proponent of international co-operation on commodity marketing questions, and the negotiation of international commodity agreements where these are found to be feasible and practicable. In fact, Australia is a signatory to all of the international commodity agreements currently in existence—wheat, sugar, tin, coffee and cocoa. Australia also participates in a variety of inter-governmental consultative organizations, such as the international lead and zinc study group, the GATT consultative group in meat, and the UNCTAD committee on tungsten.

Australia's attitude to the question of commodity trading is well summed up in the first (1974/5) *Annual Report* of the Department of Overseas Trade, (p. 23):

> Australia favours arrangements involving both producing and consuming countries, believing that such arrangements can provide market growth opportunities for exporting countries (many of which are developing countries) and predictability of supply for importing countries at remunerative, fair and stable prices.

This noble objective, however, is not likely to be easy to attain. Since the success of OPEC in increasing the price of oil, the producers of other products have yearned to imitate the oil price cartel. But it is difficult to find another product with the same monopoly selling position as oil, and at times even the wall around oil threatens to break.

Australia is already a member of two producer organizations—the International Bauxite Association and the Association of Iron Ore Producing Countries. It is also an associate member of the Intergovernmental Council of Copper Exporting Countries. In joining such bodies, Australia has made it clear that it will not be a party to any form of international blackmail in resources trade, and also insists that resource-deficient countries should have access to markets at fair prices.

Australia is in a position of being both a substantial producer and substantial user of bauxite, iron ore and copper, unlike other countries who are basically producers only. Undeveloped or developing producer countries tend to emphasize pricing arrangements, while the resource hungry stress access to supplies. Sometimes these two attitudes cannot be reconciled on a multinational basis but only by bilateral negotiations, and Australia has taken bilateral action with the U.S., Japan and the EEC on such matters as beef market access, import duties on lead and zinc, and stockpile disposals. But the hard bargaining likely to be pursued by Japan through MITI (mentioned before) may well require that Australia's approach be different in the future.

Over four-fifths of Australia's exports and imports are with four trading partners–Japan, the European Economic Community, developing countries and the U.S. In fact, if the traditional market 'The United Kingdom' is added, all that remains is the relatively captive market of New Zealand, and the centrally planned economies, where at the moment some are customers for Australia's commodities, but it is difficult to find suitable products in exchange. The centrally planned economies do business on a government to government basis and find it difficult to understand why the Australian government or its agencies such as the Meat Board or the Wheat Board can do business on the basis of selling, while there is no government organized basis for buying. The existence of the projected Australian Overseas Trade Corporation would have helped in the promotion of trade in these areas but, unfortunately, the measure was defeated in a conflict between 'ideology' and the defence of 'free enterprise'. We cannot expect the centrally planned economies to buy from Australia without there being some matching of Australia buying from those countries.

Australia's existing major customers (Japan, the U.S., the EEC and the developing countries) are all capable of acting out of national interest when it suits them, rather than being great respecters of the market system. On Australia's part, while wool, wheat and sugar farmers probably claim to have been highly individualistic, they certainly have not been averse to some forms of orderly marketing. Iron ore producers also have found recently that it was no disadvantage to act in concert as sellers. And there were periods in the past when for some primary products–wheat, sugar and dairy products are examples–Australia had an artificially high home price to make up for that part of the total production sold overseas at prices often not sufficient to cover total costs.

The situation now is markedly different, and Australia is one of the few countries left in the world capable of being a food exporter on a substantial scale. Simultaneously Australia can help feed the rich world and the poor world, but the conditions of selling to either group are not likely to be easy. Nor, hopefully, has Australia yet reached a situation of 'triage' where it has to choose between one group and the other. However, successful marketing in both is going to demand a great deal of goodwill on all sides in the future.

Conclusion

For some two years the author served as Australia's representative on 'the Committee of Twenty', charged with the task of endeavouring to secure international monetary reform. Various proposals always foundered between two great obstacles, national sovereignty and the use of special drawing rights (SDR's) as a viable international currency. Those who are strong enough economically believe that the internal strength of their own currency is the most important and are not prepared to concede that any international body should regulate their exchange rates. There is a reluctance to revalue when a country should, and a tendency to hold off devaluing until it is essential, when it is then inevitably done in an atmosphere of panic.

Those who are weaker economically believe that, to a degree, their situation is determined by the absence of fair prices for their international exports, denying them adequate foreign exchange to acquire the necessary goods, techniques and capital and social equipment to diversify their economies. The lesser developed countries wanted the SDR's to be used as a form of credit creation that would transfer real resources from the rich to the poor, the resources which the poor think the rich have. Perhaps the rich are really rich: but the transfer is not going to take place by any magical 'link'. It will only occur when the rich consciously acknowledge the seriousness of the disparities between the lucky countries and the luckless countries, and concede that poverty anywhere is a menace to prosperity everywhere.

References

[1] Policies for Development of Manufacturing Industry—A Green Paper, vol. 1, *Report* (AGPS, Canberra, 1975).

[2] *Annual Report* (1975/76), Australian Department of Overseas Trade (AGPS, Canberra, 1976), p. 71.

[3] *Review of Marketing and Agricultural Economics*, March/June 1976, pp. 41-2.

[4] *Annual Report* (1975/76), Australian Department of Overseas Trade (AGPS, Canberra, 1976), p. 54.

H. W. ARNDT

11 Foreign Investment

Australia has been a capital-importing country since 1788. Like the previous wave of immigrants, the ancestors of the present Aborigines, British people took possession of an almost empty continent. But unlike the earlier immigrants, they brought with them western civilization, technology and capital. For most of the nineteenth century, overseas capital for private investment in rural industries, mining, housing, manufacturing and commerce came with the immigrants or as British deposits with Australian banks, while public investment in railways, ports, irrigation, public utilities, schools and hospitals was financed largely through loans raised in London by the governments of the several colonies. When, with the Great Depression of the early 1930s, the inflow of loan capital dried up and export earnings fell catastrophically, servicing the accumulated foreign debt became a major problem. Australia never defaulted, but the experience left a legacy of popular animosity towards overseas creditors and fear of foreign borrowing.

The 'Open Door'

A new era began in 1945. Australia had emerged from World War II determined to prevent a return to the mass unemployment of the depression years, sensitive to the longer-term implications for her national security of the changes in the world power structure the war had brought about, but also full of optimism about a future of rising living standards for a growing population. A large-scale immigration programme, and efforts to attract the overseas capital needed to support it, were central to this vision of Australia's future.

It is worth recalling the spirit of that time, and there is no better source than the early post-war writings of D. B. Copland. Convinced of the 'strategic urgency of increasing our population rapidly' and of the desirability of 'broadening the cultural inheritance of our people', he warned of the problems entailed in a planned 4 per cent annual rate of population growth—'a colossal rate of increase'. 'The problem before us is the capacity of the Australian economy to absorb a planned increase of 4 per cent, to maintain our standards of living and to provide all the capital equipment for so rapid a growth of population.' He derided an 'anti-borrowing psychology'.

> In the old days if we went in for a big migration programme we resorted to external borrowing . . . Then we fell into a depression, and in our thinking we never recovered from it. We still live in fear of overseas borrowing . . . If capital equipment is available . . . this country will be justified in borrowing lavishly if she cannot otherwise finance the purchase of it . . . The risks of borrowing are well covered by the prospective returns.[1]

While Copland and others were still thinking mainly in terms of 'borrowing', the Labor prime minister, J. B. Chifley, was already focusing on the benefits to Australia of American direct investment.

> I do not think [he told the 1949 annual conference of the New South Wales Branch of the Australian Labor Party] that even the Australian people realize the enormous expansion that is taking place in secondary industries, . . . nor are they able to contemplate the confidence and faith which not only producers and manufacturers of this country but of other countries have in the potentialities of this country. That is true of American industrialists who want to bring factories or branches here. Indeed only last week we reached an agreement which will bring a new type of manufacture here. Similar arrangements in conjunction with American holders of patents and licences are being made which should be of considerable benefit.[2]

Three years later, the Menzies government authorized a treasury *Statement of Policy in Relation to Overseas Investment in Industry in Australia* which confirmed the bipartisan consensus that 'the participation of overseas capital in the development of industrial enterprises is welcomed' and gave assurances to overseas investors that no limitations would be imposed on their freedom to remit earnings, though not to repatriate capital.[3]

This, broadly, remained Australian policy on overseas investment for two decades, from the end of the war to the mid-1960s. It was a policy of positive encouragement of overseas investment—'overseas' because it included British which was not then regarded as 'foreign'—chiefly in manufacturing industry and later increasingly in mineral exploration and development, 'particularly where it is of a kind likely to help in the balanced development of Australia's resources and brings with it the skill and "know-how" needed'.[4]

It was not a policy of unqualified *laissez-faire*. All inflow of capital from non-sterling area countries and all remittances abroad required exchange control approval, though this was usually granted. Of most substantial projects the authorities were well aware because overseas investors found it necessary to negotiate beforehand with state governments and Commonwealth departments about a host of conditions imposed and concessions sought, from access to land and zoning regulations to taxation matters, royalties, decentralization and other subsidies, tariffs and import restrictions, and many more. Certain tertiary industries, banks, news media and civil aviation, somehow secured for themselves complete protection from foreign competition on special grounds of 'national interest'. But with these relatively minor qualifications, official policy on foreign investment until the late 1960s was fairly described as a policy of the 'open door'.

The Rise of Economic Nationalism

Economic nationalism has always been latent in twentieth-century Australia, as in most other countries, but there is little evidence of open hostility towards foreign investment before the early 1960s.

When General Motors-Holden paid its first dividend in 1955 there was a hubbub which no doubt had economic-nationalist overtones. But the outcry reflected, apart from sour grapes among those who would have liked a share in the profits, chiefly anti-capitalist resentment of high profits of any sort—Dr Evatt took the occasion to attack the GMH 'colossus'—and some concern about the implications for the Australian balance of payments of a sharp rise in remitted profits.[5]

It was on this and other *potential* economic costs that academic and other public discussion of foreign investment largely turned in the following years.[6] Fears that income due overseas would impose a serious burden on the balance of payments subsided when it became apparent that the ratio of profits due abroad to exports, which had been rising rather alarmingly, reached its peak in 1958–9 and declined during the 1960s under the impact of soaring mineral exports.[7] Much the same applied to official and unofficial concern aroused around 1959 by evidence of widespread restrictions imposed by overseas companies on export franchises of their Australian subsidiaries; what seemed a serious worry in the late 1950s, when the burden of making up for lagging rural exports was thought to rest on efforts to expand exports of manufactures, largely lost its urgency with the expansion of mineral exports during the 1960s.[8] The 1959 report of the Tariff Board drew attention to the problem of transfer pricing, but in the following years it came to be recognized that this, while not entirely controllable, could be adequately looked after by the taxation commissioner.[9]

By 1963, when E. L. Wheelwright gave the first fairly comprehensive account of foreign investment in Australia, he made much of a list of 'potential' conflicts between the interests of overseas investors and the Australian national interest.[10] But there was very little, if any, evidence of any *actual* adverse economic effects. This, however, did not, and has not since, stemmed the tide of economic-nationalist sentiment. A prescient commentator said in 1960:

> Whilst agreeing broadly with the *economic* assessment, . . . in the long run, the non-economic issues may in fact become the important ones. A serious deterioration in our balance of payments would of course throw the economic issues into sharp relief. This may or may not happen; but the emotional and sentimental issues arising from the equity ownership question are likely to be chronic. Is there not a danger that they may bring repercussions unlikely to benefit either the foreign owners of capital or the Australian economy?[11]

At first, emotional hostility to foreign investment in Australia was confined to the extreme left where it was just one facet of the struggle against capitalism and imperialism. When the historian of *British Imperialism and Australia* joined forces with the most prominent radical economist of the next generation to sound the tocsin about the dangers of foreign investment, they were already able to quote a fair number of left-wing authorities inside and outside the federal parliament.[12] But from about 1960 economic-nationalist sentiment also began to be heard from the right. Among the most forceful voices was that of the deputy prime minister and leader of the Country Party, Mr (later Sir) John McEwen who, as early as February 1960, made his position clear: 'We want US business here with all its magnificent skills of management at all levels. But we don't want to be taken over. We will *not* be taken over.'[13]

To some extent the debate in Australia echoed controversy about foreign ownership and control in Canada and elsewhere. In Canada, concern about threatening 'foreign domination' had been vocal for some years and had been given weighty endorsement by the Royal Commission on Canada's Economic Prospects which, in its final report of November 1957, had recommended pressure on American companies to sell some part of their equity stock to Canadians. By the time the Menzies government, primarily in response to public discontent with 'stop-go' and demands for some form of long-term planning, appointed a Committee of Economic Inquiry in 1963, the costs and benefits of overseas investment had come to be regarded as a sufficiently topical issue to be included, with many others, in its terms of reference.

The report of the Vernon Committee which was published in May

1965 conceded much to the critics of overseas investment. While stressing that 'overseas investment has . . . been a force assisting the growth of the economy', it came to the conclusion that 'an increase above the recent level of "new" overseas investment is to be avoided if possible'.[14] Its main concern was on account of the balance of payments which, on the basis of an excessively pessimistic projection, it expected to be burdened by a rapidly rising ratio of income due overseas to export earnings. But it was also exercised by the prospect of 'a substantial increase in the proportion of overseas ownership of Australian companies'. While deprecating a 'simple nationalism, which is sometimes irrational and narrow', it also warned that 'such feelings go deep and cannot be ignored'.[15]

The Committee did not think it wise or practicable as a general rule to force a degree of Australian equity participation in overseas subsidiaries operating in Australia. But it recommended that all overseas take-over bids for Australian companies should require specific government approval; that foreign exchange control approval for foreign investment be made subject to some satisfactory undertaking from the company concerned that it would not rely unreasonably on funds raised by borrowing in Australia; and that the sterling-area exemption from the requirement of formal Reserve Bank approval of overseas investment be abolished.

For some more years, while Menzies remained prime minister and during the brief reign of Harold Holt, official policy, largely guided by treasury opposition to economic-nationalist measures, stood fast. Mr Holt did indeed adopt one of the Vernon Committee recommendations, when it issued 'guide-lines' in May 1965 to discourage overseas companies from borrowing in Australia. But this was done in response to restrictions on capital outflow imposed by the U.S. and British governments and was primarily designed to protect Australia's balance of payments against the risk of a sharp drop in the inflow of overseas equity capital.[16]

The atmosphere changed markedly when Mr John Gorton succeeded Mr Holt as prime minister in December 1967. Much more sensitive than either of his two predecessors to the appeals of economic nationalism, he found himself thinking about foreign investment on much the same lines as Mr McEwen, still deputy prime minister, though he tended to speak and act more impulsively. In September 1968, he startled the country by deciding, on his personal initiative, to protect the MLC life insurance company against a rumoured foreign take-over and thus 'prevent the people's savings from falling into foreign hands'.[17] Early in 1969, in a speech to the Australia Club in London, he likened Australia's past attitude to foreign investment to that of a puppy that wants its tummy tickled and proclaimed Australia's continuing desire for foreign investment but, in some respects, 'on our own terms'.[18] In May 1969, when an earlier suggestion that stock exchanges should allow companies to restrict the voting rights of foreign-held shares had fallen on deaf ears, amendments to render take-overs more difficult were made to the companies ordinances of the Australian Capital Territory and Northern Territory, the only parts of Australia under federal jurisdiction in these matters.[19] A further gesture came in June in the form of a bill which reduced the oil search subsidy to companies with less than 51 per cent Australian equity.[20]

The practical and legal difficulties which Mr Gorton encountered in his efforts to develop a more selective approach to foreign investment delayed the formulation of a new policy and were reflected in the form it took when it was finally announced in September 1969. No attempt was made to legislate for minimum local equity requirements or legal control of take-overs. Instead, both objectives were to be promoted by moral suasion and inducements, with the May 1965 'guide-lines' on local borrowing by foreign companies as the chief vehicle. Under the complex formula, the proportion of their capital requirements which subsidiaries of foreign companies were to be allowed to meet by borrowing in Australia would vary with the Australian share in their equity capital, and a 'take-over code' was adumbrated but, in the absence of any clear Commonwealth powers to take legal action, the government could merely 'reserve the right to try and prevent any takeovers which it felt were against the national interest'.[21] For the first time, the government also formally claimed the right to restrict entry for foreign capital into certain enterprises 'of national importance'.[22]

To the more ardent advocates of drastic action, all this seemed 'pretty mild stuff'.[23] But it was the first attempt at intervention of a general character to limit foreign ownership and control. It was followed by two further significant steps before the fall of the Gorton government in March 1971. One was the realization of Mr McEwen's scheme for a large public corporation, provided with substantial initial capital from the Commonwealth, which would borrow money overseas and invest it in mineral and other development projects, thus increasing Australian ownership; one of Mr McEwen's last acts before his retirement from politics in December 1970 was to pilot through parliament legislation to set up the Australian Industry Development Corporation. The second was emergency legislation, following discoveries of large uranium deposits in the Northern Territory, to limit foreign ownership, in line with the 'take-over code', to 15 per cent of the equity of the two Australian companies concerned.

The displacement of Mr Gorton by the former treasurer, Mr William McMahon, as prime minister seemed for a while to herald a return to the earlier more relaxed official attitudes to foreign investment. But political pressures, generated by 'an atmosphere of rising emotional, even hysterical, reaction to real or imagined overseas takeovers'[24] and to other aspects of foreign investment, became increasingly irresistible for a government that, for other reasons, found itself in many political difficulties. In November 1971, the treasurer, Mr Snedden, announced that he had ordered his department to prepare a White Paper evaluating the impact of the open-door policy on foreign investment. In December a rare joint initiative of the ALP and DLP secured the establishment of a Senate Select Committee on foreign investment which began its hearings in June 1972, with Senator Murphy as its first witness. The treasury document, which was tabled in parliament in May 1972, gave a comprehensive summary of available statistics and analysis of the economic issues but refrained from suggesting policies.[25]

At the end of September 1972, the McMahon government, facing a losing battle in an election campaign fought by the ALP on a platform of which 'buying back the farm' formed an important plank, announced a package of measures on capital inflow. But most of these served a different purpose, to stem the inflow of portfolio capital which was undermining domestic monetary policy and pushing Australia into currency appreciation.[26] The only component of the package directed at restraining foreign ownership and control was the establishment of administrative machinery for vetting of take-over bids, incorporated a few weeks later in the Companies (Foreign Take-overs) Act of November 1972.[27]

Socialist Economic Nationalism

Maximum local ownership of Australian industry had been an objective of the Australian Labor Party for some years when it came to power in December 1972. By this time, the focus of the foreign ownership debate had swung from manufacturing to mineral development which, during the 1960s, had become the most dynamic sector of the Australian economy, but had in the process come to be largely owned by the overseas companies or joint consortia that supplied much of the needed capital and technology. By this time, also, fears about the danger of exhaustion of non-renewable resources and particularly about a looming energy crisis had been given worldwide currency by the Club of Rome sponsored study on *The Limits to Growth*. This, in turn, encouraged the OPEC group of oil-producing countries to form the cartel which in November 1973 quadrupled the world price of crude oil. In many quarters, in Australia as in other affluent countries, the stress was now on environment and the 'quality of life', with economic growth at a discount. In

Australia, mineral policy was further complicated by the issue of Aboriginal land rights. All these currents contributed to the resources policy which became one of the chief preoccupations of the Whitlam government in its three years of office.[28]

The initiative in formulating the government's foreign investment and resources policies, for most of the period, was in the hands of Mr R. F. X. Connor, the minister for minerals and energy, and Dr J. F. Cairns, the minister for overseas trade. Both were ardent nationalists and convinced socialists who saw in government ownership and control of mineral development the only effective means of reducing foreign in favour of Australian ownership and of achieving other desirable policy objectives. For two years, until their crusade was held back by constitutional difficulties, hampered by mounting economic problems of 'stagflation' and finally overtaken by the tragicomedy of the 'loan affair', they sought to realize the demand, voiced many years earlier by Fitzpatrick and Wheelwright, for a 'socialist economic nationalism'.[29]

All through 1973, decisions to implement this policy came thick and fast. In January, federal export controls were extended to all minerals, raw and processed. In March, exchange control approval for foreign investment in real estate was suspended–the Melbourne *Age* commenting approvingly that Mr Whitlam had 'unfurled the banner of militant economic nationalism'[30]–and a private project for construction of natural gas pipelines was halted pending establishment of a National Pipeline Authority. In April, the government announced decisions to establish a Petroleum and Minerals Authority 'for exploration, production and refining' and to expand the Australian Industry Development Corporation. In May, the subsidy for oil exploration was abolished, existing tax concessions for mineral prospecting withdrawn, and a new treasury division on foreign investment and take-overs set up. In July, Mr Connor halted negotiations for a natural gas plant in South Australia, demanding 51 per cent Australian equity. In August, following demands for strong action against multinational corporations at the annual conference of the ALP, Mr Whitlam denounced multinational corporations in Ottawa, claiming that Australia was 'not its own master';[31] all remaining special tax concessions to the mineral industry were withdrawn. In September, Dr Cairns put forward a scheme for a 'National Investment Fund' to enable the AIDC to 'buy back Australia'.[32] In October, Mr Connor announced a new policy of government control and compulsory acquisition of the entire output of natural gas and condensates of the Woodside-Burmah field on the Northwest Shelf; and in Tokyo the prime minister explained that henceforth all four energy industries (oil, natural gas, coal, uranium) would be closed to new foreign equity investment and that uranium development would have to be 100 per cent Australian-owned, though this extreme position was modified a few weeks later by reference to Australian control rather than ownership. In December, legislation to set up the Petroleum and Minerals Authority was introduced, and the treasurer, Mr Crean, announced that new foreign investment in insurance companies would be unwelcome.

During 1974, as Australia began to feel the effects of the world recession that followed the OPEC coup while still experiencing accelerating domestic inflation, the impetus of the Labor government's resources policies slowed down. Some new initiatives were still taken. In May, a report on Aboriginal land rights recommended against any development of the Naberlak uranium deposit without Aboriginal consent; in September, Dr Cairns announced that Australia would join the newly formed International Bauxite Association, in terms which gave the impression that Australia favoured OPEC-type producer cartels; and in October, Mr Connor issued a statement reserving to the government all rights to uranium exploration. Meanwhile, however, much of the government's resource policy legislation had run into opposition in the senate and as the damaging economic effects on mineral exploration and development of the changed climate for foreign investors, of much less favourable tax treatment and of the worsening general economic situation became increasingly apparent, the government began to reconsider some of the more extreme positions it had taken up. Early in November, just before a visit by the Japanese prime minister, Mr Whitlam issued new guidelines which withdrew from insistence on 100 per cent Australian ownership in uranium development and recognized the need for risk funds in exploration. But it was the 'loan affair' which, by discrediting the two extreme exponents of socialist economic nationalism in the cabinet, paved the way for a more moderate stance.[33]

A New Consensus?

In September 1975, after the dismissal of Dr Cairns and shortly before the resignation of Mr Connor, the Labor government issued a new statement on policy which went a long way in moderating and clarifying its policies on foreign investment and mineral development. The statement explicitly recognized that 'Australia will, for the forseeable future, continue to require foreign capital, including equity capital' for the development of its resources; only 'within this over-riding goal' and as 'a major longer term objective' did it declare itself in favour of 'the promotion of Australian control and the maximum Australian ownership compatible with our long-term capital requirements and our need for access to markets, advanced technology and know-how'.[34] When, three weeks later, the Liberal and National Country Parties issued their own agreed statement on the subject, it proved almost identical in its formulation of objectives and indeed of policy in most respects. Like the Labor Party statement, it listed, among specific policy objectives, 'maximum Australian ownership and control of national resources', 50 per cent Australian equity in new projects (75 per cent for uranium) and prohibition of foreign investment in certain sectors.[35]

Thus, the traumatic change of government of December 1975 made less difference in foreign investment and resource policy than might have been expected. The new government was clearly more sympathetic to private enterprise and even more anxious than the Whitlam government in its last months to make it clear to potential overseas investors that Australia still looked for overseas equity capital. But, equally clearly, the new government had no intention of reverting to the pre-1972 open-door policy. As one newspaper editorial saw it, 'the foreign investment pendulum has at last swung back to a centre position which takes reasonable account of nationalist sentiment on the one hand and economic development on the other'.[36]

Cui Bono?

But what is a *reasonable* compromise between nationalist sentiment and economic development?

Let us be clear that what is at issue is not the area of potential conflict between the interests of overseas investors and the economic interests of this country. There is little cause for disagreement about government regulation or surveillance of foreign investment to ensure an adequate share in the profits for Australian taxpayers, whether in the form of income tax, royalties or infrastructure investment, to minimize the risk of tax evasion through transfer pricing, to secure compliance with rules to protect the environment and also presumably, though this leaves more room for debate, to influence the directions of investment according to national economic policy priorities. The issue is what price, in terms of economic development, should be paid to satisfy nationalist sentiment against foreign ownership and control of Australian industries—for its own sake, as a matter of national pride independent of economic or other considerations.

Economic nationalism, it has been said, is a consumption good, a public good like defence, education and social security.[37] If people, in order to have more of it, are prepared to make some sacrifice of per capita GNP or economic growth, or even of defence, education or social security, that is their right. It is not for the economist to pass judgement. Fair enough. But the economist is perhaps entitled to ask *cui bono*? Who are the people who reap the benefits in this trade-off and who are the people who bear the costs?

Obviously, there is no clear-cut, objective or sure answer to this question. Who is to say how much value individual Australians attach to local ownership of Australian industries? Few of us are quite without feelings of national pride, few of us do not glow just a little when we hear that an Australian athlete has won a gold medal at the Olympic games or that an Australian has been awarded a Nobel prize. But the economic sacrifices that each would personally be willing to make for such pleasures probably differ greatly from person to person, and between moods and circumstances.

It is also unquestionable that there has been a marked change in public attitudes, in Australia as in other affluent countries, towards economic growth. Compared with the 1950s, economic growth has been greatly downgraded as an objective of economic policy in favour of other desiderata. People have been told, and many have come to believe, that it is worth sacrificing some economic growth in order to conserve non-renewable natural resources, to reduce pollution, to enhance the quality of life, to ensure a more equal distribution of income and wealth, to safeguard humanity against the risks of nuclear energy development or to protect the interests of Aborigines and other underprivileged minorities. Why not also in order to reduce foreign ownership and control?

But again, *how much* has economic growth come to be downgraded by *how many* Australians? Considering the dire economic straits in which Australia, more than most other western countries, finds itself because of the unremitting struggle for larger shares of the cake of GNP between labour, capital, farmers, pensioners, taxpayers and other interest groups—a struggle of which two-digit inflation is the most conspicuous symptom—it would not appear that a greater detachment from the benefits of economic growth has as yet taken hold of the majority.

Part of the problem is of course the common human failing of wanting to have one's cake and eat it too and, as a particular species of this genus, the collective schizophrenia that makes most of us strong supporters of more government expenditure for all manner of worthy purposes and strong opponents of more taxation to pay for it. Another part, which helps both to explain and to rationalize the apparent schizophrenia, is the almost universal belief that, in justice, someone *else*, for example the rich or the city people or the easterners or the mainlanders, should pay the cost.

This latter propensity is particularly relevant to economic nationalism in general and to opposition to foreign ownership in particular. Economic nationalists tend to believe that it is foreigners who can, and should, be made to pay. If they happen to be radical nationalist socialists, they are likely to believe that foreign investment is an instrument of imperialism and that the costs of a policy to reduce foreign ownership and control would fall wholly, or primarily, on those agents of imperialism, the multinational corporations.

Another point is the observation frequently made with reference to contemporary environmentalism, that the environment is a good with a high income elasticity of demand.[38] Concern for the environment partly reflects the degree to which the more basic needs for food and shelter and conventional necessities have been met in the affluent countries and is therefore more strongly felt and more vocally expressed by the relatively affluent than by the less well-to-do within these countries. This generalization would not seem to hold for nationalism in the political sense of jingoism, since jingoism appears to be inversely correlated with education. But casual observation suggests that *economic* nationalism, insofar as it is not, like crude protectionism, a rationalization of sectional economic interests, may, on the contrary, make a special appeal to the educated and especially to intellectuals who, as Schumpeter observed,[39] have in western countries become antipathetic to the business ethic and who have little personal reason to count the costs of economic nationalist policies.

Finally, if it were possible to demonstrate that the costs of satisfying Australian economic-nationalist sentiment could be imposed on foreigners, would that settle the issue?

One of the victims of the emergence of anti-growth attitudes, and of hostility to direct foreign investment, in the past decade has been the post-war Australian policy of economic development based on large-scale immigration. The social costs of the immigration programme have been given greater weight relative to its economic benefits and, insofar as direct foreign investment had been a means of meeting the capital requirements of rapid population growth, the resulting increase in foreign ownership has come to be regarded as one of the social costs of the programme. The implication would appear to be that, if abandonment of the immigration programme could be shown to be on balance in the interest of the present generation of Australians and their descendants, the cost to those who would be deprived of the opportunity of migrating to Australia would count for nothing.

Or, to take a more obvious illustration, if one of the consequences of measures to limit foreign ownership and control should be a slower rate of development of Australia's mineral resources, and thus a reduction in supplies or an increase in costs of the mineral products concerned to foreign countries, would this be irrelevant to the trade-off?

Australians are not alone, in a world of nation states, in treating the national interest as the ultimate touchstone of all aspects of national policy. It is almost universally taken for granted that we are entirely within our rights in restricting imports from low-wage countries or charging the highest price we can for our minerals or, should we judge it to be in our national interest, in keeping our uranium ore in the ground. Offensive as this habit of mind may seem on moral grounds, it does not matter very much in practice provided care is taken to distinguish between short and long-term, between narrow and enlightened, interpretations of Australia's national interest.[40] It is arguable, for example, that a small nation of fourteen million people in possession of a large continent containing a not inconsiderable proportion of the world's reserves of non-renewable resources would find it in its own enlightened self-interest to develop these resources with due regard for the needs of other countries as well as its own.

When all this is said, there is still much room for debate about the reasonable compromise between nationalist sentiment and economic development. But it may serve as a warning against underestimating the costs of gratifying nationalist sentiment, costs not necessarily to ourselves but to others less affluent, less secure and less able to press their claims.

References

1 D. B. Copland, *Inflation and Expansion* (Cheshire, Melbourne, 1951), pp. 46, 53-4.

2 A. W. Stargardt (ed.), *Things Worth Fighting For: Speeches by Joseph Benedict Chifley* (Melbourne University Press, Melbourne 1952), pp. 61ff.

3 Quoted D. B. Copland and R. H. Barback (eds), *The Conflict of Expansion and Stability* (Cheshire, Melbourne, 1957), p. 252.

4 *Overseas Investment in Australia* (Commonwealth Printer, Commonwealth Treasury, Canberra, 1960), p. 3.

5 Cf. E. Penrose, 'Foreign Investment and the Growth of the Firm', *Economic Journal*, June 1956.

6 D. M. Hocking, 'The Contributions of Overseas Companies to Australia's Post-War Industrial Development', section G (ANZAAS, Melbourne, 1955); H. W. Arndt, 'Overseas Borrowing: The New Model', *Economic Record*, August 1957; R. J. Cameron, 'Comment on Overseas Borrowing', ibid.; G. D. A. MacDougall, 'The Benefits and Costs of Private Investment from Abroad: A Theoretical Approach', *Economic Record*, March 1960; J. O. N. Perkins, 'Some Fallacies About Overseas Borrowing', *Australian Quarterly*, June 1960.

7 H. W. Arndt, *A Small Rich Industrial Country: Studies in Australian Development, Aid and Trade* (Cheshire, Melbourne, 1968), p. 33.

8 H. W. Arndt and D. R. Sherk, 'Export Franchises of Australian Companies with Overseas Affiliations', *Economic Record*, August 1959; D. T. Brash, *American Investment in Australian Industry* (Australian National University Press, Canberra, 1966).

9 D. T. Brash, op. cit., p. 219.

10 E. L. Wheelwright, 'Overseas Investment in Australia', in A. Hunter (ed.), *The Economics of Australian Industry* (Melbourne University Press, Melbourne, 1963), pp. 150ff.

11 H. F. Bell, 'Attitudes to Overseas Investment', *Australian Quarterly*, September 1960, p. 51.

12 B. Fitzpatrick and E. L. Wheelwright, *The Highest Bidder: A Citizen's Guide to Problems of Foreign Investment in Australia* (Lansdowne Press, Melbourne, 1965).

13 Quoted H. F. Bell, op. cit., p. 50.

14 *Report of the Committee of Economic Enquiry (Vernon Report)* (Government Printer, Canberra, 1965), vol. I, p. 285.

[15] Ibid., p. 288.
[16] Reserve Bank of Australia, *Annual Report 1965* (Sydney), p. 19.
[17] *Age*, 25 September 1968. Part of this and the next two paragraphs is taken from the author's chapter on 'Foreign Investment' in G. Greenwood and N. Harper (eds), *Australia in World Affairs 1966-1970* (Cheshire, Melbourne, 1974).
[18] Quoted *Australian Financial Review*, 26 February 1969.
[19] 'Foreign Investment', *Bank of New South Wales Review*, July 1976, p. 9.
[20] *Age*, 4 June 1969.
[21] *Age*, 17 September 1969.
[22] Ibid.
[23] Editorial, ibid.
[24] *Australian Financial Review*, 19 September 1970.
[25] *Overseas Investment in Australia*, Treasury Economic Paper no. 1 (Commonwealth Printer, Canberra, May 1972), see also the comment by T. W. Swan, *Economic Record*, June 1972.
[26] Cf. *Australia* (OECD Economic Survey, Paris, December 1972).
[27] 'Foreign Investment in Australia', in *Australia* (OECD Economic Survey, Paris, April 1974), appendix I, p. 49.
[28] Cf. H. W. Arndt, 'Australian Resources Diplomacy', in B. D. Beddie (ed.), *Advance Australia—Where?* (Oxford University Press, Melbourne, 1975).
[29] B. Fitzpatrick and E. L. Wheelwright, op. cit., p. 4.
[30] *Age*, 21 March 1973.
[31] *Age*, 3 August 1973.
[32] *Age*, 7 September 1973.
[33] Cf. H. W. Arndt, 'The Economics of the Loan Affair', *Quadrant*, September (1975); for details, see P. Kelly, *The Unmaking of Gough* (Angus & Robertson, Sydney, 1976).
[34] *Age*, 25 September 1975.
[35] 'Foreign Investment Policy', The Liberal and National Country Parties, Press Release, Canberra, October 1975; the special provision relating to uranium was announced later, *Age*, 2 April 1976.
[36] Age, 26 September 1975.
[37] A. Breton, 'The Economics of Nationalism', *Journal of Political Economy*, vol. 72, no. 4 (1964).
[38] W. Beckerman, *In Defence of Economic Growth* (Jonathan Cape, London, 1974), p. 49.
[39] J. A. Schumpeter, *Capitalism, Socialism and Democracy* (Allen & Unwin, London, 1943), chapter 13.
[40] Cf. H. W. Arndt, 'Aid and the Official Conscience', *Australian Quarterly*, December 1969.

F. G. DAVIDSON

12 Brigden, Vernon, Rattigan, Jackson[1]

The Brigden Report, published in 1929, was meant as a warning,[2] though a warning against excessive protection and therefore very different in emphasis from the Jackson Committee's warning about the 'deep-seated malaise' of the Australian manufacturing sector in 1975.[3] The Vernon Report of 1965,[4] though less easy to characterize, had intellectual links with the Brigden Report. The Rattigan Report (1973) was brief compared with the other three,[5] but a mention of it is essential to the story of the three major reports.

Brigden

By 1927, when the 'Informal Committee' which produced the Brigden Report on *The Australian Tariff* was set up by Prime Minister Bruce, industrialization had been under way for more than half a century. 'The War' may not have directly accelerated it. But wartime dislocation had led to extensions of the manufacturing sector 'under a "natural" protection', in the Brigden Committee's words (p. 100), 'sometimes amounting to an embargo'. Nevertheless, the Greene tariff of 1921 was intended, as Greene said, to 'protect industries born during the war' as well as to 'encourage others that are desirable, and . . . diversify and extend existing industries'.[6] Under the Bruce-Page ministry, which took office in 1923, further tariff increases followed. By 1926 the Tariff Board was alarmed about extreme protectionism and the vicious circle of increases in tariffs and arbitrated wages. (Regular indexation of the basic wage began in 1922.)

Bruce, who had a large interest in a leading firm of importers, was only a moderate protectionist, and he shared the Tariff Board's alarm about rising wages. Like the McMahon government in 1972 and the Fraser government in 1976, the Bruce-Page government in 1928 amended the Arbitration Act to try to increase the influence of 'economic' considerations. The fall of the Bruce-Page government in

October 1929 was precipitated by an attempt at curing the malaise of the 1920s by actually abolishing federal arbitration.

In the prefatory note to their report the Brigden Committee claimed to have pursued their inquiry 'quite unhampered by any preconceived opinions of what results would come of it. We have been able to greet the unseen with a cheer . . . quite regardless of which controversial view it supported.' Reviewing the Brigden Report in the *Economic Record* for November 1929, Viner praised Bruce for having sponsored 'a disinterested and non-political inquiry by competent and unbiased economists into the merits of a policy to which his party and his country are so strongly committed'. In his foreword to the report, Bruce commended 'the obvious impartiality of mind which distinguishes the approach to every phase of this vast subject'.

In fact the impartiality of the Brigden Committee was less obvious than their moderation. The first number of the *Economic Record*, which appeared in 1925, carried an article in which Brigden expressed a moderate protectionist view strikingly similar to that of the report in 1929. In presenting this view he of course argued against free trade: 'The effects of free trade would be to reduce the standard of living in a growing population engaged upon primary production until it could compete with manufactured imports'. In other words, under free trade the primary sector would be better able to compete for labour against the manufacturing sector. There would have been a rise in the value of land and greater inequality of income, which would have tended, Brigden concluded, showing no doubt Pigou's influence, 'to diminish the utility of the total amount'.[7]

Brigden's argument was not novel. At the beginning of the century the English politician Joseph Chamberlain claimed that protection would benefit the British working class. Pigou, in *Protective and Preferential Import Duties*, published in 1906, agreed that in principle protection could benefit, absolutely as well as relatively, a factor specialized in a protected industry.[8]

The Brigden Report may well have been what Bruce wanted. The committee considered (p. 140) that the tariff had been an effective means to 'the basic Australian objective': 'the largest white population at the highest standard of living'. However, 'the present costs of protection are dangerously high' (p. 144). The main text concluded (p. 145): 'It cannot be too strongly emphasized that only by improved efficiency and consequent reduction in prices in the industries now protected can resources be set free for protecting new industries'. But, as regards the tariff, what Bruce wanted bore no relation to what happened in the next two or three years: duties were greatly increased. On the other hand, with advice from Copland (whose opinions on wage policy were shared by other members of the Brigden Committee), the Arbitration Court which Bruce had tried to abolish reduced Australian costs by a 10 per cent cut in the basic wage.

Ineffective as it was in relation to immediate tariff policy, the Brigden Report can be regarded as influencing general discussion of protection in two respects.

First, the income-distribution argument (which Brigden had put forward in 1925 and which the committee adopted in modified form) though it was not novel, passed through the Brigden Report into some of the most admired lucubrations of academic tariff analysis, including the famous article on 'Protection and Real Wages' published by Stolper and Samuelson in the *Review of Economic Studies* in 1941. In Australia Evans, an economist placing himself in the Brigden tradition, made an attempt to assign orders of magnitude to the income-distribution effects of the Australian tariff over the period 1958–9 to 1968–9.[9] His results suggested that aggregate capital, aggregate labour and skilled labour would have done better under free trade, but that the tariff benefited female labour and unskilled labour. However, as Evans emphasized, his calculations involved weak data and drastic simplifications.

The second 'contribution' of the Brigden Report is to less ambitious discussion. It is unfortunately very alive in Australia today. The Brigden Committee made a calculation of the costs of protection by estimating how much it would have cost to import what was in fact produced in Australia behind protection. They suggested that in 1926–7 protected production could have been bought from overseas for £36 million less than it cost in Australia. But the committee do not seem to have asked whether, if Australia had set about the extra importing, the exchange rate of the Australian pound could have been held. The obvious answer is that it could not have been held, but if the exchange rate of the Australian pound had been lower the 'excess costs' of protected production as compared with imports would not have appeared so 'dangerously high'. In other words, in this context an exchange rate assumed to be unaltered would be a misleading measure of the cost of greatly increased imports. (An exchange rate actually sustained by capital operations such as international borrowing or even by exports—uranium perhaps—might be judged even more misleading by someone whose 'social welfare function' condemned the borrowing or the uranium mining.)

An assessment of the cost of imports expressed in a monetary unit which implies that those imports are not being made is not nonsense in all contexts. The Vernon Report, while rejecting the idea of measuring the social cost of protection, used the Brigden method to calculate what it called the subsidy equivalent of the tariff. Again, the Brigden estimate might not have been nonsense if the committee had used it only to emphasize an *upper* limit to the likely cost of actual protection. But the estimate is nonsense in the context in which the committee offered it and in the contexts in which, despite the Vernon Committee's explanation, anti-protectionists often quote such estimates today.

The Brigden Committee used a 'partial equilibrium' approach where 'general equilibrium' (bringing more closely together the estimates for particular goods and including the foreign exchange market) was required. A general equilibrium calculation, even with over-simplifying assumptions, might have been so complicated as to be impracticable. But to quote Keynes's hackneyed maxim, perhaps the committee should have chosen to be vaguely right than precisely wrong.

It is, indeed, doubtful whether, even with computers and modern techniques, any calculation of the cost of a country's protective system can be worth much. Even if a hypothetical free-trade economy is elaborated, and the reality is compared with it, other things are still assumed equal which no one would assume equal if his calculation did not depend on it. As the Jackson Report remarked (vol. 1, p. 165), 'this type of study still rests on basic assumptions which may not fit easily into the complex real world'. Calculations often suggest (Evans's general equilibrium analysis of Australian protection is an example)[10] that protection costs fairly little, often decidedly less in proportionate terms than the Brigden Committee estimated. This conclusion is, of course, unpalatable to many economists, and a 'theory' about going back on assumptions that other things are equal when the results are unpalatably favourable to protection (or monopoly) has been successfully marketed during the last eleven years. Known as the theory of X-efficiency, it is also indicated for difficulties with the orthodox theory of the firm brought on by getting to hear about joint-stock companies.[11]

Vernon

The malaise which led to the setting up of the Vernon Committee in 1963 would certainly have been regarded by some people as deep-seated. By others the malaise would merely have been traced back three years, to the almost complete removal of the quantitative restrictions to which imports had, with varying severity, been subject during the 1950s. In 1961 Menzies was said to be consoling himself by reflecting that the unemployed, whose numbers had risen rapidly, would have voted Labor anyway, but the election at the end of the year left him with a Representatives majority (after providing the Speaker) of only one.

Perhaps the insecurity of the Liberal-Country Party coalition would in any case have strengthened the smaller party against the larger. Moreover McEwen, the leader of the Country Party, was minister for trade and industry. In the federal bureaucracy, so much expanded since the days of the Brigden Report, his department was treasury's bitter rival in the making of economic policy.

Already in the mid-1950s the Tariff Board had asked for a general survey of protection. In the crisis of the early 1960s the idea of a new enquiry into protection gathered more support. Crawford, the former secretary of trade and industry who had recently moved to the Australian National University, advocated much wider terms of reference, and his view prevailed. But treasury was spared a Crawford Committee, though Crawford was one of the five members.

In an extremely interesting thesis,[12] Glezer described that apparent paradox of Australian politics, the emergence of a Country Party minister as spokesman for protection of manufacturers: Hotelling's application of his minimum differentiation theory of duopoly (published in the *Economic Journal* in 1929) to the Democrats and Republicans is well known. And Glezer described how, for some years at least, 'our Jack' continued to be trusted by rural interests.

Towards the end of 1962 protectionist pressures led to the resignation of Melville, the chairman of the Tariff Board. As Melville's successor, McEwen and his department secured the comptroller-general of customs, who seemed likely to be as docile in accepting McEwen's policy as he would be ingenious and authoritarian in enforcing it. His name was Rattigan. Customs and excise was taken over by one of trade's chief policy makers, Carmody, who in 1976, before the 17½ per cent devaluation and 'managed float' of the Australian dollar and before the splitting up of treasury, was to become secretary of the prime minister's department.

The chairman of the Committee of Economic Enquiry seemed, hardly less than Rattigan, a McEwen man. Among his many activities as an advocate of higher protection, in general and for chemicals in particular, Vernon had presented an estimate of the Brigden cost of the tariff in 1951–2: his conclusion was that the tariff level had fallen to only about half what it had been in 1927. The Tariff Board had linked their desire for 'another complete investigation into the costs of protection' to a polite rejection of the results of Vernon's 'long and painstaking investigation'.

Whatever others may have hoped for, treasury and McEwen were no doubt largely at one about what they wanted the Vernon Committee to say. Arguments that high protection was necessary to avoid unemployment, especially now the adolescents who represented the post-war 'baby boom' were coming on to the labour market; that, irrespective of the pattern which demand would have shown in a free market, manufacturing must be stimulated (at the expense of the tertiary sector) to get more rapid productivity growth; that planning and achieving such growth (on the lines believed to have been followed in Japan and France) should be given much more emphasis, and avoidance of inflation much less—this kind of thing would hardly have pleased McEwen more than it would have gratified treasury enemies of the committee after two years of listening to rumours and sharpening the knife for economic fallacy. It seems that when the Vernon Report arrived treasury were satisfied that it was in this sense what they wanted it to be.

Menzies, in his presentation of the report to the Representatives, seemed to treat it with calm disdain. One example of his attitude might seem justified: his reference to the 'so-called projections'. The committee had made projections of gross national product and gross national expenditure, both of which must be the resultants of supply and demand. Projected GNP and GNE were then compared, rather as if they represented supply and demand respectively, that is to say ignoring the problem of identifying supply and demand 'schedules'. The committee did not improve the exercise by adopting the unphilosophical distinction, beloved of demographers, between projections and forecasts: as Lydall pointed out, so far as the projections were not forecasts the report should not have had a section on their 'policy implications'.[13] But, instead of emphasizing the identification problem and dismissing both projected GNP and projected GNE as arithmetic and midnight oil, some of the report's enemies seemed to take sides with GNE, seen as standing for consumer sovereignty, against collectivist GNP, seen as favoured by the committee.

In general a dispassionate reader of the Vernon Report might have expected treasury to welcome it as a justification of righteousness out of the mouths of those who had come together to persecute righteousness. For the report showed much concern about inflation: so far from regarding the population 'bulge' as justifying employment-creating protection, it expounded the orthodox view that population growth tends to cause excess demand. As to the intersectoral issue—the kind of employment that would be available:

> The work force will increasingly be finding employment in the tertiary industries and, because productivity as we are measuring it cannot be expected to rise so fast in those industries as elsewhere in the economy, this will tend to hold back the rate of increase in G.N.P. This does not mean that the movement is to be deplored. It merely means that the community will be demanding and receiving more of the goods and services concerned (p. 446).

Much more explicitly than the Brigden Committee, the Vernon Committee recommended moderation in wages. While stopping short of any automatic rule, the Vernon Report went a long way towards advocating the 'gearing' of money wages to productivity.

In contrast with Copland's success in 1931, the Vernon Committee's views on wages met forensic defeat. In the 1966 wage case the employers used the report to reinforce their argument. However, as one justification for quasi-'gearing', the report had urged that the national accounts for 1948–9 to 1961–2 showed 'virtually no correlation between the rate of increase of wages and changes in wage shares' (p. 126). But figures released a little later showed the wage share falling during a period of wage moderation. Three of the committee's members, subpoenaed and examined by Hawke, the union advocate, admitted the importance of the new figures and agreed that the problem of wage determination might need to be looked at afresh.

As a discussion of protection, however, the Vernon Report appeared to be influential. Though outside the arbitration room perhaps no one would have described the report as impartial, its treatment of protection can, like that of the Brigden Report, be described as moderate.

By the time of the Vernon Report, Corden had brought many Australian economists to accept the idea of a general-equilibrium 'second best' of tariff *uniformity*: the cost of the tariff might be more related to its variability from one type of imports to another than to its general level (which to a large extent might only influence the exchange rate or the balance of payments). The uniform tariff underlay the tariff proposals of the report as productivity 'gearing' underlay its proposals about wages. The report explicitly emphasized another idea which Corden had made familiar, the effective rate of protection. In other words the committee suggested that systematic allowances could be made for the fact that a producer can be protected by cheapness (low protection) of his materials as well as by duties on his product. Estimates of the effective rate of protection were offered for some industries. In this respect the committee was, for an official body, well up with the times.

However, within a year or so academic writers, including Corden, were emphasizing possible defects in actual calculations of effective protection (essentially misplaced assumptions of other things equal and failure to bridge the gap between partial and general equilibrium). The Vernon Report was innocent of such doubts. Their practical importance is, it is true, open to dispute. Must rules for reform of an actual situation be as difficult to formulate as the 'counterfactual' free-trade economy necessary to an unqualifiedly general estimate of the cost of protection? Where else but in general counterfactual comparison can immediate rules find acceptable justification? Yet what is the alternative to rules?

The Vernon Committee's quasi-expression of the uniformity idea took the form of suggesting that a rate of something under 30 per cent (in nominal, not effective, terms) might give a benchmark below, or not greatly above, which industries should be encouraged; others should not be encouraged. Within two or three years the Tariff Board announced the adoption of something very similar –'points of reference'. They were expressed in terms of effective protection, which could be expected to be generally higher than corresponding nominal rates. Industries with effective rates of 50 per cent or more were normally to be contained, while a fairly liberal attitude was to be adopted towards industries with effective rates of 25 per cent or less. To compare the points of reference with recent estimates that *average* effective rates available to *large* groups of industry ranged up to 97 per cent in 1968–9 is to understand the collapse of Rattigan's popularity with manufacturers. Nevertheless in 1971 the Liberal-Country Party government approved a systematic review of the tariff by the Board, the completion of the review being scheduled for 1978.

Rattigan

The Rattigan Committee was expert, official and confidential; it was set up in June 1973 by a letter from Whitlam, and its *Report on possible ways of increasing imports* was signed less than three weeks later. The letter to Rattigan explained that Whitlam and Cairns, the minister for overseas trade and for secondary industry, had been discussing an increase in imports as a means of restraining price rises at a time when the balance of payments was strong. The letter recognized that it would be desirable that tariff changes made for macro-economic reasons should accord with longer term objectives in tariff policy; they might, for instance, anticipate some of the results of the systematic review.

In a sympathetic account of the Vernon Report's views on protection–written it is true before Rattigan had emerged as a tariff reformer and on the assumption of a fixed exchange rate–Corden had largely excused the Vernon Committee (given their cautious view of balance-of-payments prospects) for their failure to face the question why a tariff was needed at all. Only external surplus combined with high employment gave the opportunity to choose free trade.[14]

International reserves in the middle of 1973 were valued at about two-and-a-half times as much as three years earlier, and in the first half of 1973 the excess of registered unemployed over registered vacancies fell by nearly 50 000 to less than 20 000. It seemed to be a Corden moment. The rapid price rise *already* taking place might be thought to involve a risk which Corden had not contemplated. But by mid-1973 exchange rates were not sacrosanct. And the Rattigan Committee contemplated that (though devaluation would be the more advisable remedy if general unemployment or balance-of-payments difficulties developed) cuts in tariffs could be reversed. They also intended that labour and proprietors affected by cuts should be given adjustment assistance.

On this basis the committee recommended that all tariffs should be reduced by one-quarter; acceptance of the recommendation was announced by the government within three days. Other, less spectacular, reductions followed.

It is not only the tariff controversialists of the 1920s who would never have expected such a stroke of liberal economic policy from a Labor government. Glezer spoke of the evaporation of Labor's tariff cohesion during the 1960s, which he ascribed as much to the influx of a new generation of parliamentarians as to the controversies over tariff-making.

The tariff cut was followed by a large rise in imports. In 1973–4 they were 46 per cent higher than in the previous year. It was 'the largest annual increase in imports, in absolute or percentage terms in current prices, since 1947–8'.[15] In the second half of 1974, with imports even higher, unemployment began to rise rapidly. What for many of us had been a triumph of liberalism began to be seen (as the removal of import restrictions had tended to be seen in 1962) as a mistake.

However, Labor's term of office had also brought a considerable revaluation of the Australian dollar: perhaps by over 20 per cent. Gregory and Martin suggested that between July 1973 and December 1974 the effect of exchange variations on imports was four times more important than the general tariff reduction. This conclusion is not so different from the implications of simple-minded arithmetic: a reduction of a quarter in average manufacturing protection of 22 per cent (nominal) might seem likely to reduce duty-paid prices by only $\frac{5 \cdot 5}{122}$ or about 4·5 per cent, only about a quarter of about $\frac{20}{120}$.

Jackson

In July 1974 the Whitlam government set up the Jackson 'Committee to Advise on Policies for Manufacturing Industry'. The members included, besides the secretary of the department of manufacturing industry, two business men, one from a big Australian firm and the other from a multinational; Hawke, who was now president of the ACTU; one of the government's advisers who had been a member of the Rattigan Committee, and Wheelwright, the 'radical' economist. The seventh member was Rattigan, whose Tariff Board had now become the Industries Assistance Commission. The membership and terms of reference recalled Cairns's book *Tariffs or Planning?* published in 1971. Rejecting red-blooded radicalism 'because a revolutary situation does not exist in Australia and those who talk as if it did talk only to themselves', Cairns had advocated 'co-operation between employers and workers, between one section of industry and another and between all these and the government'.[16]

Could a consensus among the seven members of the Jackson Committee be expected, except on such italicizable matters as '*change* and the need to *adapt to change*'? Rattigan did not sign the Jackson Report. But on the importance of a subject which has attracted increasing attention in many countries, the seven members did agree: the quality of work life, which is no doubt particularly deplorable in some small firms. The Jackson Report helped to publicize the problem, and Rattigan said that he shared his colleagues' concern. Effective action, that truly benefits the least-privileged migrant workers, is less certain. Perhaps something can be hoped for from the fact that, even from the narrowest point of view, bad working conditions are often inefficient.

The first section of the report's summary spoke of the 'immediate financial crisis' of Australian manufacturing. That there should have been such a crisis is not surprising. Between the beginning of 1974 and October 1975, when the committee reported, the wage explosion raised the index of male award rates by over 50 per cent. It is true that the Whitlam government devalued by 12 per cent in September 1974, and from about that time began to reverse the liberalization of trade, putting temporary quotas and other restrictions on many imports. But a fierce squeeze was applied to credit. Between February 1974 and October 1975 the ANZ Bank factory production index (excluding power) declined by 10 per cent.

The Jackson Report went on to its assertion (vol. 1, p. 1) that 'in Australian manufacturing there is a deep-seated and long-standing malaise'. One of the main proofs offered that the malaise was long-standing was persistent decline in profitability: a commissioned appendix to the report (vol. 3, pp. 69-115) suggested that the trend of the real return on investment in manufacturing after correction for 'accounting distortions' had been downward since 1963–4.

Though the Jackson Committee declared themselves 'for lower rather than higher tariffs' (vol. 1, p. 9), they urged that 'reductions should be spaced over a period of five to fifteen years depending on the industry concerned' (vol. 1, p. 177). And 'the idea that a particular level of tariff is a desirable end in itself should be moderated' (vol. 1, p. 9). Reflecting the Whitlam revaluations, the report emphasized the exchange rate (vol. 1, pp. 10-11).

The Vernon Committee's pessimism about the balance of payments was due to not foreseeing the mineral boom. To the Jackson Committee the mineral boom was an intersectoral worry. Export successes by the mining and rural sectors would lead to revaluations and therefore to a squeeze on manufacturing (vol. 1, pp. 179-80). (It would be tempting to call this intersectoral problem a Brigden issue if the Brigden Committee's message for policy had not been a warning against increases in protection for the manufacturing sector.) The Jackson Report recommended that, in deciding on changes in the exchange rate, the 'authorities should consider fully their implications for [manufacturing] industry policy' (vol. 1, p. 10); the possibility of multiple exchange rates was mentioned (vol. 1, p. 122). (Of course other people have been worried about the effect of mineral exports and revaluation on the rural sector.[17]) A submission quoted by the committee had raised the question (posed by Vernon before 1963): ' "where do you create jobs for those who want them?" ' The submission suggested that 'the only answers are in the tertiary section (already the fastest growth area) and in manufacturing'. Unlike the Vernon Committee, the Jackson Committee seemed to endorse the implication that acceptance of the tertiary sector, or reliance on it, might be excessive in this respect (vol. 1, p. 180).

If revaluation was therefore to be avoided, another question presented itself: 'what should be done if [overseas] balances keep accumulating?' (vol. 1, p. 10). The Vernon Committee had felt some anxiety about the long-term effects of overseas investment in Australia on a weak balance of payments. The Jackson Committee suggested that the reserves which might accumulate as a result of a persistently strong balance of payments might be used to 'buy back the factory' (to cover repurchase of foreign interest in firms operating in Australia) as well as to encourage Australian investment abroad (vol. 1, p. 11).

The Jackson Report did not limit itself to a new policy towards the manufacturing sector. It proposed machinery to make the policy work, notably a system of 'Industry Councils', on which, recalling *Tariffs or Planning?*, 'governments, firms, unions, consumers and other industry groups would be represented' (vol. 1, p. 18).

Shortly after the main text of the Jackson Report was presented to Whitlam, and two days before Whitlam's dismissal, Rattigan submitted his objections. He disputed in particular the diagnosis of long-standing malaise and the proposal for industry councils. The councils, he reasonably concluded, would be dominated by the manufacturing firms, trade unions and industry bureaucracy, who would favour the interests of the manufacturing sector against other sectors or the community as a whole. On the other hand, Rattigan's criticisms did not dispose of the belief that real profitability in manufacturing had on the whole been falling since the mid-sixties.

Nevertheless, Rattigan's objection that his colleagues had confused short-term economic conditions—a short-term recession compounded by inflation—with long-term trends seemed justified. Since recession usually reduces the share of profits more than the share of wages, the time to judge the need for special measures to restore profits in the manufacturing sector would surely be after a strong attempt to cure the recession than was made either in 1975 or in 1976. It might be that the economy would adapt itself successfully to a generally lower profit share just as, before the period invoked in the Jackson Report, it seemed, on the admission of the Vernon witnesses, to have adapted itself to a lower wage-share. The other difficulties of adjusting to a structural squeeze on the manufacturing sector might also turn out to be chimerical.

The Jackson Report has been criticized as superficial. Yet the text, though sometimes sententious, was often informative and, as with the Vernon Report, there were many useful appendices. But in one respect the superficiality was undeniable. From one point of view—a point of view important not least to the Labor Party—Australia's chief economic problem in the 1970s has been the problem of cost inflation (including attempts, under both Whitlam and Fraser, to remedy cost inflation as if it were demand inflation). Wages are at least a major aspect of cost inflation, and on wages the Jackson Report came close to the impartiality of silence. It is a hackneyed question. It is also a question on which the six signatories could hardly be expected to agree in their report, whatever advance towards mutual understanding they achieved in writing it. But to explain the report's evasion does not explain it away. This remained one of the Jackson Report's intellectual shortcomings, compared with the Vernon and indeed the Brigden Report.

The Jackson Committee recommended that a White Paper on manufacturing should be presented 'within say six months' (vol. 1, pp. 21-2). A White Paper by the Fraser government is expected early in 1977. Newspaper leaks suggest that, though unlikely to accept industry councils, the White Paper may propose arrangements for easing adjustment to structural change. Moreover several measures taken in 1976, including modification of company tax and devaluation, are in the Jackson spirit. Thus of the three major documents which this Chapter has discussed—each concerned in varying degrees with protection and intersectoral competition—two, the

Vernon and Jackson Reports, have some claim to be in the main stream of Australian economic policy making. But policy significance is even more ambiguous and difficult to assess than intellectual power.

References

[1] For helpful comments I am grateful to L. Glezer, R. G. Gregory, J. E. Isaac, W. R. Stent and D. H. Whitehead, but naturally they cannot be blamed for the final version.

[2] J. B. Brigden, et al., *The Australian Tariff: An Economic Enquiry* (Melbourne University Press, 1929).

[3] Commonwealth of Australia, *Policies for Development of Manufacturing Industry* vol. 1 (Australian Government Publishing Service, Canberra, 1975); vols. 2-4 (Australian Government Publishing Service, Canberra, 1976).

[4] Commonwealth of Australia, *Report of the Committee of Economic Enquiry* (Government Printer, Canberra, 1965).

[5] Commonwealth of Australia, *Report on possible ways of increasing imports* (Australian Government Publishing Service, Canberra, 1973).

[6] J. B. Brigden, et al., op. cit., p. 149.

[7] J. B. Brigden, 'The Australian Tariff and the Standard of Living', *Economic Record*, vol. 1 (November 1925), pp. 29 and 44.

[8] A. C. Pigou, *Protective and Preferential Import Duties* (Macmillan, London, 1906) pp. 58-9.

[9] H. D. Evans, 'Income Distribution, Welfare and the Australian Tariff', *Australian Economic Papers*, vol. 10 (December 1971), pp. 106-111.

[10] H. D. Evans, *A General Equilibrium Analysis of Protection. The Effects of Protection in Australia* (Basic Books, Amsterdam, 1972) pp. 109-112.

[11] H. Leibenstein, 'Allocative Efficiency vs. X-Efficiency', *American Economic Review*, vol. 56 (June 1966), pp. 392-415.

[12] L. Glezer, The Making of Australian Tariff Policy: 1960-1972, La Trobe University, 1976.

[13] H. F. Lydall, 'The Economy as a Whole: Policies for Growth', *Economic Record*, vol. 42 (March 1966), pp. 152-5.

[14] W. M. Corden, 'Protection', *Economic Record*, vol. 42 (March 1966), pp. 133-4.

[15] R. G. Gregory and L. D. Martin, 'An Analysis of Relationships between Import Flows to Australia and Recent Exchange Rate and Tariff Changes', *Economic Record*, vol. 52 (March 1976), pp. 10 and 21-2.

[16] J. F. Cairns, *Tariffs or Planning?* (Lansdowne Press, Melbourne, 1971), pp. 63-4.

[17] See R. G. Gregory, 'The Green Paper on Policies for Manufacturing Industry: A Review', *Australian Journal of Management*, vol. 1 (October 1976), pp. 71-3.

L. R. WEBB

13 Criteria for Micro-economic Policy

Advocates of the merits of completely unhampered market processes might regard this chapter as a redundant exercise. For on their view about the proper place of government in the economic order, little micro-economic intervention is required. On the other hand, those whose preference is strongly for government intervention will be disappointed, for the discussion points to some of the complexities of micro-economic policy and indicates that economists are far from reaching agreement about relevant criteria.

The chapter discusses six issues about which there is significant disagreement. The list is certainly not intended to be exhaustive. Moreover, particular institutions and policy problems are not systematically dealt with. Instead, the chapter focuses on the economic aspects of policy and skirts around legal, institutional and historical considerations.

Economic Rigidification Versus Free Market Forces

Underlying much contemporary debate about social and economic issues is a fundamental disagreement concerning the relative importance of economic rigidification on the one hand and allowing the economy to adjust to the free play of market forces on the other. By economic rigidification is meant policies or measures which have the effect of maintaining the economic status quo. The disagreement is long standing, one of the most familiar examples of course being the debate between free traders and protectionists in the international trade policy area. While protectionist policy is not necessarily concerned to maintain the status quo in terms of a particular allocation of specialized factors of production receiving real rates of remuneration approximately similar to those received in the past, there is no doubt that it often takes that form.

In a recent address Ronald Henderson drew attention to another example of this underlying disagreement.[1] In a free market system, retirement incomes and provision for various types of emergency are left to the resources of individual citizens and groups acting either for themselves or for others through charitable organizations. Recognition of the inadequacies of this approach to provision of retirement incomes and welfare services has led many, including Henderson, to favour the so-called 'needs' approach to welfare provision. This involves an attempt to measure basic needs (for health services, unemployment benefits, retirement income, and so on) and to provide payments out of public revenues sufficient to cover these needs.

As Henderson points out, another increasingly popular response to the recognition of the failure of the market mechanism to provide basic needs for some people in the community has been to recommend payments out of public revenues designed to maintain the living standards of citizens *at levels to which the individuals concerned have become accustomed.* Social service payments which are earnings-linked and indexed, for example a pension which is a fixed proportion of real earnings at retirement (or over a specified period leading up to retirement), are examples of the second approach. Henderson sees the Hancock recommendations about national superannuation[2] as being of this type. In terms of the distinction drawn here they represent an approach which seeks to maintain at least some elements of the community's real income through time. From another aspect they represent a shift of some income streams in the community out of the category of those which depend on continuing individual initiative and good management, not to mention luck, into a category of shielded incomes.

Of course there is only an imperfect analogy between welfare schemes which tend to maintain people in the life-style to which they have become accustomed, and protective devices such as tariffs which might be intended to have the effect of maintaining the profits of particular firms and industries at levels experienced in the past. Protection maintains or may be aimed at maintaining a particular allocation of factors of production, as well as a certain pattern of factor incomes, whereas schemes which relate retirement benefits to earnings at retirement are not in any immediately apparent way concerned with the production side of the economy. Nevertheless, the analogy is worth pursing to underline the widespread lack of consistency in attitudes in the community towards economic and social issues. Thus a person's willingness to accept the outcome of market forces on production by no means implies willingness to accept such outcomes on income distribution. One can imagine, for example, that some individuals or companies which depend on tariff protection might not be in favour of unemployment benefits being designed to maintain intact the incomes of unemployed workers at the levels which they received in their most recent employment.

Similarly, company executives might be enthusiastic about government-sponsored earnings-related superannuation, while at the same time think they are whole-heartedly committed to the principle of free-market competitive capitalism.

In short, most people, not surprisingly, prefer a ratchet effect to operate whereby improvements in their own economic position are possible but deterioration is restrained. Free market forces generally receive enthusiastic support from those whose opportunities they enhance and opposition from those who suffer, or feel likely to suffer, depleted circumstances. At the same time few people, certainly very few economists, would dispute the proposition that the functioning of the market mechanism requires that prices, employments and outputs be allowed to move down as well as up.

The disagreements about the relative importance of status quo preservation and free market forces may be summarized in the following table. The two types of policy (status quo maintenance and free market forces) are considered in relation to a second distinction, namely that between the resource allocation and income distribution aspects of the economic process.

TABLE 1

Method	*Function*	
	Resource Allocation	*Income Distribution*
Free market forces	A	B
Status quo preservation	C	D

The four types of approach which follow from the classification provided by Table 1 are all represented in Western economies today. Indeed, the phrase 'mixed economies' might be best used to describe this type of mixture, for it is perhaps a phenomenon which goes further towards explaining the major difficulties confronting these economies than does the mixture of public and private sectors to which the phrase normally applies. No less a critic of excess government than Professor Hayek acknowledges that the public sector must exist alongside the private sector to provide certain public goods which a purely market system would fail to offer in appropriate quantities. At the same time he is totally opposed to attempts by governments to overcome the problem of inflation by the use of income and prices policies which rely on what he calls the concept of 'social justice'. Hayek's interpretation of 'social justice' is closely related to the concept of economic rigidification, as the following quotation from his recent lecture at the University of Melbourne indicates.

> Whatever meaning social philosophers have attached to this concept, in the practice of economic policy it has almost always meant one thing, and one thing only: the protection of certain groups against the necessity to descend from the absolute or relative material position which they have for some time enjoyed. Yet this is not a principle on which it is possible to act generally without destroying the foundations of the market order . . .
> It is one of the paradoxes of the present world that the communist countries are probably freer from the incubus of "social justice", and more willing to let those bear the burden against whom developments turn, than are the "capitalist" countries.[3]

Comparative Wage Justice

An instance of procedures or recommendations about microeconomic policy in Australia which seem to exemplify, in terms of Table 1, attempts to achieve status quo preservation, is the principle of comparative wage justice. This is firmly established in Australian industrial relations policy and procedures. The Conciliation and Arbitration Commission has indicated its importance in the following words: 'That employees doing the same work for different employers or in different industries should by and large receive the same amount of pay irrespective of the capacity [to pay] of their employer or industry is well embedded in Australian industrial thought.'[4]

The view has been expressed that comparative wage justice is compatible with the free play of market forces in the markets for factors and goods. In terms of Table 1 this amounts to saying that D is compatible with A and B. Economic theory, however, offers no guarantee of such compatibility.[5] For example, in a free market economy differential changes in labour productivity between two industries employing, say, fitters and turners, might lead to a rise in wages in the more productive industry, or no change, or even a fall, the actual result depending on the characteristics of the demand for the products of the industries, the pricing behaviour of the firms concerned and the degree of mobility of labour between the industries. It follows that the enforcement of comparative wage justice by arbitration or collective bargaining might generate disequilibrium (excess demand or supply) in markets for goods and factors of production, not only in the industries immediately affected by arbitration, but also in related areas of the economy.

Prices Justification

Attempts to moderate inflation by prices justification also tend to involve considerations both with respect to resource allocation and income distribution which relate to historical and comparative data.

To the extent that these considerations are influential they tend to push the economy into row 2 of Table 1. Thus, for example, a proposal to grant a firm a particular price increase because the increase is needed to maintain the firm's profit rate near levels experienced in the past, or near levels experienced currently by other firms in similar circumstances (however that similarity might be assessed), is an example of status quo criteria. This example has been referred to as 'comparative profit justice' and it has been argued that it is incompatible with criteria for prices justification derived from competitive market processes.[6]

One can sympathize with the tendency of price surveillance authorities to resort to comparisons when seeking some 'navigation aids' to guide them to the notion of a justified price, or price increase. And certainly there are some points in any attempt at prices justification at which comparative studies will usually be desirable. For example, the evaluation of risk premium figures for the purpose of calculating the cost of capital will involve classifying industries into groups within each of which risk conditions are broadly comparable. Even so, there is certainly no basis in economic reasoning for the proposition that, in general, market forces are compatible with attempts to preserve profit relativities between industries, any more than there is for the analogous proposition with respect to wages.

If we put together Mathews-type proposals[7] for business tax indexation and prices and incomes policies geared to preserving various price and wage relativities (in the interests of moderating rates of change in absolute prices for commodities and factors) we have an image of modern capitalism which is far removed from anything which is known to be reconcilable with the free market mechanism. The large-scale corporation, with capital maintained intact by internal financing facilitated by tax indexation based on age-coefficients of capital assets,[8] with a relative wage structure imposed by forces external to the firm and with a profit rate maintained intact by a prices board or tribunal, seems like a giant oil tanker, pursuing a set course, unable to change direction except over a long distance.

This is, of course, an exaggeration, but the caricature may help to highlight leading problems in economics today. These may be characterized as follows. In a market order, the nexus between absolute and relative price determination on the one hand, and that between the functions of resource allocation and income distribution on the other, are preserved intact. (In other words, the one set of transactions determines absolute and relative prices, income distribution and resource allocation.) Prices and income policies, inflation-proof accounting, status-quo oriented welfare schemes, and so on, are examples of schemes designed to solve an economic or social problem by operating on one side of one of the two nexus, often in complete disregard of the consequences flowing through to the other side which may frustrate or compromise the initial objective. Thus, prices and incomes policy might try to restrain absolute price increases while interfering as little as possible in relative price determination. However, minimum interference often translates into status-quo preservation, and in a changing world the attempt to maintain relativities might be no less an interference in the determination of relative prices than an attempt to change them in a specified way.

If the community wants to achieve certain degrees of status quo maintenance, moderation of the rate of inflation of absolute prices, and at the same time efficiency in resource use, then it will have to find ways of breaking the two nexus mentioned. This seems to delineate major areas for economic research in the future. For example, if the Prices Justification Tribunal is a political necessity (as appears to be the case), economists should be turning their attention to the problem of separating the inflation-control aspect of the Tribunal's role from the relative price determination aspect which, willy-nilly, is bound up with its continuing task of monitoring the cost-push inflation process. Finding answers to such problems may well involve economists joining forces with sociologists, political scientists and students of institutional structure and change.

Average Practice versus Best Practice

When industries are arguing cases for government support or protection, and government agencies are appraising these arguments, there is a tendency for the discussion to be based on data which reflect average experience for the industry. One of the most important examples of the use of data which averages the experience of groups of firms is the calculation of effective rates of protection. A typical procedure for calculating the effective rate of protection for an industry is to use a weighted average of tariffs for the industry's products and the *combined* input structure for producing these products. The result for the industry is a weighted average effective rate of protection of the results which would be obtained by calculating effective rates on a product- and plant-specific basis.

Against this, the desirability of calculating effective rates which are specific to particular plants arises because efficiency may vary substantially between the different plants involved in an industry. While an industry may have, say, a high average level of effective protection in relation to other industries, the average may conceal relatively low rates of effective protection for firms at the efficient end of the industry's efficiency spectrum, and extremely high rates for the least efficient members of the industry. A similar phenomenon might apply within a particular firm, so that its most efficient equipment (which may or may not be the most recently installed) experiences a low effective rate of protection at current prices for inputs and output, while the equipment which is on the verge of being scrapped will for the same price data exhibit relatively high effective rates of protection.

The average of effective rates for a multi-plant firm and/or multi-firm industry is an extremely suspect statistic for purposes of micro-economic policy. Suppose, for example, that as part of its process of tariff review a tariff authority is using a target band of effective rates (or in the Industries Assistance Commission terminology a set of 'reference points') where the rates have been calculated on an industry basis. It is possible that an industry's average rate of protection lies above the upper limit of the target band, while the most efficient plant or plants in the industry have effective rates lying below the lower limit of the target band. Such an industry would be a candidate for reduced tariffs if industry average data are used, whereas it may reasonably be argued that, because of the high relative efficiency of its more efficient plants, it should be a candidate for greater stimulus to new investment via higher tariffs.

Leaving aside considerations of tariff protection, entrepreneurs in a competitive industry would, when deciding about the appropriateness of new investment in the industry, make their appraisal on the basis of current best-practice technology. If investment in best-practice plant appears attractive, under competitive conditions it will be implemented regardless of the impact of the new investment on the operating profitability (or quasi rents) of previously installed equipment. Under such competitive conditions data which represent industry averages are not calculated by the participants in the industry, since they are not relevant to each firm's decisions. It is difficult to justify their use by government authorities when they are appraising, say, arguments for and against protection.

Considerations similar to the above are relevant to the work of the Prices Justification Tribunal.[9] Under competitive conditions the impact of, say, an increase in the wage rate on the price of a firm's or industry's product will depend not on the industry's average input-output coefficients for labour but on the coefficients associated with best-practice plant. If a price surveillance authority approves price increases which reflect average input-output coefficients, then they may well be agreeing to price increases greater than those which would occur under a competitive regime.

One implication of the proposal that best-practice costs should be the subject of investigation by bodies such as the Industries Assistance Commission and the Tribunal is that the scope of their inquiries should relate to industries rather than particular firms. The procedure whereby firms rather than industries notify the Tribunal of proposed price increases runs counter to this principle. The Industries Assistance Commission generally deals with industries, but there is scope for its inquiries to include a more detailed investigation of costs at the plant level with a view to identifying best-practice data.

In criticism of proposals such as these, it is almost always insisted that the data demands of a best-practice approach are far too great to be practical and that industry averages, such as are available in the form of input-output tables, should be used as a second best. But this seems an unsatisfactory position. The empirical importance of inter-firm variations in efficiency can be judged only in the light of detailed knowledge of the cost structure of the industry concerned. Basevi's view about tariff appraisal seems correct, namely that 'meaningful and sound results can come only from the "case studies" approach'. In this approach

> . . . information is brought to bear at the most detailed level not only on tariff rates, coefficients of production and other variables and parameters . . . , but also on the whole set of institutional, industrial and market characteristics that matter for the analysis of the production at hand.[10]

The point is that we can ascertain whether the use of industry averages is likely to be misleading only *after* we have compared average data with the best-practice data. Thus we might as well seek the best-practice data in the first place.

Stability versus Instability

Public discussion of micro-economic policy frequently contains statements to the effect that a more stable economic environment is better than a less stable one. Expression of a preference for greater stability seems to ignore the findings of some interesting work in micro-economic theory which has established that, in certain circumstances, individual firms and consumers may receive more profits and consumer's surplus, respectively, in a more, rather than less stable environment. In particular the Waugh-Oi theorem shows that a perfectly competitive firm operating under conditions of price instability, but with high predictive ability, will make larger profits over a given number of periods of operation than would be made if price were steady at a value equal to the average of the fluctuating prices.[11]

The literature on the effects of instability indicates that a distinction should be drawn between stability and uncertainty (or predictive ability). Much of the stated preference for stability is probably, on closer inspection, a preference for greater certainty in the economic environment. The stock exchange speculator for example, would no doubt like to be more certain about future price movements, but does not wish for stability of prices as such. Indeed, if prices did not fluctuate, there would be no scope for speculation at all. Even so, many individuals and organizations find that they cannot exploit instability to make greater surpluses but on the contrary would be better off, given their predictive ability, in a stable world. In these circumstances it is common for an approach to be made to the government to achieve intervention designed, in effect, to provide insurance schemes funded from public revenues. The distinction between instability and uncertainty should play an important part in determining government responses to requests for stabilization schemes. If the government can operate in such a way as to reduce the degree of instability in the economic environment (irrigation facilities are one way in which this might be achieved) the case for intervention is much stronger than in a situation where all that is being achieved is a shift of the consequences of limited predictive ability from those involved in a particular industry to the taxpaying community.

Many versus Few

Trade practices and antitrust legislation rarely state but often presume that economic behaviour will more closely approximate desired goals of efficiency and equity if there are a large number of competitors or participants in an industry. Standard courses in micro-economics have no doubt done much to embed this notion in the minds of those who are concerned with industrial policy. Such courses often give the impression that micro-economic efficiency is simply a matter of numbers in the sense that, at one end of the numbers spectrum there is perfect competition and price equal to marginal cost, at the other extreme monopoly with prices greater than marginal cost, while inbetween there are types of market organization ranging from monopolistic competition through oligopoly to duopoly with the degree of approximation of price to marginal cost progressively diminishing.

There is no support for such simplistic thinking in economic theory. Last century, for example, Bertrand showed that even a pair of competing duopolists might, on certain assumptions about their rivalrous behaviour, tend towards a situation where price equals marginal cost. Again, a monopolist might for various reasons prefer not to equate marginal cost and marginal revenue while at the other extreme of the numbers spectrum a large group of competitors might find ways of organizing an industry association with effects similar to those associated with classical monopoly theory. To take another example, prolonged price warfare between oligopolists might produce a price lower than marginal cost for significant periods of time. Large numbers are therefore, neither a necessary nor sufficient condition for micro-economic efficiency and, especially in the context of large-scale modern technology, it may be doubted whether the number of firms provides even a helpful first approximation to an appraisal of relative efficiency.

These considerations suggest that trade practices legislation and its implementation should not be mesmerized by such statistics as concentration ratios, market shares, number of firms in the industry and so on. Of course it would be wrong to suggest that these numbers play no part in an analysis of industrial conduct and performance. But the use made of them should be non-mechanistic and cautious, and suitably supplemented by detailed knowledge of industries derived from thorough case studies.

Co-ordination versus 'Unco-ordination' in Economic Policy

There appears to be some inconsistency in economists' views about the desirability of policy co-ordination. In the macro-economic policy area a good deal has been said about, for example, the alleged dominance of the treasury and the need for a greater diversity of sources of economic advice for government, which would presumably make co-ordination more difficult since it is likely that one department can co-ordinate its advice more effectively than can two or more departments. We also have the proposal of the Coombs Commission to create a department to oversee long-range economic planning, and the creation by the present government of a department of finance to take over part of the work of the treasury.

In contrast, in the micro-economic policy area the most frequent complaint seems to be about the excessive number of departments and authorities responsible for developing and implementing policy. In particular, the independent operations of the Industries Assistance Commission, Prices Justification Tribunal and Trade Practices Commission have been seen by some observers to be a source of undesirable diversity in the generation of micro-economic policy and costly duplication of effort by firms required to prepare returns and other materials for the purposes of the separate organizations. The recent grouping of the three authorities in the one department has modified but not eliminated such criticism.

The Jackson Committee entered a strong plea for more co-ordination of micro-economic policy and indeed of micro-economic behaviour. The recommendations of the Committee reflect their view that policy toward industry should be developed by participatory and co-ordinated processes.

> there should be a framework of industry strategy available as a guide to action, against which detailed policy can be checked for consistency, which is visible to all policy-makers, inside and outside the Government, and which is directed to meeting visible objectives. Government departments, commissions, and agencies should take note of, be guided by, and justify their actions in the light of that framework of strategy; as should decision-makers in firms, unions, lending institutions, and elsewhere in the community.[12]

On the other hand, on the subject of policy co-ordination the *Report* of the task force on economic policy, prepared for the Coombs Commission, sounded a suitably cautious note:

> Most people regard co-ordination as so unarguably a good thing that it is always easy to argue persuasively that more co-ordination is necessarily better. Similarly, it is always easier to suggest that a lack of co-ordination exists than to demonstrate that co-ordination does take place. Lack of adequate co-ordination is often suggested as the explanation when things go wrong; in many cases the cause of the problems is elsewhere.
>
> Co-ordination, like most actions, involves costs as well as benefits. Consequently, proliferation of co-ordination mechanisms or agencies, or the addition of new co-ordination functions to existing agencies, may add more to the lack of co-ordination than to the resolution of problems. It may also reduce the quality of policy making.[13]

When discussing the harmonization of policy, it is important to distinguish policy objectives and actions taken to implement policy objectives. Few would dispute the need to co-ordinate the various actions that might be taken, possibly by different authorities, to achieve a common objective (although the task force would no doubt suggest that cost-benefit appraisal should govern the degree of effort put into the design of co-ordinated procedures). It does not follow, however, that there is anything in principle wrong with a situation where authorities with *different* objectives are not closely co-ordinated. The theory of economic policy, which has been developed mainly in relation to macro-economics, is relevant here. In the context of the theory the assignment principle makes the point that, provided there are sufficient, but not too many, instruments to achieve the targets or objectives of policy, and provided the instruments are properly assigned to the targets, it is possible that the authorities controlling each instrument may act without consultation and still achieve the desired results.

Thus, in the micro-economic policy area one might propose the following 'assignment' of instruments and authorities to targets (Table 2). The list is only a sample and the assignment, which will not be defended here in detail, is based on the proposition that instruments should be allocated to the objectives on which they bear most directly.

TABLE 2

Instrument	*Objective*	*Authority*
Trade practices legislation	To promote overt competition	A trade practices authority
Prices justification	To check the relationship between prices and costs	A prices justification authority
Tariffs, subsidies and so on	Efficient resource allocation between traded and non-traded production sectors	A protection review authority

The objectives listed in the table are of course interrelated, a fact which no doubt accounts for a good deal of the preference which has been expressed in Australia for a greater degree of co-ordination of government intervention with respect to these objectives. Nevertheless, given our imperfect understanding of the relationships between the overtness of competition and the efficiency of resource allocation, given the costs of co-ordination of policy implementation, given the dangers of concentrating power in government in too few hands, and given the lessons of the assignment literature in the theory of macro-economic policy, there seems to be at least as much to be said for an arrangement such as shown in Table 2 as for one which allocates all the objectives listed in Table 2 to one authority.

Competition versus Government Enquiry as Sources of Economic Data

In the lecture entitled 'Competition as a Discovery Procedure', to which reference has already been made, Hayek said:

> It is difficult to defend economists against the charge that for some forty or fifty years they have been discussing competition on assumptions that, *if* they were true of the real world, would make it wholly uninteresting and useless. If anyone really knew all about what economic theory calls the *data*, competition would indeed be a very wasteful method of securing adjustment to these facts.[14]

Hayek described competition 'as a procedure for the discovery of such facts as, without resort to it, would not be known to anyone, or at least would not be utilised.'[15]

The progressive auction would probably be accepted by Hayek as an example of market competition operating as a discovery procedure. The house vendor who uses a progressive auction would not otherwise know the market value of the house. Also, the successful bidder does not know until the auction is completed (a) that he will succeed, and (b) at what price he will succeed. The winning bid may well be less than the winner's own reserve price, it will not be less than the seller's reserve price, and will probably be unique to the particular bid sequence which eventuates (in the sense that another run of the auction might have yielded a different sequence and a different winning bid). In the event of two or more bidders having the same reserve price, we cannot even be sure that a hypothetical second run of the auction would yield the same winner.

While the auction process is an example of a discovery procedure in Hayek's sense, it is also one which suggests that we should in this context interpret the notion of discovery rather broadly. The phrase 'discovery procedure' might be taken to imply that there are facts to be discovered—as there is oil in the ground awaiting discovery—and that competition is a means for their discovery. Such an interpretation is too narrow, for competition does not only 'discover' facts which are already, as it were, in existence awaiting discovery. As the auction example indicates, competition determines or invents certain phenomena which do not exist independently of the competitive process. In addition to the points we have already noted about a competitive auction, whereby a particular winning price is linked with a particular competition, we may note that even the reserve prices of individuals at an auction might be influenced by the excitement (or lack of it) generated by the auction itself. More generally, the shapes, sizes and performance of everything from cars to watches reflect the effects of competition as a discovery *and* invention procedure.

The competitive progressive auction might seem rather a special type of competition for the purpose of gaining insights about the market mechanism. It is usually used for the sale of items, or lots, which are unique in one or more respects and which certainly do not conform to the textbook notion of a standardized commodity. Even if competitive procedures such as the Dutch auction and the competitive sealed tender are included as devices closely related to the progressive auction, the impression might still exist that odd, or at least unusual, market procedures are being dealt with. However, there is in fact an important similarity between the auction/tender procedure and the methods by which prices are set in those parts of the economy concerned with the production and distribution of flows of standardized commodity (cornflakes, cars, toothpaste, air travel) and which are more commonly the subject of analysis by economists. To establish this point will involve taking a short excursion into an aspect of price theory.

Consider the standard textbook representation of a monopoly. The diagram always contains explicit cost and demand functions. Students may well be forgiven for forming the impression that marginal cost, for example, is something about which the firm can be definite, provided it can obtain the relevant information about input prices and production techniques. However, as recent work on marginal cost emphasizes there is an important sense in which marginal cost is a matter of opinion.

The sense in which marginal costs represent matters of opinion, and in relation to which significant differences of opinion might normally be expected, may be illustrated by reference to the concept of amortization charges. When a firm is considering whether to invest in a new piece of equipment it is necessary for it to make several predictions about the course of key variables in the future. It must predict the future movement of the price for its product since, of course, price represents one of the constraints on the unit amortization charges which the firm hopes to receive through the working life of the plant under consideration. A prediction of the future movement of price will in turn entail a prediction about the rate of technological progress in the industry and the degree and nature of competition in the industry. The firm must also predict changes in operating costs for the plant in the future which in turn entails predictions about rates of wear and tear and the movement of factor prices. Thus if marginal cost is broken down into operating cost and amortization or unit capital charge, it appears that while the former may be a relatively precisely ascertainable number, the latter depends on a set of predictions about which opinions may differ widely. A firm taking an optimistic view in the sense that it expects future prices to be relatively high and/or future operating costs to be relatively low will require a smaller unit capital charge in the earlier years of the new plant's operation than would a firm taking a more pessimistic view. The more optimistic firm will therefore be likely to announce or accept a lower price; in effect it is putting in a more competitive 'bid' for a share of the market for its product.

This is the point at which it is important to see the connection between the overt bidding procedures of, say, the tendering process, and the implicit bidding process entailed in manufacturing industries. In a competitive process the prices which are set by firms making new investments may be likened to bids in a tendering process. In preparing a bid, a tenderer adds to his estimate of direct costs a profit margin which it is judged yields some chance of winning the contract and at the same time a suitable rate of return. In choosing a 'suitable' profit margin the tenderer will have to make estimates of the number of other contracts for which success is likely as the value of other work carried out may have a bearing on both the costs associated with the project under consideration and also on the amount of profit which should be sought from each project. This, the 'cost' of a contract for a 'one-off' project is a bid involving matters of opinion as is also the case with marginal cost for a manufactured commodity.

What are the consequences for micro-economic policy of the two observations which are made in this section? These are that (1) competition is an information generating (not merely an information discovery) process, and (2) for many commodities the production of which involves the use of durable capital, the pricing decision has elements in common with bidding procedures and incorporates estimates derived from expectations about future events.

First, in relation to the first observation, it is clear that authorities which are concerned with price and cost data should not regard this data as something which exists and which can equally well be discovered by government-sponsored questionnaire as by the varied procedures of the private sector. When a firm is completing a questionnaire which asks for, say, cost data, it may be asked to organize numbers in a way which bears no relation to its own decision-making. In terms of the concept of competition as a discovery-cum-investment procedure, the government questionnaire represents another kind of discovery-invention procedure. And although it may be intended by the authorities to yield the same data as firms use themselves, it is by no means sure that it will succeed.

Secondly, if marginal cost is more often than not a matter of opinion there may be significant qualifications to be made to some of the standard propositions of welfare economics. Suppose we draw a standard long run supply curve as the lateral sum of a set of long run marginal cost curves. The curves may be used, according to widely accepted practice, in combination with a demand curve to produce estimates of producers' and consumers' surplus, i.e. of net economic welfare.

Now suppose that opinions about the future become more optimistic. The supply curve, reflecting marginal costs, shifts downward and net economic welfare increases, the increase being shared between producers and consumers. Measures of community welfare, at any rate those of the partial equilibrium type, seem then to be dependent on opinions about investment prospects.

Whose opinions are relevant to the calculation of marginal cost? Those already in the industry will certainly have opinions. Those who might wish to enter the industry may have opinions which because of barriers to entry they may not be able to ventilate or implement. The government itself may generate an opinion, for example through an IAC or PJT inquiry. Where there are barriers to entry or where for any other reason it is suspected that monopoly profits exist, it is appropriate for there to be government sponsored processes of auditing and checking private sector calculations. Cost data generated by a public inquiry should be regarded as an alternative view of cost, discovered by processes separate from but complementary to those of the private sector.

As suggested at the beginning of this chapter it is easier to find difficulties in micro-economic policy formulation than it is to offer solutions. In particular it is difficult to state principles which are sufficiently general to enable one to propose major rationalization of institutional arrangements affecting micro-economic policy. If a single conclusion is to be drawn from the observations offered here it is that government action should be based, as in many areas it already is, on detailed case-studies of particular firms and industries. High quality case-studies are expensive in terms of manpower, and they also lead to a tendency for piecemeal rather than across-the-board policy formulation. However, in the present state of knowledge these disadvantages are offset by the advantages associated with case-studies. Not the least of these advantages is the broader acceptance by participants in industry of proposals which reflect thorough study of practical situations.

References

[1] R. F. Henderson, 'Criteria for Welfare: Needs or Earnings', Address to Victorian Branch of Economic Society of Australia and New Zealand, 1976.

[2] *A National Superannuation Scheme for Australia*, Final Report of the National Superannuation Committee of Inquiry, pt. one (Australian Government Publishing Service, Canberra, 1976).

[3] F. A. von Hayek, 'Competition as a Discovery Procedure', Address to Combined Melbourne, Monash and La Trobe Universities, October 1976 (mimeograph). pp. 9-10.

[4] 25 *Industrial Information Bulletin*, 2022 at 2028.

[5] See R. Manning, S. Richardson and L. R. Webb 'Market Forces and the Principle of Comparative Wage Justice: Discord or Harmony?', *Australian Economic Papers*, December 1972.

[6] See B. R. Parmenter and L. R. Webb 'Prices Justification and Microeconomics', *Australian Economic Review*, 2/74.

[7] *Inflation and Taxation*, Report of Committee of Inquiry into Inflation and Taxation (Australian Government Publishing Service, Canberra, 1975).

[8] Ibid., chapter 14.

[9] See B. R. Parmenter and L. R. Webb, op. cit., p. 58.

[10] G. Basevi, 'Aggregation Problems in the Measurement of Effective Protection', in H. G. Grubel and H. G. Johnson (eds), *Effective Tariff Protection* (GATT and Graduate Institute of International Studies, Geneva, 1971), p. 132.

[11] F. V. Waugh, 'Does the Consumer Benefit from Price Instability', *Quarterly Journal of Economics*, August 1944 and W. Y. Oi, 'The Desirability of Price Instability under Perfect Competition', *Econometrica*, January 1961.

[12] *Policies for Development of Manufacturing Industry*, A Green Paper, volume 1, Report to the Prime Minister by the Committee to Advise on Policies for Manufacturing Industry (Australian Government Publishing Service, Canberra, 1975), p. 7.

[13] *The Processes of Economic Policy Making in Australia*, Report to the Royal Commission on Australian Government Administration by the Task Force on Economic Policy (Australian Government Publishing Service, Canberra, 1975), paras. 10.3 and 10.4.

[14] F. A. Hayek, op. cit., p. 1.

[15] Ibid.

W. B. REDDAWAY*

14 The Prices Justification Tribunal

One central idea underlies the approach of this chapter, which was written in August 1976: we live in a world in which economic judgements are difficult to make, and cannot be made at all exactly. There are many reasons why this statement is particularly applicable to a body like the Prices Justification Tribunal, some of which will be developed as the chapter proceeds. But one should be stated at the outset: the data which the Tribunal would like to have are not easy to define; they keep changing, they take time to prepare, and most of them can only come from a highly interested party. Moreover, the prices which are being discussed will apply in the future, and most of the data inevitably relate to the past: this alone raises acute problems, since obviously one cannot have daily decisions by the Tribunal in the way that the market price of rubber is varied every day (or indeed every hour). This single fact suggests that one should not be too ambitious over what a body like the Tribunal should attempt to achieve, and one should not expect a high degree of precision from it.

The Tribunal as a Check on Inflation or on the Abuse of Market Power?

The Tribunal was created essentially as an instrument in the fight against inflation. Moreover, it was given a highly independent status, and not conceived as one part of a co-ordinated set of instruments, which would be operated according to a joint strategy. This emphasis on 'fighting inflation' as a justification for creating a Prices Justification Tribunal was unfortunate. So long as it operated 'on its own', and not as part of a package of policies (hopefully endorsed by trade unions and other bodies), its effect on the speed with which

* The author was a consultant with the Prices Justification Tribunal during July-August 1974, and a part-time member of the British National Board for Prices and Incomes between 1967 and 1971; this chapter represents his own ideas and does not in any way commit either of these organizations.

prices rose could only be small, even on the assumption that its 'verdicts' were accepted. The anti-inflation basis led naturally to the idea that its operations should, in one way or another, be made to apply over as large a field as was practicable, and should be aimed at resisting price increases by any means which might be made to appear legitimate: the Tribunal's staff almost inevitably tended to see it as their duty to concentrate on picking holes in the case made for an increase and getting its size reduced.

However, one can make a case for having some sort of review body to enquire into the price-behaviour of companies which appear to have substantial market power, which has nothing whatever to do with inflation. In times of generally stable prices it has been normal in most countries to have some kind of supervision of public utility companies for just this reason: and they are far from being the only companies which might be held to have excessive market power.

Naturally, the fact that such a case can be made does not mean that the policy should automatically be adopted: there are costs involved–notably the expenses of the review body and the diversion of company executives from their normal activities to dealing with the enquiries. Moreover, the difficulties of doing the job may lead to bad decisions by the review body, which may inhibit enterprise and investment; the inevitable mistakes may bring the Tribunal's whole activity into contempt, and lead companies to give distorted evidence and evade (or ignore) the decisions. The guiding principle in devising and operating such a system should be to set limited objectives, which are likely to be achievable in practice, rather than to aim at doing everything which would be desirable in a world of perfect information with an all-wise Tribunal.

How, then, does the case for having a review body to deal with market power in non-inflationary conditions relate to the case for a prices tribunal in times of inflation? There is–or should be–a great deal in common. The case for scrutinizing possible abuses of market power clearly does not disappear in a time of inflation, and if the Tribunal tries to do much more than deal with such abuses, the results of the further activity are likely to produce consequences more unfavourable than favourable (at least so long as it is thought of as acting on its own, rather than as part of a package).

Inflation does, however, have two really important effects on the actual operation:

(a) The fact that costs are rising in an inflationary period raises a whole host of additional complications about how to judge what does constitute an abuse of market power, or–if one prefers it–a justified price. It also greatly increases the need for *speedy decisions.*

(b) On the other hand, the fact that most companies will be wanting to raise their prices at fairly frequent intervals provides a very simple method of bringing the Tribunal into action, and gives it an almost dangerous degree of power to impose a vast 'fine' on a company by the very 'innocent' action of saying that there should be a Public Inquiry. This action does not necessarily imply that the Tribunal considers the price increase to be *un*justified, merely that the matter is important and should be investigated in public.

To this one might add that the need to do something about rising prices may lead many people to feel more prepared to accept (or indeed *demand*) some direct action on prices, despite its imperfections: but it is doubtful whether this point should be given any significant weight, unless the Tribunal is clearly made part of an integrated package.

Problems in Non-Inflationary Times

Since the problems involved in having a review body in non-inflationary times are *simpler*, it seems useful to start by examining these. Given below is a list of rather dogmatic points, which are made with full heed to the dictum that one should 'play for low stakes'–i.e. aim at something which is manageable, even if it does not achieve everything which is theoretically desirable.

(a) The government should give the Tribunal an easily intelligible definition of the area in which it is to seek abuses of market power, and something analogous to 'companies or groups of companies with a turnover of more than $20 million' seems appropriate. Size is not an automatic guide to potential market power, but abuses by small companies (for example, the sole motor-repairer operating in a district) will simply have to be left to the restraint of potential competition, or disregarded as *de minimis*. Similarly total turnover is not an ideal guide to the relevant type of size–*diversification* in a big company may mean a lack of market power on any one thing, and *value added* may be more relevant than turnover. But the criterion needs to be familiar and easy to establish.

(b) There has to be a decision whether the Tribunal is to report solely on the *past* performance of a company, or in some sense also to consider its future plans, notably about prices. In the interests of comparability with the Tribunal, the latter is assumed.

(c) There has to be a means of bringing the Tribunal into action on a particular company, since one cannot rely on the company having to approach the tribunal over a proposed price increase. It would be possible to leave it to the government to refer cases to the Tribunal, as happened with the National Board for Prices and Incomes in Britain. But for present purposes it seems better to assume that all companies with a turnover of more than $20 million have to register with the Tribunal, and each is allocated a date in the year on which it has to report to the Tribunal the prices which it intends to charge over the next year, with corresponding past prices. (For companies selling a vast range of products the report would be in terms of average percentage movements for categories of goods, with the prices of a few leading items specified in cash). It would then be for the Tribunal to decide which companies would have to justify these prices at a Public Inquiry (or in some alternative forum), ending with a report by the Tribunal: the Tribunal would be free to cover only a part of a company (for example the steel section of BHP).

(d) The Tribunal would *not* be held to have 'approved' the prices proposed by companies which were not selected for an inquiry:* it is clearly beyond its powers to form a definite opinion on every company, and any attempt to cast its net too widely is likely to reduce the value of its work. Correspondingly, there would be no compulsion on companies to send in elaborate 'justifications' for their price proposals, though they would be free to do so if they thought it would reduce the chance of a Public Inquiry: the only compulsory submission would be a copy of their latest accounts, and an outline of movements in their prices over the last three years.

(e) How, then, should the Tribunal decide which companies to examine? Its basic object should be to find *important* cases of abuse, so it would be natural to concentrate on companies known to be operating in not-very-competitive markets, which are large, and which sell things of real economic importance to the community; the company's accounts, its price-history and complaints from customers may give further clues. It is however, important that *all* companies should feel that they *may* be examined, so it would be wise to have some system of taking a small proportion of companies more or less at random—and to let it be well known that such a system *is* followed. The whole thing is, indeed, somewhat like a customs check. Everyone must go through the shed; everyone *may* be examined; but the customs officers have various systems for concentrating most of their efforts on cases which are more likely to produce useful results. Above all, the fact that a company is not examined does *not* imply that the customs are certifying that it has no contraband.

Difficulties over Criteria

This leaves open the crucial question of the criteria by which the Tribunal should decide whether a price (or set of prices) is or is not justified. Even without the added complications caused by inflation,

* It seems to be most unfortunate that the Tribunal is often described as having 'approved' price-increases when it does no more than issue a statement that it will not hold a Public Inquiry: in 1974/5 such notices were issued without any change in the original price-notification in about 80 per cent of cases. Logically, such a notice may merely mean that the Tribunal does not consider it worthwhile to have a public inquiry for a small luxury item, even though the price-increase seems unjustifiably large.

the main emphasis must be laid on the inevitable imprecision of the Tribunal's decisions, and the possibly conflicting–and non-commensurable–criteria which may seem applicable. Since much has been written about this, only a few illustrations are given. A number of these spring from the fundamental question whether an abuse of market power represents the charging of a price higher than the one which would prevail in a world of strictly atomistic competition, or whether other factors come in–for example, 'fairness'.

This issue is fundamental to the practical problems which arise out of *fluctuations* in the level of demand for an industry's product. Under atomistic competition a fall in demand typically means that the price falls to something like prime cost, but a tribunal which said that a company's proposed prices were unjustifiably high because they would not produce large losses would certainly not be considered 'fair' and such decisions would not be observed.* At the other extreme, most economists would feel very uneasy about a Tribunal which regarded it as 'justifiable' to raise prices in the face of falling demand, in an attempt to maintain some 'fair' level of aggregate profits (with the corollary that prices 'must' be cut if demand becomes unusually active even if the company cannot meet all of it). Some compromise–perhaps based on what is thought to happen with an average degree of competition–might appear more hopeful. But it is not easy to make this at all precise: does it, for example, mean charging a price which gives the same surplus over prime cost per unit of output, leaving the effects of changes in sales volume to show up proportionately in aggregate gross surplus *before* overheads, and more than proportionately in surplus *after* overheads?

Even if one could ignore fluctuations in demand, however, it is notoriously difficult to decide what constitutes a 'right' or 'fair' level of profits for a company, because it is so difficult to value old assets, and because varying degrees of managerial efficiency (or even sheer luck over research) should somehow come into the picture.

Sometimes one tries to escape from the above dilemma by applying the new investment test–'what price would make it just attractive to build a new factory on a green-field site?' But this test may be *irrelevant*, if there is no likelihood of anyone doing so (for example because demand is not growing, or because it would be more attractive to expand existing factories); and there are problems over what charge should be made to the new factory for the use of

* In many cases a company can *formally* comply with a decision on prices, but evade them in substance by giving worse quality, worse service, smaller discounts and the like: this 'flexibility' provides some safeguard against over-harsh decisions which the Tribunal may make for any reason. But in the case envisaged one would expect an open revolt, which might well destroy the whole effectiveness of the Tribunal. If an instrument like the Tribunal is applied too vigorously, it breaks in the user's hand.

trade secrets, and so on, developed in the existing one. Moreover, the method involves a maximum of problems over data, which can often come only from the company affected, and do not relate to actual operations.

Then there are all the awkward consequences which arise out of technical progress and/or mechanization. It would clearly be wrong to say that a company was justified in continuing to charge the old prices if an unpatentable discovery made by somebody else had greatly lowered its expenditure per unit of output on labour, or fuel, or raw materials, without involving the company in any capital expenditure; at the other extreme, it would clearly be wrong to insist that the whole of such savings in prime costs should be passed on to the consumer if they reflected the results of capital expenditure–*some* allowance for depreciation, interest and profit on the latter must be made. But *how much* is it 'justifiable' for a monopolist to allow for these purposes, especially if the new capital reflected the results of the monopolist's own research? How fast should the expenditure be amortized, when further discoveries may render it obsolete? Is it 'justifiable' that successful research and development should earn big enough surpluses to cover the costs of unsuccessful research and development as well, *plus* a margin to give an incentive to do research? And how does one translate any principles into figures when the data are variable through time, hard to come by, and derived from an interested party whose research department may be highly inefficient?

This list of problems over criteria (which could easily be extended) poses an awkward dilemma: if the tribunal is to be respected, should it take up a definite stance on some of them (or say which ones are to prevail over others), or should it merely list some of the problems and say that each case must be considered in the light of its own facts? And how far should it go, in individual reports, in showing how it arrived at a conclusion when the various approaches pointed to different answers? Clearly the further the Tribunal can go in the direction of candour, without creating too many embarrassing precedents, the better. Perhaps it should also be added that the Civil Service Arbitration Tribunal in Britain, regularly reported the arguments of the parties and then simply gave its own judgement: the three members could often agree on the figure while disagreeing fundamentally on the reasons.

What does seem clear, however, is that if one establishes a price review body of this broad kind in non-inflationary times, it should have the very modest aim of providing a limited check on abuses of market power, by presenting an impartial review of the position in a number of cases and relying–as the Tribunal does–on the force of public opinion and on companies' desire to be seen to conform, rather than on any penal sanctions. We do *not* live in a world in which atomistic competition either exists or is regarded as generally desirable, and there is a case for having a watch-dog of this kind, in the interests of securing a better degree of co-operation between classes and individuals in making the economy work. But the watch-dog should not be regarded as capable of precise judgements: it may be able to point to some cases of flagrant abuse, but it should *not* be thought of as a *price-fixer*. Where the tribunal considers prices to be unjustifiable it should not, in my view, be under an *obligation* to say what would be justifiable: typically the 'verdict' should, I think, be in one of these forms, which recognize the imprecision of the conclusions:

(a) The prices proposed seem to the Tribunal to be unjustifiably high by a substantial margin.

(b) *Ditto*, but with 'small' for 'substantial'.

(c) The Tribunal has no comment to make on the proposed prices.

The company would be under obligation to announce publicly what it intended to do in the first two cases, and would be allowed to consult the Tribunal privately before doing so: but the Tribunal would not have to take a public stance on the exact set of prices which it considered to be justified, even if it allowed the company to quote its private views in general terms. It might be wise for the company to be permitted to say no more than that the Tribunal had no comment to make on the revised prices: the absence of such a statement would lead to obvious inferences.

Complications Caused by Inflation

A period in which costs are rising by more than (say) 10 per cent a year creates problems for a company which sells at 'administered' prices even if its freedom is not limited by any such body as the Tribunal. It has to decide broadly whether it is going to fix prices by reference to replacement costs, or historic costs plus its traditional mark-up, or estimated future costs, or perhaps historic costs plus an extra margin:* and it has to decide *how frequently* it will raise its prices—is it better to have many small increases or a few large increases (or perhaps large increases at different times for different parts of the business)?

These problems naturally have a counterpart for a review body like the Tribunal, but they look somewhat different. To put it crudely, if it adopts a tough attitude in assessing what constitutes a justified price in relation to the facts as they existed at time T, then

* This may be aimed at allowing for the non-use of replacement costs and/or at making the price start a bit on the high side, so that it can continue to be used when on the low side.

that price will be seriously too low within a short period, because costs will have risen: the company will suffer unjustifiably (with possible effects on employment and investment discussed below), and it will be back with another price notification very speedily —thus overloading the Tribunal. (If the decision does not become effective until (say) three months after time T, then the price will already be too low when it becomes effective. Even if the price includes an allowance for 'delay costs', to compensate the company for having had to charge the old price rather than the new one during those three months, this does not provide against a rise in (say) raw material prices since time T; this burden may perhaps be compensated at the *next* review as impact costs, but the company will still have an incentive to bring another claim speedily.) The tough decision may *seem* like a triumph in the fight against rising prices, but it is liable to prove a Pyrrhic victory.

What, then, should the policy of the Tribunal be? To my mind, it would be wise for the Tribunal to state unambiguously that it accepts the principle of replacement cost rather than historic cost as giving the proper starting point. There are of course difficulties over applying the principle, both to fixed assets (notably where the type of machine now being installed has changed radically) and to materials (forward contracts, seasonal stocks, and so on); but it seems best to be unambiguous about the type of concept to which one is seeking an approximation. The alternative of starting from historic costs and then being 'generous' in dealing with the various unquantified items seems a poor tenth best—though there may be *something* to be said for regarding this factor as an unspecified off-set to the assumption that a company will give itself the benefit of the doubt in presenting data and in interpreting the decision (which also cannot feature explicitly in the report).

Why, then, should the Tribunal not go further and broadly extrapolate the rise in (replacement) costs so as to arrive at an average level for (say) six months or a year after time T and decide what prices are 'justifiable' on that basis? So long as the Tribunal is acting 'on its own', such a procedure seems unwise on the crucial item of wages: whether the tribunal published its assumptions or not, they would be liable to prove very embarrassing in relation to the work of the Arbitration Commission.

Let us assume, therefore, that the Tribunal would receive notifications in the way provided by the 1973 Act, and judge some of them in terms of the criteria suggested in the previous section, but explicitly adopt the criterion of replacement cost (and profits considered 'right' in relation to replacement capital). The cases to be investigated would be selected in the way outlined in section 3, but in considering the company's price-history the Tribunal would have more regard to the cumulative increase over the last three years than to the size of the increase now proposed (and the latter would have to be converted to an annual rate, since applications come after varying periods). At the inquiry there would be no presumption that the previous price was justified: the widespread view that the investigation should be concerned only with cost-increases since that price was introduced would be replaced by a clear recognition that it is the proposed price which is to be considered, not the price-increase.

The main function of the Tribunal would, as before, be to look for abuses of market power. Such action may help the general fight against the free-for-all process of cost inflation, by buttressing an appeal for moderation with an assurance that the big boys are not being allowed to get away with murder: the process might be made more effective if a real package deal could be organized. What else can such a Tribunal do to help in the fight against inflation?

The answer is, 'not much'. By making it apparent that employers who negotiate sweetheart agreements with their work force may not be able to convince the Tribunal that these extra wages constitute a justification for higher prices, the Tribunal may stiffen the resistance of employers to union pressures:* this may do something, but its value really depends on the attitude of the various wage-fixing bodies and on the establishment of a general consensus in favour of moderation. It is always possible that a tribunal decision that a price-increase is not justified because of a company's 'inefficiency' (for example its practice of supplying too much bread on sale or return, or its prestige advertising) may lead to cost-saving—as, of course, *may* happen when a tough price is imposed by *any* outside force, such as foreign competition. It is also possible that companies will seek to avoid the trouble and expense of price-applications by tightening up their methods: but this is a rather feeble off-set to the manifest expense and disturbance caused by making applications which are unavoidable.

Finally, a word of warning about the possible mistakes of a Tribunal operating in inflationary times. One thing that inflation clearly does is to increase the danger of decisions having a persistent downward bias. In the absence of inflation, one might well fear that a review body would tend on the whole to be too soft in its verdicts, if only because the company's case will be well presented and based on better information than is available to 'the other side' (even if there *is* another side): on top of that, harsh verdicts may be evaded by

* It is interesting that, since 1975, companies in Britain which agreed to a larger wage-increase than was provided in the 'voluntary' wage policy of the day have not been allowed to take account of *any* of the wage increase for price-fixing purposes. The temptation to an employer to give way in the interests of good industrial relations has indeed been reduced, and the union may, at least on occasions, see that successful pressure to exceed the norm would lead to the employer's bankruptcy.

quality changes, worse service, and so on. But with inflation the delay factor is operating to make the prices actually charged too low, and there may well be a general tendency to judge the success of the Tribunal by the extent to which it holds down prices. The general confusion about historical and replacement cost may lead to companies' cases being badly presented in this respect and to wrong principles being used by the Tribunal. Published profits, based on historical costs, add further to the confusion.

Therefore, it is necessary to emphasize the dangers of holding down prices to a level based on historical costs. For simplicity let it be assumed that the profit margin is in fact kept equal to the original percentage of sales (ignoring for example, the possibility that the company will thwart the Tribunal's intention by lowering quality). In the simplest case, then, this system of pricing means that the money values for the enterprise's capital and profit (as conventionally measured) remain unchanged, and their real value progressively declines. This development could in principle be combated by the elimination of dividends, and/or the issues of new shares and/or the raising of loans—though it would clearly not be easy for a company to combine all three of these, and the *supply* of funds for taking up shares and/or loans might well be small if most companies were earning little real profit and trying to follow this policy. It is much more likely that the outcome will be a liquidity squeeze, under which the companies cut out most expenditure on fixed capital (including replacements) and concentrate on trying to minimize the fall in the real amount of their working capital and prevent it from enforcing a fall in physical output. A natural corollary is a pruning of the labour force, which has some advantages if it means the introduction of genuinely improved methods, but which may well mean postponement of maintenance and research, or simply a reduction in output to keep the wage-bill down to what is available.

It may be argued that there are reasons of equity, whereby the entrepreneur should only be able to keep the money value of his assets stable, since that is all that the bond-holder or depositor in the savings bank can do. However two wrongs do not make a right. One could alternatively argue that the savings bank depositor at least receives some compensation in a higher rate of interest; but when the indirect consequences of historical cost pricing to the economy are so unpleasant, perhaps the previous verdict is more apposite.

Conclusion

This chapter has dealt mainly with the difficulties which inevitably confront a body like the Prices Justification Tribunal: one might be tempted to conclude that it should be abolished, because the mistakes which it will inevitably make in practice are likely to outweigh any theoretical benefits from its operations. Constitutionally, however, if one is an economic optimist, one would rather conclude in favour of reform on more modest lines. The dangers of being too ambitious with a prices policy have been learned in many countries, and a more modest objective and procedure could be adopted, based explicitly on replacement cost: hopefully, this could be made part of a manageable and concerted policy on incomes as well as prices. There is a real need to control inflation, and it is quite certain that Australia will not establish 'the unfettered role of genuine free markets'. A combination of a good fiscal policy, a good monetary policy and a concerted prices and incomes policy may be the most effective strategy: to mix a metaphor, two wrongs do not make a right, but two rights may also fail to make a right, unless combined with a third right.

P. J. DRAKE

15 Intervention in the Securities Markets?

In 1967 the stock exchange prices of Australian corporate securities—led by metal, mineral and engineering stocks—rose overall by over 50 per cent. Thus began a share market boom which lasted for about four years. Large numbers of local and overseas investors were attracted into Australian securities. Many others were indirectly involved in securities through investments made by superannuation and pension funds, unit trusts, mutual funds, and so on, to which they had subscribed. The boom led also to a rapid increase in the number of people engaged in stockbroking, underwriting, merchant banking, investment counselling and other related activities. Inevitably, those involved in the market's boom were caught in its subsequent demoralization and collapse.

During the boom period the securities markets were subject to many strains. Pronounced day-to-day fluctuations in share prices became common; remarkable price rises occurred in particular mining stocks (led by Poseidon N.L.); the volume of trade increased dramatically; and eventually the mechanism of securities transfer (conducted through brokers' offices and share registries) broke down under the weight of transactions. These events were marked especially by an influx to the market of over-optimistic, inexperienced and uncritical share traders, and opportunities arose for profitable manipulation and sharp practice on the stock exchanges and in the new issues market.[1]

Following adverse publicity about several episodes towards the end of 1969, much disquiet was expressed about the conduct of affairs in the securities markets. Discussion welled up and came to a head in federal parliament in March 1970, when the senate established a select committee charged

> ... to inquire into and report upon the desirability and feasibility of establishing a securities and exchange commission by the Commonwealth ... to act speedily and efficiently against manipulation of prices, insider trading and such other improper or injurious practices as the Committee finds have occurred or

> may occur in relation to shares and other securities of public companies, and to recommend . . . such legislative and administrative measures by the Commonwealth as will, having regard to the constitutional division of legislative power in Australia, enable the utmost protection of members of the public and the national interest.[2]

The Senate Select Committee on Securities and Exchange discovered serious and widespread malpractice and incompetence in the securities markets. It therefore recommended measures aimed at obtaining 'fundamental reform' of the conduct of securities trading.

Public discussion, engendered by events of the boom and its collapse, by the inquiries of the Committee, and by legislation attempted in 1974–5 by the Labor government, has concentrated on weaknesses and inadequacies in the structure and operations of the securities markets and on various legislative proposals for reform. In this chapter a somewhat broader approach is taken, beginning with an outline of the economic role of securities markets in a modern mixed economy, proceeding to a digest of the Senate Committee's *Report* and subsequent events, and concluding with a discussion of the purpose and nature of official intervention in the securities markets.

The Functions of Securities Markets

In any period of time, the value of a nation's aggregate investment (real capital formation and additions to stocks) is formally identical to the value of its savings (unconsumed income) plus or minus capital movements from or to the rest of the world. But *individual acts* of saving and investment are seldom alternate sides of the same coin. In the main these acts are separated, either because those who save are not those who undertake investment or because those who both save and invest do not do so simultaneously and in identical amounts. It follows that, in any economy where decisions about saving and investment may be made freely and independently, the transfer of resources from savers to investors requires some institutional channels. These are supplied by financial intermediaries and by the securities markets. Intermediaries, as the term suggests, borrow from some and lend to others. Securities markets provide the framework in which companies and government may issue marketable securities (shares, debentures, bonds) in exchange for cash and in which the issued securities may subsequently be bought and sold freely to effect changes of ownership.

The so-called 'secondary market', centred on the stock exchanges, where securities may be sold for cash (irrespective of whether or not the sellers then purchase other securities) is of paramount importance. Without it, few companies could expect to raise capital on the new issue market, for the ability of most firms to float new issues depends on the back stop of a market in which those shares can be traded. The secondary market provides a way in which the individual owners of securities can achieve liquidity without reducing the liquidity of the firms and governments whose shares, debentures and bonds are traded. The modern system of company finance owes as much to the saleability of shares and so on in the securities markets as it does to the fundamental advantage of limited liability.

In addition to providing a channel between saving and investment, the securities markets may lead to increased aggregate savings in so far as securities are bought with income that otherwise would have been consumed. Further, and distinct from any effect they may have on the level of saving, the securities markets contribute to an increase in the volume and intricacy of financing, thus extending the scope for specialization and division of labour in the financial world. These developments lower the real costs of investment and improve the allocation of capital resources.

The securities markets also influence the allocation of resources more directly. The disposition of the funds which are attracted to new issues of securities is made broadly in accordance with the returns expected from ownership of the competing new securities—private or public—on offer. The expected returns (which may eventuate as interest, dividends or capital gains) are determined by the standing and anticipated profitability of enterprises. These characteristics are reflected in the market values of existing securities.[3]

Finally, those who are engaged or employed in the activities of the securities markets may increase their knowledge and skills from the experience. This point embraces many possibilities: we may mention that entrepreneurial and trading talents can be developed from experience in the markets, that employees of broking and banking firms may learn the skills which later enable them to establish their own financial enterprises, and that 'external economies' arise to the extent that knowledge gained in any one form of activity or enterprise in the market may be fruitfully deployed elsewhere in the financial sector.

From this sketch of the economic functions of securities markets, it appears almost axiomatic that a market would benefit Australia, where private enterprise accounts for some two-thirds of gross capital formation and about half of this private sector investment is undertaken by companies, principally by a relatively small number of firms which raise capital publicly and have their securities traded on the stock exchanges. Unfortunately, as a review of the senate *Report* will now illustrate, Australian securities markets have lately been so abused that the benefits promised by economic theory have been put in jeopardy.

The Report

The Senate Select Committee on Securities and Exchange (the Committee) met first in April 1970 but its *Report* was not published until 1974. This unexpectedly long interval arose because the Committee, on looking into various events in the securities markets, uncovered a tangle of activities which was both complex and startling. Consequently, it took a great deal of time (to say nothing of ingenuity, determination and authority) to unravel facts and analyse the issues which emerged. Not surprisingly, therefore, the *Report* consists preponderantly of a detailed account and indictment of unsatisfactory practices, providing the justification for the Committee's strong recommendations for fundamental reform: 'The importance and seriousness of the issues cannot be appreciated without a concrete understanding of circumstances which exist . . . It has therefore been necessary to provide a substantial amount of specific information to substantiate the Committee's findings.' (1.5)

The *Report* is detailed indeed: it is some 850 pages long and is backed up by a companion volume of documents and three volumes of transcript public evidence. Although long the *Report* is written in a lucid, brisk and engaging style, and its authors show a fine touch of dry humour. The introductory chapter lays constant emphasis on the need to '. . . ascertain facts and, having done that, to record them in the interests of helping to promote an adequate understanding of the securities industry' (1.2).

In chapter 2 the *Report* plunges into the first of its case studies: an account of insider behaviour in the Poseidon boom. This is a main chapter in several respects: its length (125 pages); the importance of the 'insider' question which is its preoccupation; and because Poseidon, as the first and most spectacular ('the share of the year—if not all time—as far as stock market performance is concerned' according to the *Times* 1969) of the boomed mining stocks, seemed to spark off a great rash of other flotations, generate remarkable investor confidence and give impetus to the whole share market. The Committee's investigation revealed casual and dishonest public reporting coupled with insider trading and abuse of confidential knowledge by those principally connected with Poseidon's mining explorations. Moreover, not only were conflicts of interest unchecked but dual roles were actively exploited for private benefit and public loss. Regrettably, the two stock exchanges most directly concerned failed to check the improper activities of their members, while the relevant state government authorities were uninterested or unable to intervene in the public interest.

Chapter 3 which is a consolidated study, markedly different from the particular cases on which the rest of the *Report* is based, presents the results of research undertaken by the Committee into the financial structure and profitability of member firms of the six principal stock exchanges. More interesting points emerge than can be reported here—we must be content to observe that broking firms are highly dependent on bank overdrafts, and therefore most vulnerable to any tightening of credit and increases in interest rates, and that the profitability of stockbroking is extremely variable from year to year. Chapter 3 is an important research contribution in its own right, providing a good example of the valuable work that could be produced by an official body empowered to collect, collate, analyse and publish brokers' statistics.

Chapters 4, 5 and 6 are case studies of three failed stockbroker firms. Here we are told again of conflicting interests, of deception (of clients, companies and the public), of inadequate capital, of the abuse of trust funds, of the incompetence and bad judgement of principals, of office inefficiency, and of laxity in the control of staff—leading to staff speculating with the firm's and clients' funds as well as their own. Again, the failure of the stock exchanges to police, restrain or discipline their members and to protect the investing public from the impropriety and incompetence of brokers is evident. 'Self-regulation' of the broking industry stands condemned by the neglect of the stock exchanges in these cases. The Committee rightly draws out the difficulties '. . . inherent in a system where the supervision of a broker's internal affairs is left mainly to those who are his competitors and with whom he is also doing daily business which involves the giving and taking of credit . . .' (5.12). The Adelaide Stock Exchange was found to have compounded its sins of omission by an act of flagrant self-interest in disposing of the proceeds of sale of the exchange seats of defaulting members. Having sold the seats of the defaulters, the Adelaide Stock Exchange allowed 'both the Exchange and the members of that Exchange to receive payment in full of the amounts they were owed by . . . [the defaulters] well before the firm's former clients received any payment of the amounts owing to them' (6.15).

In chapter 7 the Committee scrutinizes the activities of investment consultants/advisers/counsellors (within and outside stockbroker firms), the financial press, and the authors of newsletters and tipping sheets. The competence and objectivity of consultants is questioned; financial relationships between stockbrokers, tipsters and journalists are noted. On the whole, the conduct of the activities discussed was judged unsatisfactory, notably because of the conflicting interests of those who advised others about buying and selling shares while being active in the market themselves. The Committee seem here to have been swayed by their particular case studies and could perhaps have made more of the benefits, noted in the *Report*, of objective investment advice (for example 7.3–6) and alert and sharp financial journalism (for example 2.5).

Chapters 8 and 9 describe and illustrate various forms of manipulation of the share market. Here recur the now familiar themes of conflicts of interest and of collusion, at the expense of the public, among parties with complementary interests.

The very important chapters 10 and 11 tackle the weighty subject of new issues, private and public respectively. Much startling and disturbing information is published for the first time, making a major contribution to knowledge about the workings of the new issues market. Among abuses detailed are: avoidance of stock exchange listing requirements; trading shares before the grant of a quotation; a company secretly selling its own shares on the exchange; improper practices in the marking of share transfers; and improper charging of brokerage. It is especially disturbing to discover that the resource allocation role of the new issue market was undermined by the device of secret issues of new stock under the guise of market sales of existing shares.

> We have shown how directors of listed companies, with the connivance of members of the stock exchanges, have sold large quantities of the new shares on the floors of the main Australian exchanges without the shareholders and the market knowing that the shares were coming on issue and that dealings in these shares were already taking place. In other cases we have shown how members of the stock exchanges themselves secretly arranged to acquire new shares in a placement at a highly favourable price compared with the market price of the existing shares, and then began the large-scale selling of these new shares at a considerable profit on the floor of the exchanges and to clients without the purchasers or the public ever knowing to this day the nature of the shares they were buying. In these placements the market had no awareness that it was dealing with an increased supply of scrip, *an increased supply that had not yet been given any formal existence* (10.105, italics supplied).

The Committee found that the rules of the stock exchanges were ambiguous on the subject of private issues; that there had been insufficient discussion of the principles involved in this activity; that often the understanding of brokers was poor and their thinking confused. All this led to marked differences in standards of behaviour among brokers, and the worst practices were sometimes defended as normal and customary. The Committee noted that the frequency of a practice does not establish its propriety and that ‘It is the closed shop system and the looseness of self-monitoring arrangements in the stock exchanges that have permitted the practices to flourish in so many varieties’ (10.104).

In the four public issues studied in chapter 11, the interests of brokers and directors again supervened over the determination of prices and the allocation of capital via a free market. The *Report* shows how privileged placements of new issues first diminished the number of new shares available to the public and then, after interest in the shares had been excited and prices had risen in response to heightened demand, the placement shares were brought into the market and sold profitably to a public whose appetites had been whetted by the initial, artificial scarcity.

Chapter 12 is a short, hair-raising tale of the financial havoc wreaked by a determined, agile and unscrupulous group engaged in activities (option dealing, investment counselling, mutual fund management) where there was not even '. . . a tradition of internal code or a structural organization attempting to improve standards of professional conduct' (12.25).

It takes the Committee 149 pages (chapter 14) to deal in an avowedly limited way (see 14.3–5) with the spectacular rise and even more spectacular fall of Mineral Securities Australia Limited (Minsec) and its associated companies. The scale of this group's indebtedness and the intricacies of its activities were without precedent in Australia's financial history.

The stated broad objectives of the Minsec group were to generate profits from share trading and employ those profits to acquire 'in the ground' mining investments. However, the group's practical strategy became confused and share trading took precedence over mining activities (partly by inclination, partly because the greater the profits made from share trading the greater the need to acquire further mineral securities in order to avoid–legitimately–the payment of taxation on the profits). Minsec's further motives for acquiring subsidiary mining companies were (a) to manipulate the market so as to trade profitably in the shares of the subsidiaries, and (b) to bleed the subsidiaries of liquid assets to finance additional share speculations. In due course, Minsec's speculations exhausted its own profits and the liquid funds of its subsidiaries; it then drew upon the resources of associated mutual funds and, finally, borrowed extremely heavily in the short-term markets, especially the inter-company market. The *Report* describes in detail the questionable practices, dangerous associations, incompetence, bad judgement, failure to heed objective advice, concealments and low standards of veracity in which the Minsec story abounds.

The Committee drew out three main issues, from the Minsec experience:

(i) the potential dangers of large corporate group activity in the securities markets

(ii) the association of mutual funds with the securities market activities of a share-trading company

(iii) the linkages between the securities markets and the short-term money markets.

On the first point, the Committee observed that insider trading has moved '. . . beyond the personal to the corporate trading level, where it can be even more misleading in its consequences' (14.132). However, the Committee admitted that there are no 'tidy remedies' against malpractice in this area: it favoured prompt and full disclosure of intra-group share transactions, in conjunction with vigilance by some statutory regulatory authority.

The Committee considered that the mutual funds problem is amenable to simpler solution and argued that '. . . there should be no overlap in memberships between the board of a mutual fund and the boards of its attendant companies . . . within the boards of the mutual fund and of the attendant companies there should not be a concentration of representation from any particular outside group . . .' (14.134–5). These minimal requirements would not, of course, guarantee the abilities of those who manage mutual funds.

Until the Minsec failure, it was not generally appreciated that the money and share markets are so closely linked that a substantial amount of money market funds could be borrowed and—without question—employed speculatively in the share markets. At first sight, there appears to be some 'distance' between the authorized money market, which is based on short-term (and mostly official) securities and conducted under the supervision of the Reserve Bank, and the securities markets (mostly shares, but also debentures and bonds) conducted by the stock exchanges and 'self-regulated'. However, these two extremes are overlapped by the 'unauthorized' short-term money market (consisting principally of inter-company loans) and are further connected institutionally (stockbrokers participating in both markets). The Committee sustained a strong argument for bringing the unauthorized short-term money market under the surveillance of the Reserve Bank; and it believed that this could be done without interfering unduly with the 'fluidity, speed and informality' of the market or giving an official commitment to 'feather-bedding' the financiers in this market (see 14.135–7).

In chapter 15, the Committee recapitulates the many regulatory inadequacies which emerged from its case studies and in chapter 16 outlines proposals for a national authority to regulate the securities markets. The essential justification for this proposal is that the Committee's case studies have shown that the existing laws, institutional rules and voluntary regulation have allowed morally undesirable and economically damaging practices to flourish in the securities markets (15.2–3).

The factual basis of the *Report* has not been shaken, nor have the

Committee's interpretations of the case studies been overturned. But several critics claimed that the *Report*, perhaps unintentionally, gave a distorted and unfair picture of the securities markets.[4]

In concentrating on specific deficiencies its whole tone is critical, to the neglect of the positive economic benefits derived from the functions which the market performs satisfactorily and which, of course, went without commendation by a Committee geared to root out malpractice. It may be argued that the Committee was misdirected in its terms of reference. These required a search for 'improper or injurious practices', and a consideration of the need for a regulatory authority to curb such practices; but the terms of reference did not demand a full enquiry into the operations of the securities markets leading to an evaluation of the system and specific proposals for improvements to it. The Committee touches on this point (1.6), but it is a great pity that the need for a thorough study of the workings of the securities markets was not given more emphasis in the *Report*.

More specifically, it has been suggested that the Committee was led to produce an inaccurate general picture of the scale and frequency of undesirable practices by both (a) its 'case study' method of investigation and analysis (selecting the bad cases and ignoring the good), and (b) its narrow temporal focus of interest (mainly 1969–70, a period of unprecedented boom, concentrated in mining rather than industrial stocks, when the sheer weight of business may have made it difficult to maintain best standards). However, the Committee anticipated such charges and had defences ready. It conceded that selective case studies were conducted but argued that the practices uncovered were widespread (1.3). It might well have added that the selected cases concerned highly publicized episodes in which undesirable practices went unchecked by the stock exchanges, and that in some cases stock exchange committeemen infringed their own rules. Nevertheless, the Committee did not fail to praise those stockbrokers who maintained high standards of integrity in conducting their own businesses and who had shown concern about malpractice (1.12).

> It should also be noted that much of this Report is not concerned with the affairs of small mineral exploration companies. In several chapters attention is directed to the activities of large corporate groups which, at the time, were in high standing in the financial markets in Australia and overseas . . . moreover . . . many of the unsatisfactory practices described in this Report occurred while the Committee was conducting its broad enquiry into the securities market and known to be doing so (1.10–11).

On the mining boom time focus, the Committee argued that the test of laws and standards of practice is that they should be able to withstand the strains of peak activity 'when the opportunities for abuse and the adoption of low standards are more readily available' (1.7).

Aftermath

Even before the Committee presented its *Report*, the Labor government had shown its intention to legislate for tight national control of the securities markets. In late 1974, after the *Report* appeared, the government, adopting the reasoning and the conclusions of the Committee, introduced into parliament a draft Corporations and Securities Industry Bill. This Bill provided for the regulation on a national basis of public companies and of the securities industry and the establishment, for those purposes, of a Corporations and Exchange Commission. Discussion of the bill—both in public and in the parliament—focused on political and legal, rather than economic, issues. There was particular criticism of the rule-making powers and extra-parliamentary authority intended for the proposed Commission and, through the governor-general, the attorney-general. The critics sustained a 'bogeyman' scare about the arbitrary and limitless nature of these powers; they also promoted the vision of an authoritarian Commission, staffed by a costly and unskilled bureaucracy, which would be likely to slow down financial operations and add needless costs to capital market transactions. Much was made, too, of the obscurity of the government's intentions in the field of company law. On the one hand, the bill contained many provisions relating to the conduct of corporate affairs; on the other a long-promised national companies act was unseen and unspecified at the time parliament was confronted with the Corporations and Securities Industry Bill. Not surprisingly, the government's plans could not carry conviction so long as they were unable to explain how the company law provisions of the bill would dovetail with those of the intended national companies act. Finally, the government was also criticized for not allowing enough time for public debate and not consulting sufficiently with parties likely to be affected by the bill.

The progress of the bill slowed down. In an amended form it eventually passed through the House of Representatives but by then too much uneasiness had been aroused, about its general wisdom and particular provisions, for it to pass readily through a finely balanced senate. The senate finally established another select committee (chaired by Senator Georges) to inquire and report on the bill. This committee had not reported by the time parliament was dissolved in November 1975 and seems to have expired. Thus, despite all the enquiry and debate about the securities markets, and notwithstanding the apparent existence of a broad political consensus in favour of some form of national regulation, there has been no federal legislation on the subject. Although there has been some relevant state legislation and a little improvement of stock exchange regulations, essentially the 'rules of the game' are still those under which the manifold abuses revealed in the *Report* occurred.

The Purpose of Regulation

Some would argue that the abuses uncovered by the Senate Committee on Securities and Exchange were so damaging to public welfare as to justify detailed government control over corporate financing and share trading, if not indeed the abolition of the stock exchanges or even of the corporate system. Any such extreme action would eliminate the opportunity for the public to be 'fleeced' in the share market by simply eliminating the market. But this would also deprive the community of the substantial economic benefits which the securities markets can provide. It is not, in my view, naive to hope for a degree of official regulation of the securities markets such as to protect investors from malpractice while at the same time allowing the issue and trading of securities to flourish.

The *Report* brought out consumer protection and improved economic performance as the two broad objectives of national policy in the securities markets (see 16.15), and these views were espoused by the Labor government when trying to pass the Corporations and Securities Industry Bill. As the *Report* rightly points out, the case for regulation rests as much on moral grounds as on economic '. . . theft has been outlawed to protect individuals, not simply because of its economic consequences' (15.2). The point was well made a century ago:

> It was a bad day for the commercial world, Mr Wickerby, when forgery ceased to be capital . . . We didn't do it, but the fact that the law held certain frauds to be hanging matters operated on the minds of men in regard to all fraud. What with the joint-stock working of companies, and the confusion between directors who know nothing and managers who know everything, and the dislike of juries to tread upon people's corns, you can't punish dishonest trading. *Caveat emptor* is the only motto going, and the worst proverb that ever came from dishonest, stony-hearted Rome. With such a motto as that to guide us no man dare trust his brother.
>
> *Caveat lex*—and let the man who cheats cheat at his peril.[5]

The moral argument for public protection finds much economic justification. Malpractices in the securities markets waste resources and undermine public confidence, thus inhibiting share trading and capital raising. Public companies in Australia have, in recent years, relied much more on internal sources (retained profits and depreciation) than on funds raised publicly for financing their capital expenditures. The best allocation of national saving is unlikely to be achieved when so much of it is not bid for on the open market. The reduction of abuse would narrow investors' risks and so enhance their willingness to participate in the securities markets. This may be expected to facilitate corporate finance and make for lower costs and better allocation in the investment process. There may come a point, however, where excessive protection of investors would impose unwarranted costs (of compliance by companies and financiers, of administration by authorities) on the economy and impede the process of capital formation. The *Report* recognizes this possibility (16.15). In supporting the senate Committee's case for regulation, one is not demanding such detailed control as would require expensive administration or would increase transactions costs intolerably. The object of intervention should be to cleanse the market, not kill it.

To give further warning against regulatory overkill, one may note that there is economic sense in the limited employment of certain practices which in extreme form were rightly condemned by the Committee. The chief of these is short-selling which may help stabilize markets in certain circumstances; for instance short sales may cool an overheated demand for a share. The freedom to sell short is also needed for the operation of share jobbing, which would be a desirable development in the Australian market. In the United States the prohibition on short sales extends only to directors, officers and 10 per cent beneficial shareholders of the company concerned. It would seem better to countenance short-selling in approved forms and perhaps limited quantities than to prohibit the practice entirely.

Insider trading is generally regarded as reprehensible. That is certainly true when it is practised as, for example, in the Poseidon episode. Nevertheless, a little cautious and qualified support for insider trading may be found among economists.[6] The substance of the argument is that informed trading pushes the price of a share towards its 'true' worth and reduces price fluctuations arising from ill-founded speculation. Undesirable insider trading should be defined with as much care and precision as possible. Care should also be taken to define 'insiders' in a way which is clear in law and operational in regulation. The net should not be spread so widely as to impede the business of banks and other financial institutions, for example, because of responsibilities they might incur in respect of the share dealings of their employees.

The insider problem leads to the more general subject of differences in knowledge, judgement and skill among participants in the securities markets. It is inevitable that these differences exist[7] and they are not economically undesirable. Nor could society afford uniform knowledge in the capital market because, for each and every participant, there comes a point where the costs of acquiring further information would outweigh its value.[8] The inevitable differences in knowledge and ability between participants in the capital market provide the very basis and incentive for trade in securities.

A powerful attraction of the securities markets is that the trader who believes himself to be more knowledgeable or cleverer than others expects to trade profitably by virtue of his superior gifts. The pure speculator is obviously seeking quick increases in his capital and is prepared to take relatively high risks for the sake of possible large rewards. At the other extreme in the market, the long-term investor in low-risk, 'blue chip' stocks is nevertheless aiming for an enlargement—albeit small but fairly sure—of his capital. Between these extremes, all investors in the securities markets are, to a greater or lesser degree, motivated by the hope of capital gains; this is one of the principal attractions of the securities markets and underpins the capital raising and resource allocation benefits that the existence of a securities market facilitates.

It is too often overlooked that participants in the securities markets are generally reconciled to losses if their transactions turn out unsuccessfully—the steady investor to small losses, the speculator to large losses, but all to some. As with a racecourse gamble, the investor hopes to gain but is prepared to lose. If taken further, the racecourse analogy suggests an approach to securities market regulation. On the racecourse, punters and bookmakers act according to their individual judgements about the likely outcome of ensuing events. No individual has perfect foresight and no one has access to all relevant information; racecourse gamblers recognize individually that their knowledge and judgement is imperfect but each wagers on it being better than general knowledge and opinion as reflected by the 'weight of money' determining the quoted odds about each horse. What the gambler requires is not that knowledge and judgement be uniformly distributed but that the racing proceedings be regulated so as to prevent *dishonest* performance and practice. Given a fair contest, the punter backs his judgement without complaint. Similarly, investors in the securities markets hope to profit individually by correctly anticipating collective behaviour. They do not ask for uniform knowledge although, like punters, they welcome as much information and comment as possible, without expecting it to be complete and definitive. Nor should investors (or punters) ask that the law should protect the foolish from the consequences of their follies. But they do expect, and are entitled to, protection against misrepresentation and dishonesty.

In all markets, and indeed in all aspects of life, knowledge and judgement are not uniform, static and distributable commodities. With this in mind, any regulatory authority in the securities markets should be concerned chiefly with obtaining honest conduct, eliminating abuses of trust and minimizing conflicts of interests. It should also encourage the publication of as much corporate information as possible, while realizing that it can never expect all information to be put before all men.

Regulation should restrain malpractice but laws should not be of such a distrustful character that they spread cynicism about the conduct of securities markets or burden '. . . all companies with deadweight handicaps to movement' (14.130). The objective of regulation should be to ensure as much scope for fund raising, share trading and the exercise of entrepreneurial and speculative initiatives as is consistent with the maintenance of fairness and honesty in handling the savings of the public.

Two Problems

This discussion has been concerned with the principles, rather than the details, of regulation. However, one should at least draw attention to two important features which those responsible for designing regulations should take into account. The first is the relative decline of individual investors and the corresponding rise of institutions which—although a world-wide phenomenon—has been very pronounced in Australia. The problems associated with privileged placements and insider trading become more difficult to handle when institutions dominate a thin market; on the other hand, it cannot be assumed from the rise of the institutions that it is no longer important for the market to be kept attractive to individual investors. This leads to the other feature, namely the retention of Australian industry— particularly minerals—in Australian ownership. If equity shareholding becomes too unattractive, difficult or costly for individuals it would be correspondingly easier for groups to effect takeovers. Mineral exploration, because of its high risk and large reward nature coupled with its relatively low costs, is admirably suited to financing with speculative money gathered in individually small amounts; in this way, small exploration companies could be financed by Australians who would own and control any deposits discovered. But if the opportunity for speculative mining companies to raise capital in the securities markets should be inhibited by over-stringent regulation, mineral exploration and ownership is likely to pass wholly to giant mining corporations, often owned abroad.

Conclusion

It is clear that self-regulation by the stock exchanges has fallen so far short of the nation's needs that even a much tighter form of stock exchange control is unlikely to command public confidence. Independent regulation is needed and this is best provided by a national government authority. Regulations should be policed strictly and the penalties for infringement should be severe. It is, however, of the utmost importance that any regulatory authority which might be established should operate on the basis of a set of rules which are clear, well publicized, designed after ample public discussion by all interested parties, and which do not discourage honest activity in the securities markets.

References

[1] A fuller account of this period and historical and institutional background may be found in P. J. Drake, 'Performance, Responsibility and Control in the Australian Securities Markets' and P. J. Drake & R. L. Mathews, 'The Securities Markets', both in R. R. Hirst and R. H. Wallace (eds), *The Australian Capital Market* (Cheshire, Melbourne, 1974).

[2] The Parliament of The Commonwealth of Australia, *Australian Securities Markets and Their Regulation: Report from the Senate Select Committee on Securities and Exchange*, vol. 1, Report (Australian Government Publishing Service, Canberra, 1974), p. V. Hereafter, this document will be referred to as *Report*.

[3] For a concise account of the uncertainties and subjectivities involved in estimating future returns, and of the influences of reputation and past performance from the allocation of funds between firms via the capital market, see G. B. Richardson, 'Ideal and Reality in the Choice of Techniques', *Oxford Economic Papers*, July 1965, pp. 295-6.

[4] For example, J. H. Valder, 'The Bill as It Would Affect Stock Exchanges and Stockbrokers', Proceedings of the Forum on the Corporations and Securities Industry Bill (Business Law Education Centre, Melbourne, 1975); H. F. Bell, 'The Securities Market—National Control or Self-Regulation?', *Economic Record*, vol. 51, no. 135 (September 1975).

[5] Anthony Trollope, *Phineas Redux* (Oxford University Press, London, 1970), Book II, p. 217.

[6] See, for example, H. K. Wu, 'An Economist Looks at Section 16 of The Securities Exchange Act of 1934', *Columbia Law Review*, February 1968; reprinted in H. K. Wu, and A. J. Zakon (eds), *Elements of Investments: Selected Readings* (Holt, Rinehart & Winston, New York, 1972).

[7] Richardson, loc. cit.

[8] G. J. Stigler, 'Imperfections in the Capital Market', *The Organization of Industry* (Irwin, Illinois, 1968), chapter 10, p. 119.

PETER KARMEL

16 The Educational System and the Labour Market

Over the past twenty years the Australian education system has undergone rapid expansion. This is so in terms of both total real expenditures and the proportion of gross domestic product devoted to education. In the mid-1950s the latter was at the comparatively low figure of about 2·5 per cent and rose steadily until it had reached 4·7 per cent in 1972–3. At this level the Australian educational effort was not high compared with other western countries, but in the two following years the proportion rose rapidly until in 1974–5 it reached 6·3 per cent; it appears to be now in the process of stabilizing–for 1975–6 the current estimate is 6·4 per cent.

The same pattern can be seen in educational activities. Over the past two decades there have been very large increases in the numbers of pupils at schools and of students in post-school institutions. While part of this increase has been caused by demographic trends, a great deal of it has been due to increased participation in secondary, tertiary and further education. Resources per student have also been rising; early in the period this was the case mainly in the universities, then in the colleges of advanced education, and more recently in the school system. However, the increased use of educational resources has not been spread evenly over the community, and some groups participate in education much less than others.

In this environment three major questions are current in debate. These are:

(a) Should the educational system be designed to promote equality of social opportunity, and, if so, what steps should be taken to protect disadvantaged groups within the community?

(b) To what extent is unemployment among the young the result of the structure of the educational system?

(c) To what extent are post-school educational expenditures giving value for money, or, more precisely, what are the priorities for marginal increases (or decreases) in educational effort; and should the pattern of activity of post-school institutions be geared to predicted future manpower requirements?

The decisions of governments to halt the acceleration in educational spending are related to these questions. There is no longer an acceptance of the view that more expenditure on education is a good thing *per se.*

The above questions relate to one of the major functions of an educational system, namely its role in locating people in the socio-economic distribution by sorting them into particular occupations. Other major functions include the development and socialization of the individual in the ways of society; the conservation, transmission and expansion of knowledge; and the custodial aspects of educational institutions whereby young people are segregated from the adult working world. It is important to emphasize that these roles of education do not themselves involve explicit goals, which may relate to educational philosophies emphasizing, for instance, personal values or social equality. The roles no doubt contain normative elements. Although the 'sorting' role of education may not obtain star billing in discussions of educational philosophy, it is indeed the function which is most central to current public debate.

A Conceptual Model

In order to discuss the three questions set out above it is useful to formulate a simple conceptual model in which the sociological and economic relationships between the educational system, the labour market and the distribution of individuals in socio-economic-cultural categories are highlighted.

The rectangles in the diagram represent the socio-economic-cultural distribution of the population at two points of time which can conveniently be designated as Generation I and Generation II. The two squares represent the educational system and the labour market. The socio-economic-cultural distribution is multi-dimensional in that it relates to such variables as occupation, income, social status, cultural background, mother tongue, ethnic group and so on.

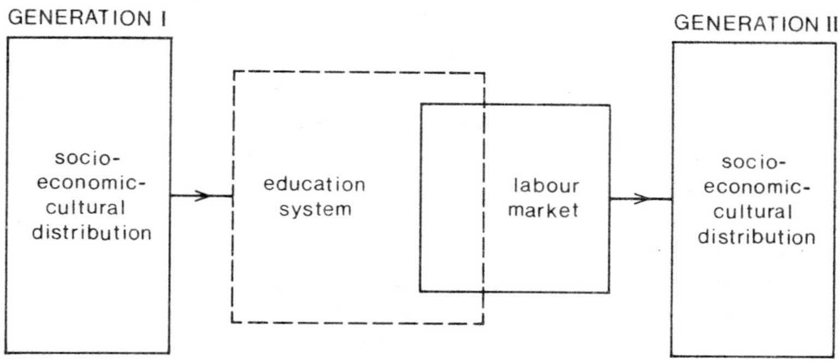

In fact these variables are interrelated in such a way that meaningful (although inexact) social orderings are possible. Within each category in the distribution individuals will have differing natural endowments, although here again it is usually accepted that there is some positive correlation between these endowments and the social orderings. There is no need here to explore the genetic *versus* environmental debate except to note that measured ability interacts with environmental factors.

Generation II are the offspring of Generation I. These offspring pass through the educational system and the labour market and are finally sorted into the distribution which is represented by the rectangle labelled Generation II. The educational system is not a monolith subject to central direction, but is a collection of many sub-systems (for example, state education departments) and individual institutions. From the point of view of the model, it is two dimensional in the sense that the system varies according to the age of the people passing through it and contains a diversity of institutions and offerings which may be selected by people of each age.

The labour market is a term for the set of relationships through which people are placed in jobs. It represents a coming together of employers (private and public) and of those seeking employment—both new recruits who have emerged from the educational system, and existing members of the work-force who wish to change their occupations. The mechanisms of the labour market also determine the wages and salaries (earned incomes) that people receive for their labour.

In the diagram, the educational system and the labour market have been drawn to overlap. This is to recognize that the movement of a new generation through the education system and the labour market into jobs is not a wholly sequential matter. Much education and training takes place on the job, e.g. apprenticeships and in-service training courses. In other cases, study in educational institutions and employment are contemporaneous, for example, part-time study at tertiary institutions; in yet other cases, study and employment alternate, e.g. sandwich courses. In recent times the interest in continuing or recurrent education and the provision of refresher or upgrading courses have increased the overlap between the education system and the labour market. In some experiments this has even extended into the school system; pupils undertake work assignments. Interest in the overlap between the educational system and the labour market has increased in recent years, and some educational innovations aim at reducing the extent to which the educational system has segregated the young from the ordinary business of life.

The educational system prepares people for the labour market in three main ways. First, it provides qualifications for those jobs which require specific vocational training, for example medical posts are only open to qualified medical practitioners, plumbers must be appropriately trained and licensed, and so on. Second, it provides education and skills for the work-force generally, thus raising both the capacity of workers to make good decisions and the standard of their performance. Third, it provides formal qualifications which are used by employers to select workers; for many jobs employers select workers by estimating the capacity of the individual in relation to the likely costs of training for the job. In these instances, educational qualifications of a rather general kind may be crucial because employers use them to rank applicants for posts; better jobs may go to those with higher qualifications or indeed to those who have undertaken more full-time education.

It is important to emphasize that, while education directed towards the first two objectives produces clear economic returns for society, education directed towards the third objective does not necessarily do so; an increase in the amount of education offered to individuals to improve their competitive position may affect only the rank order of the individuals and not add to society's wealth. However, from an individual's point of view, education for this purpose is of great importance, as less desirable employment or unemployment would be likely without it. This education probably has a high private and a low social rate of return.

The conceptual model is useful not only for understanding the 'sorting' role of the education system, but also for clarifying notions of social equality. Thus a comparison of the socio-economic-cultural distribution of Generation II with that of Generation I gives an indication of the extent of social mobility. In a rigid class society the place in society of the parent determines the place of the offspring; the landlords are the sons of landlords and the labourers are the sons of labourers. In a perfectly mobile society (i.e. where there is equality of social opportunity) the parents' rank or occupation has no effect on that of the offspring: the socio-economic distribution of the parents of, say, doctors, is the same as that for the general population. Biases within the educational system and the labour market produce a clear correlation, observed in western societies, between the socio-economic distributions of Generation II and Generation I: people whose parents are higher in the socio-economic scale are more likely to be higher in the scale themselves than those whose parents are lower in the scale.

There is clear evidence that the location in the socio-economic-cultural distribution of the parents of Generation II individuals affects the latter's attainment in the educational system in such a way that families which are higher in the scale tend to have offspring whose educational attainment is higher. In addition, as individuals proceed through the education system, decisions have to be made from time to time on the direction in which they will move; for example, what type of school they should attend; what course options they should select; whether to proceed with another year of secondary schooling; whether to proceed to institutions of technical and further education, colleges or universities; and if so, in which courses. The educational system is thus a complex switching configuration; and in many instances a switch to a particular track may make it difficult or impossible to switch to another track at a later date. The switching decisions themselves are affected by educational attainment and by the socio-economic position of the Generation I families. Again, there is evidence that families higher in the scale tend to make decisions which facilitate their offspring moving into positions higher in the scale.

Given the nature of western society it is thus likely that there will be less than perfect equality of social opportunity, and that, although there may be some inter-generational mobility, considerable advantage will attach to having parents who themselves are located relatively high in the socio-economic scale. The degree of this inequality of social opportunity will itself depend on the nature of the educational system and the labour market as well as on the inherent inequalities between the home backgrounds of Generation II individuals. Institutional changes in the educational system, particularly in reducing the rigidity of the 'switching' arrangements, and in the labour market, particularly in relation to the use of educational qualifications as a selecting mechanism for jobs, may decrease inequality of social opportunity.

Equality of Social Opportunity

In discussions on equality and education, it is important to be clear whether the reference is to equality of *outcomes* or equality of *opportunity*. No society produces an exact equality of outcomes. The question of how much inequality a society is prepared to tolerate is an important political issue.

The socio-economic-cultural distributions in the conceptual model involve inequalities of outcomes. It is certainly the case that the distribution of educational attainment or income or power in both Generation II and Generation I displays variation. One question that arises is whether the operations of the educational system in conjunction with the labour market produce more equal or less equal outcomes in Generation II than in Generation I. This is the question of whether the educational system has an equalizing effect on the distribution of income. It has been commonly supposed that, since people with more education earn higher incomes, the increasing participation of the population in education should result in a general levelling up of incomes. There is no clear evidence on this issue and it must remain an open question. The explanation of the lack of clarity probably lies partly in the large number of factors (of which education is only one) influencing the distribution of income and partly in the way in which educational qualifications are used to order people in the labour market rather than to produce specific skills with determinate market values.

Although the educational system may not have a large impact on reducing inequalities of outcomes in society, it may do something to reduce inequalities of opportunity. Can the educational system affect the extent to which the ranking of a Generation II individual is dependent on family ranking in the Generation I distribution? This is the question of equality of educational opportunity. The lower the correlation *via* parent/offspring relationships between the Generation II and Generation I distributions, the greater is the equality of social opportunity. Equality of educational opportunity is the contribution that the educational system makes towards equality of social opportunity and greater social mobility.

Inequality of social opportunity probably lies largely outside the educational system and is rooted in family and cultural backgrounds. However, the structure of the educational system may be such as to reinforce handicaps imposed by family circumstances, and may render educational decisions of the individual irreversible, thus steadily reducing the range of options available to those whose socio-economic status inhibits social mobility.

Restrictions on the volume of educational opportunities at the post-school level may themselves reduce social opportunity. Thus, if there are limited numbers of places available in courses which are likely to lead to posts high in the socio-economic scale, opportunities for social mobility are likely to be inhibited. This is particularly the case if the method of selection into courses itself already favours those whose families are high up the socio-economic scale. For example, selection for university courses, which depends on high achievement in matriculation examinations, favours those in higher socio-economic classes. However, restrictions in post-secondary opportunities need not reduce social mobility if steps are taken to establish quotas of places for the disadvantaged, or if alternative criteria for selection are used. It is important to emphasize this, for otherwise there would be a direct conflict between improving social opportunity and restraining expenditures on higher education.

Modifications of the educational system and its relationship to the labour market cannot be expected to eliminate social inequalities. They may, however, open up opportunities for groups that are currently disadvantaged and produce a fairer society. Moreover, they need not involve an open-ended commitment to more and more tertiary places. Without going into detail such modifications might include consideration of:

(a) Emphasis on the basic skills of reading, writing and numbering at the primary level so that all children completing a primary education have a competence in those skills. Without this competence, young people suffer an almost insurmountable handicap in society;

(b) Educational provision designed to provide more resources for disadvantaged groups rather than the present arrangements which tend to offer more resources for the already advantaged;

(c) Consideration of the nature of the curriculum in upper secondary education so that vocational training and work experience soften the sharp division between schooling and work;

(d) New methods of training for the skilled trades, including reform of the apprenticeship system;

(e) Diversity of educational offerings so that the socially mobile may move by smaller steps into activities acceptable to them;

(f) Provision for the return into the educational system of those who have dropped out at an early age;

(g) Means for providing job opportunities for early school-leavers to increase experience and skills;

(h) Special opportunities for disadvantaged groups in post-secondary education.

In some instances, in order to improve the fairness of our educational system, major new programmes may be required, but it is often simply a question of choosing policy options which move in the direction of equality of opportunity rather than against it.

Unemployment Among the Young

Increasing unemployment among the young has been a common phenomenon in western countries over the past decade. This is illustrated for Australia in the diagram below, which compares unemployment among the 15 to 19 years old group with unemployment among the adult work-force.

It can be seen that although adult unemployment has risen over the last decade from something under 1½ per cent to about 3½ per cent, unemployment among the young has risen very much more steeply and its incidence is now some four times greater than among the adult population. The significance of increasing unemployment among the young depends on its duration. If it is simply the result of all young people taking rather longer to find a job, it is clearly less serious than if it stems from a fraction of young people remaining

UNEMPLOYMENT RATES

(The unemployed in each group as a percentage of the civilian labour force in the same group)

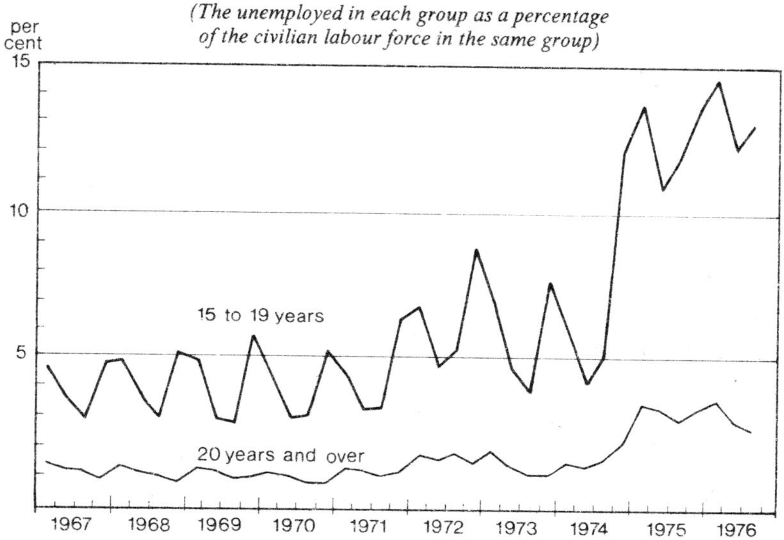

more or less permanently out of jobs. In the Australian situation, the average duration of unemployment among the young is at present of the order of eighteen weeks, which is much the same as the duration of unemployment among adults in the work-force.

In a tight employment situation, difficulties in obtaining jobs will occur particularly at the point of entry to the work-force, so that a relatively high incidence of unemployment among the young is to be expected. It follows that the gap between the unemployment rates of the young and of the rest of the work-force will tend to be wider the lower the overall level of activity. Moreover, employers faced with relatively plentiful labour may prefer older and more experienced workers to school-leavers; the increasing participation of married women in the work-force has certainly been to some degree in direct competition with the young. To the extent that employers use educational qualifications to select workers, the incidence of unemployment among the young will fall with special severity on the less skilled. Under these circumstances any general raising of educational qualifications does not solve the difficulties of the relatively unskilled in obtaining employment; everyone has to be somewhat better qualified to maintain their place in the queue. If unemployment is due to an insufficiency of aggregate demand, changes in the educational system or the labour market will not eliminate it; they may, however, change the nature of the unemployment. Thus an increase in the skills of the young may result in shifting the incidence of unemployment from the young to other groups of workers.

The above remarks relate to unemployment among school-leavers; there is also the question of unemployment among tertiary graduates. Until recently this does not seem to have been a major problem in Australia.[1] It is true that significant numbers of graduates appear to be dissatisfied with their jobs which they regard as inappropriate to their educational qualifications. This, however, is a reflection of the relatively higher educational qualifications among the additions to the work-force compared with the work-force generally. In a given industrial structure, the production of more and more graduates inevitably means that graduates must accept positions lower in the job hierarchy.

While unemployment among the young may, to a significant extent, be a reflection of the general level of economic activity, it may also be the result of two other factors. The first is structural maladjustment. For example, it is possible that the substantial expansion of tertiary education may have produced a surplus of persons with high level white collar qualifications at a time when there is an insufficient supply of skilled tradesmen. There is some evidence to this effect in the Australian situation. Whether this is due to the relatively poor provision of educational facilities for blue collar occupations, or to the preferences of young people and their families, or to an outdated apprenticeship system, cannot be known without further examination. Modifications in educational facilities, including the apprenticeship system, will almost certainly be necessary to eliminate structural maladjustments of this kind.

The second factor which might produce unemployment among the young relates to the low productivity of the unskilled and poorly educated. An employer will not be prepared to pay a wage to a young person where the employee's anticipated contribution to the enterprise is worth less than the wage. Employers incur costs in on-the-job training, and they may not be willing to employ people who are unlikely to become reliable members of the work-force or are ill-equipped to learn. In particular, the raising of juvenile wage rates towards adult rates militates against employing young people. To improve the employability of the young may require a better preparation in basic literacy and numeracy and also measures to make up for their lack of work experience. Even so, improved employability among the young will not reduce total unemployment unless aggregate demand increases.

In this general area the main issues include:

(a) The employability of the young who have the least education. For example, should their employment be subsidized as an offset to employers' costs of training them for jobs?

(b) The whole question of apprenticeship training. For example, should the output of apprentices be geared to the current willingness of employers to accept them or should it come more under the control of the educational system? There are major industrial questions involved in this.

(c) The desirability of additional educational resources being directed towards the technical and further education sector rather than to the university or college sectors.

(d) The response of the labour market to the increasing participation of married women in the work-force. In particular should part-time employment be facilitated, for example, by Box and Cox arrangements in which two persons undertake one job.

(e) The development of improved careers guidance services. In itself this may imply a greater degree of knowledge of future labour market conditions than is possible.

(f) The question of the relationships between the educational system and the labour market, including the effects on the labour market of the rising educational standard of new recruits to the work-force. There is also the question of the role of educational qualifications in providing credentials for jobs.

Priorities in Educational Expenditure

To some extent the demand for education stems from its power to widen the life experiences of the individual. This is education for its own sake and, in the economist's term, represents the *consumption* element of education. For many whose lives are involved in the provision of education it is the most important reason for education, but it would be unrealistic to suppose that it is the main motive force in the trend towards more and more education. This motive force stems from the *investment* aspects of education.

From the point of view of the individual, education gives an opportunity to acquire skills which command high values in society, and parents and teachers often urge young people into particular educational avenues simply for this reason. From the point of view of society, specific skills and general education yield economic returns. While it may not be possible to measure the exact contribution of education to economic growth, there is no denying that the broad expansion of education has contributed to economic progress and that higher levels of education, both in general and in terms of specific skills, have been an integral element in technological progress. Nevertheless, education is not always concerned with providing skills which are prerequisite to the performance of particular occupations; it frequently provides credentials of a general kind which give individuals an advantage in seeking jobs over those whose credentials are lower. In a world in which there is a tendency for students to spend more time in educational institutions simply to maintain their places in the queue, the trend towards more education becomes self-perpetuating and, while yielding returns to the private individual, may not necessarily produce an equivalent economic benefit to society. Although this may seem an argument against open-ended expansion of post-school education, it is important to realize that restrictions on educational opportunities are rightly seen by an individual as restrictions on the opportunities offered for upward social mobility; if we all have to run to keep in the same place, the one who cannot run must fall behind.

Primary education is, in effect, universal. Secondary education is close to universal at the lower levels, but only about 35 per cent of young people complete high school. Nevertheless it has been generally accepted in countries like Australia that there should be no limitation on the number of places available in secondary schools so that all may complete secondary schooling. There remains the question as to how much education should be provided in the post-secondary area. (That is, omitting pre-school education which is not discussed here.)

It is often said that, on principle, tertiary education should be available to all qualified people who wish to undertake it. In itself this statement is question-begging because the definition of 'qualified' is arbitrary. Moreover, since individual faculties at individual universities are finite, there is no conceivable way in which students can have complete freedom of choice of course and institution. Nevertheless, until recently, tertiary places have been provided at a level to meet student demand in aggregate, subject, of course, to restrictions in particular faculties in particular institutions. The provision of tertiary places in Australia has been geared to social demand rather than to manpower considerations, although manpower requirements have been taken into account in the provision of expensive facilities where there is a clear one-to-one relationship between academic qualifications and the practice of a profession; for example medical, dental and veterinary schools. The Australian attitude was clearly expressed in *Tertiary Education in Australia.*[2]

> The possibility of conflict between individual aspirations and community needs may arise, however, in regard to some types of specialized training. Should the nation make facilities available to all students wishing to become doctors or engineers or lawyers, if it is doubtful whether the community will need this number? The nub of this question lies in the meaning of 'need'. It is possible, of course, to attempt to forecast the demand for skilled manpower of various kinds. Such forecasts must be hazardous. Future requirements depend on the future level of national production, on future production techniques, and on the future wants of the

population. While it might be desirable to attempt to predict shortages of various kinds and to take steps to overcome them, the dangers of the reverse operation are great. The consequences of producing an unnecessary shortage are much more serious than those of producing an unnecessary plenty.

The Committee believes that, in general, conflicts between students' aspirations and community needs should be allowed to be resolved by the operation of supply and demand in the market. Students' aspirations are not insensitive to the scale of remuneration and job opportunities for different callings. Consequently, shortages and surpluses tend to produce corrective forces. In fields involving higher education, there is a lag of some years between entry and graduation so that this year's output of graduates tends to be related to the state of the market four or five years ago. This leads to some maladjustments in the supply and demand for highly trained labour. The Committee believes that research into future labour requirements is useful both for aiding the decisions of students and of educational institutions and for guiding business and government; it does not subscribe, however, to the view that entry of students into the various courses of higher education should be restricted by forecasts of future needs. Such a policy would not only run the risk of grave error, but it would also restrict educational opportunity to an undesirable degree.

The Martin Report was written in the belief that 'higher education should be available to all citizens according to their inclination and capacity.'[3] The committee rejected the view that there was 'some smaller fraction of the population to which higher education should be restricted.' The interruption to the triennial programme for universities and colleges of advanced education which occurred in the middle of 1975 and the guide-lines issued by the Commonwealth government in May 1976, however, suggest that the view rejected by the Martin Committee now more nearly accords with the realities of government budgeting. In both its *Fifth Report* and *Sixth Report* the Universities Commission took the view that the size of the tertiary sector was a matter for political decision.[4] This has now been confirmed by the guide-lines in which the government has indicated the magnitude of the tertiary sector that it will support.

There remains the question as to how priorities should be determined for educational expenditure. Massive changes in expenditure can hardly be contemplated without interfering with the historical continuity of the educational system. For practical purposes the question must relate to changes at the margin. One approach to this question (and the one favoured by many economists) is that expansion or contraction of the relevant sectors of the educational system should be guided by the social rates of return to educational expenditures (or alternatively by calculations of cost-benefit ratios).

However, calculations of social rates of return are difficult to make with any degree of accuracy, and indeed, are based on a number of heroic assumptions about the nature of the economic world. These include:

(a) The lifetime earnings of persons with given levels of education are calculated from cross-section data of age-income profiles. It is assumed that these can be applied to a new generation of qualified persons. However there is no reason to believe that these profiles will hold over a generation in which the fundamental supply and demand conditions of people with a particular level of education differ from those of the time at which the cross-section data were tabulated. Also, the variance in the pattern of lifetime earnings is assumed away, but there is a finite probability that additional education may actually make an individual worse off.

(b) The differentials in earnings due to different levels of education are assumed capable of separation from those due to ability, socio-economic class and other background variables. However, such attribution of differentials to the one variable *education* is extremely difficult because the relevant variables are all strongly intercorrelated.

(c) Incomes are assumed to reflect social values. This implies all the assumptions of the competitive model–many, if not most, of which are not valid in the real world. Quite apart from this, it ignores the powerful conventional elements in salary and wage determination, particularly in the professional and skilled areas.

(d) If educational qualifications are used to select individuals into jobs (i.e. if there is *job* competition rather than *wage* competition) income differentials according to qualifications may have little meaning in terms of social values.[5]

(e) Externalities are assumed away so that the benefits of one individual's education on other individuals or on society at large have to be left out of account.

(f) Likewise the value of education for its own sake, i.e. the consumption aspect of education, is left out of account.

(g) On the cost side, the calculation of the opportunity costs of undergoing education assumes that the earnings forgone can be aggregated. This is a difficult assumption to sustain.

It would indeed be a brave administrator who based his decisions on educational development on calculations of social rates of return or cost-benefit ratios. There may, of course, be cases where serious shortages in the supply of specific forms of skilled manpower make a high social rate of return patent, for example, the training of computer programmers during the period when computers were being introduced on a large scale. These needs, however, are usually obvious and do not require rate of return calculations.

The dubious validity of rate of return or cost-benefit analysis stems mainly from the measurement of benefits. Calculations of costs of educational developments can be made relatively accurately. It is thus possible to pursue questions of cost effectiveness without their being subject to the same qualifications as are involved in calculations of benefits. Whether or not particular educational outcomes can be achieved more cheaply, or whether a given expenditure on education can be made to yield greater outcomes are important questions which should be pursued. They extend to issues relating to rationalization of educational institutions and the avoidance of unnecessary duplication between educational courses. It would also seem reasonable to subject expensive educational ventures to more stringent tests than cheap ones; decisions on extending medical education should be subject to greater rigour than decisions on extending the teaching of the humanities. To the extent to which the provision of post-school education is in response to student preferences, it would be reasonable to meet those preferences more readily in the case of cheaper than of dearer courses.

An alternative approach would be to gear the pattern of activity in post-school institutions to manpower requirements. A common criticism of post-school education in Australia today is that the educational system produces large numbers of people with qualifications which are not strictly relevant to their future occupations. In particular it is alleged that too many are produced with generalist degrees while there are too few skilled tradesmen.

It is important to distinguish between those qualifications which are specific to the practice of a particular profession or trade and those which are general. Manpower requirements have always been a consideration in determining the number of places in courses of the first kind. It is possible that manpower aspects should be taken into account in a wider range of courses. However, it is important to bear three things in mind: first, the relative risks involved in making positive or negative errors in predictions of manpower requirements must be taken into account; second, if educational opportunities are geared precisely to manpower requirements, governments may find themselves with commitments to employ the products of particular courses; third, emphasis on the vocational aspects of courses may result in producing numbers of people with narrow skills: where these skills become surplus, the redeployment of the individuals concerned may be difficult.

The qualifications required for certain professions and trades are quite specific. However, there is a wide range of qualifications which do not necessarily lead to the particular profession for which the qualification is designed; for example, many people with qualifications in education or in law do not become teachers or practise law. As far as these qualifications are concerned, it would be extremely difficult to determine numbers of students by manpower predictions. Under the most favourable circumstances, manpower predictions have a wide range of error; predictions of requirements for people with generalized qualifications are particularly hazardous since they involve charting the future course of economic activity and technological progress. It is difficult to avoid the conclusion that the amount of post-school education to be provided is a political decision which must contain arbitrary elements. It involves an assessment of the value to society of having a more highly educated population and of the aspirations of individuals, who are entitled to attempt to better themselves.

An example of the issues that would have to be faced if educational planning were to be directed by manpower considerations arises from the potential surplus of teachers referred to in the recent report of the Schools Commission.[6] It is clear that a continuation of the present inputs of students into teacher training institutions combined with the recent experience of teacher turnover and of the re-employment of former teachers will, in the 1980s, produce much larger numbers of teachers than can be employed with pupil/teacher ratios that can reasonably be expected to be funded by the Commonwealth and state governments. There is a number of possible responses to this situation:

(a) The training institutions might reduce intakes sharply;

(b) State education departments might accelerate moves towards eliminating special scholarships for teachers, thus discouraging young people from wishing to be teachers;

(c) State education departments might reduce the re-employment of former teachers, thus maintaining their demand for new graduates;

(d) No special action might be taken, leaving the market to act as a self-regulating device;

(e) Governments might provide sufficient funds to employ all available teachers at increasingly favourable pupil/teacher ratios.

A manpower approach would place emphasis on the first of these responses. It is not, however, obvious that this ought to be the response. An alternative, for which a strong argument could be made, would be to eliminate special scholarships and to permit young people to enter teacher training institutions if they wished to and to take their chance of obtaining jobs as teachers (that is, a combination of the second and fourth response).

Conclusion

The conceptual model set out at the beginning of this chapter is a description of the role of the educational system in sorting people into jobs. In order to assess its effectiveness in this role, criteria have to be established. For example, these might relate to the promotion of social opportunity, the avoidance of structural unemployment among the young, the efficiency of the education system, the provision of educational opportunities to meet the aspirations of young people, or to other social objectives. In the final analysis the amount of public resources to be devoted to the educational system is for political decision. However, an understanding of the relations between the education system and the labour market and of the possible social objectives which provide goals for the educational system, is a prerequisite for making that decision a properly informed one.

References

1 See Universities Commission: *Sixth Report* (Australian Government Publishing Service, Canberra, 1975), paras 4.53 to 4.62.

2 'Martin report': *Tertiary Education in Australia: report of the committee on the future of tertiary education in Australia to the Australian Universities Commission* (Melbourne, 1964-5), paras 1.42 and 1.43.

3 Ibid., para. 1.41

4 See *Fifth Report*, para. 3.17, *Sixth Report*, para. 5.9.

5 See L. C. Thurow, *Generating Inequality* (Macmillan, New York, 1975), chs 4 and 5.

6 Schools Commission, *Report: Rolling Triennium, 1977-79* (Australian Government Publishing Service, Canberra, 1976), pages 106-7.

MARK PERLMAN

17 The Editing of the *Economic Record* 1925–1975

Introduction

My essay with Naomi Perlman, prepared in 1974, analyses points of focus of the economics literature published in English language journals, 1970–4.[1] In that effort we were principally interested in two questions: (1) what could be said about the points of subject-matter focii during the early 1970s and (2) how much was empiricism, as distinct from apriorism, coming to dominate the choice of methods. By the time this chapter is published, our 1974 study with all its data and interpretive qualifications will not only have become available, but will have, quite likely, been subjected to further critical scrutiny.

The present essay takes up the first of these questions and applies it to a single journal over a much longer time period. It does not touch the second question. The journal is the *Economic Record*; the time period is the half-century 1925, when the journal first appeared, until 1975. The objects of this exercise are basically two: (1) to present a description of the way a significant portion of Australian academic economic interest, the written journal as distinct from book-length efforts, developed over a period when the University of Melbourne and later a combination of the University of Melbourne and the Australian National University, were emerging as major exporters of economic analysis (to say nothing of economic analyzers); and (2) to give an analysis of the contents over a long time period of a journal, because doing so offers an opportunity to speculate on the interaction between the development of the discipline and the administrative organization of the article selection process. These questions are of clear concern to economic policy in Australia, since the *Economic Record* has served for so long as an influential outlet for policy analysis and advice.

It is a commonplace that academia is full of authors of essays turned down by editors. To them, the process of selection seems, if not actually biased, certainly irrational. As one who has been for almost a decade an editor of a major journal, albeit one covering mostly bibliographic contributions, I believe that I can draw some demonstrable conclusions by discussing the half-century history of the *Record*. These conclusions may have some utility to frustrated academic authors. They may even have some utility to journal editors.

In drawing these conclusions, of course, one has to make the assumption that editors can substantially influence the offerings to journals, and that journal content does not simply reflect the current interests of those making submissions. This is an important caveat because, while a strong editor is undoubtedly able to influence the contents of a journal, the role of demand as contrasted with that of supply should not be overemphasized. One reason why the relative importance of subject areas changes from one editorship to another is that the preoccupation of the profession changes; for example, interest in economic stability gives way to interest in economic growth; and so on. Also, in a small country such as Australia, some subject areas are under-represented. Despite these qualifications, however, it is possible to speculate on selection processes.

Objects of Journals

The *Economic Record* has been published principally at the University of Melbourne, although Canberra has long been represented in the editorial team and more recently has been apportioned an explicit joint editorship. In 1925 the University of Melbourne's academic self-perception seemed antipodal. Indeed, it appeared to believe itself to be so far out of the catholic mainstream in economics that it was, as it were, a monopoly in its own pool. Its audience was Australasian; moreover it was Australasians who included not only university academics but also responsible men of political and commercial affairs. 'Their' journal was intended to focus on what they thought they could do something about. Thus, it seems, from its inception, the *Economic Record* was perceived as a main-line publication which was, nonetheless, aimed at providing its clientele with information and analyses giving perspective to the practical realities of an isolated antipodean society.

To put this matter in a negative way, the *Economic Record* does not seem to have reflected anyone's overwhelming desire to improve Australasian economics pedagogy. Consequently, except for the indirect contribution it may have made to the tone of the intellectual life in the Melbourne faculty of economics and commerce (as it came eventually to be called), its contents do not begin to explain the flow of brilliant theoretical economists turned out regularly in the University of Melbourne's economic honours degree. If anything, it was an outlet for only some of the Melbourne teachers, for only a very few of their other Australian colleagues, and for a number of people not confined to economics pedagogy.

All journals, and the *Economic Record* (as its development is examined) is no exception, reflect both the effects of the emergence of the discipline as well as the current editor's power, goals and taste. By power one means simply, does the editor alone make selections or does he merely chair an editorial board, which argues (and ultimately usually compromises between) competing views? Under some conditions, editors clearly have greater power; under other conditions, less. These conditions involve not only personalities but also the various *Weltanschauungen* peculiar to specific times. History, Carlyle believed, is the acts of great men. Sometimes. At other times it is the relative inaction of committees, grounded or paralyzed by division.

One question that the editorial leadership of any journal immediately and continually must handle is whether the journal shall be specialized, that is, focused deeply on a small number of topics, or whether it should be broadly comprehensive and appeal to several 'intellectual publics'. In so far as the journal is *the* (or even a) publication of a national (or as in this case, bi-national) economic society, there seem to be obvious pressures to provide a broad spectrum of coverage. There can also be simultaneously specialized journals; they are likely to be found in the areas of agricultural economics, managerial economics, labour economics, industrial relations, economic history and economic policy. What often results is a practical compromise with a so-called 'general' journal eschewing articles in several major sub-fields (where alternative outlets for publication exist) and focusing on the remaining 'priority' areas. But whose priorities?

To some editors (or to some editorial boards) there are now established priority fields like: (1) economic theory, (2) monetary economics, (3) fiscal economics, (4) international economics, (5) economics of price stabilization and/or national product growth. To these 'traditional' priority fields are occasionally added (depending upon how seriously one takes such work in research institutions as the University of Chicago, Harvard University, Cambridge University, and the Massachusetts Institute of Technology) other priority areas like (a) labour economics, (b) economic development, (c) the epistemological redirection of the whole discipline, (d) econometrics, and (e) mathematical economics. To other editors, priorities seem to be transitional. Contemporary priorities may be established by transitory national emergencies like wars, international economic integration, or seemingly uncontrollable stagnation or stagflation pressures. Other sources of contemporary priorities may be more of purely intellectual rather than public policy origin. The appearance of a basic new idea (or 'paradigm' to use a recent Kuhnian cliché) may encourage a set of Schumpeterian innovational waves. My space is limited and the imagination is active; suffice it to let the broad outlines of the point be sketched. One self-imposed overriding editorial limitation, however, may be the avoidance of what is called 'non-productive' or 'tendentious' controversy. Jacob Viner once told me that it was not hard to be original if one never read anything nor worried about being wrong. By way of contrast, some editors put a high priority on not publishing anything that is 'wrong'; consequently they probably eschew opportunities to seek creativeness.

Finally, there is a question of taste. Here, I refer not only to literary elegance or one form of its apotheosis, algebra, but also to a favouring of either empiricism or apriorism, of either speculation or dispassionately accurate description, of either *tours de force* in the application of new techniques so as to stimulate the imagination or to practical, mature and sophisticated judgements so as to extend the frontiers of accepted, conventional wisdom.

The Economic Record

Revenons à nos moutons, which in this case is the analysis of the *Economic Record*. I have used as my analytical matrix the *Journal of Economic Literature* classification scheme developed by an American Economic Association select committee in the mid-1960s and by the *JEL* editors thereafter. Its use has its limitations, for just as each generation needs to rewrite history to its own uses, so each generation needs to create new classification schemes. Admittedly, therefore, using the current (1970s) scheme to analyse literature one or two generations back may do an injustice to earlier eras, but it is an injustice hard to avoid. At least one is aware of the danger.

During the half century starting in 1925 there have been in the case of the *Economic Record* four principal editorial eras. The first, under Professor Douglas Copland, lasted from 1925 to 1946. Copland, for those too young to remember him, was a New Zealander whose lengthy career in Australia affected most aspects of Australia's economic policy from the 1920s until the late 1950s. He was professor at the University of Melbourne; he was deeply involved in the 1931 Imperial Conference on Tariffs held in Ottawa; he played a key (probably misunderstood) role on the much-criticized deflationary premiers' plan of 1931; he dominated pricing policy during World War II; he was in a real sense the creator (and founding vice-chancellor) of the Australian National University; and he was later high commissioner to Canada. These were but the peaks of achievement in a career sparkling with accomplishments.[2] Although he had a bi-national editorial board at the *Econ-*

omic Record (among whose members there were some scholars of note), it is probably accurate to say that the *Economic Record* during his editorship largely reflected his own set of professional priorities. It also clearly incorporated ideas he thought stimulatingly controversial.

Copland's successor as editor was Mr G. A. Weller, who had actually been doing the job *under Copland's guidance* for some time.[3] Weller was editor (and consequently the second period lasted) from 1947 until 1954. Weller, as I recall him, lacked aggressive intellectual independence. He did not seem to dominate the editorial board (he appeared to be more a recording secretary than a meeting chairman), nor did he seem to have much taste for what one might call the 'animating fruits of intellectual disagreement'. Particularly was this the case, it seems to me, about controversy in monetary economics, which was his own area.

The third period editorship (1954–68) was led, but probably not dominated, by Professor R. I. Downing. Besides having had a University of Melbourne training, Downing had been an undergraduate at King's College, University of Cambridge, at the time when John Maynard Keynes's influence held sway. He had been something of a Copland protege but, as I knew them, Downing was clearly more the aesthete. This set of aesthetic interests was stronger, I believe, than his advocacy of any particular set of economic policies. In this one sensed he differed from his mentor. The foregoing is not to suggest that Downing was simply a cultural dilettante. On the contrary, he had considerable experience with the wartime Australian governmental economic agencies, and a long-time relationship with the International Labour Organization. At the time of his death (1975) he was jointly research professor and chairman of the Australian Broadcasting Commission (something he clearly prized). As an editor he preferred to share work, if not actually to farm much of it out, and over the years he designated a small number of Melbourne faculty colleagues as assistant and associate editors. As I recall Downing, he was fully conscious of his own cosmopolitanism; my surmise is that Downing's perception of his role as editor was basically independent, but that this independence was self-limiting by virtue of his wide range of personal interests and activities. This range of passionate interests was much wider than Copland's and encompassed a great many more things clearly apart from some strict views of the scope of the science of economics. What stimulated his interests was often tangential to the topics most economists, even those with far-ranging perceptions of the limits of their field, expected to find in the journal.

By 1970, when Mr A. H. Boxer was acting editor, we begin to approach the fourth period of editorship. In 1968 Boxer and

Downing had been joint editors. In 1972 Professor C. S. Soper was designated acting editor. In 1973 the joint editors were Boxer (again), Professor S. J. Turnovsky (of the Australian National University) and Professor L. R. Webb (of the University of Melbourne). There was always at least one, and sometimes more, assistant and/or associate editors. During this fourth period the flavour of the journal seems (to me) to be hard to characterize, from which I surmise that policy is set by compromise in committee or by reference to what is perceived to be a responsibility to cover the wide spectrum of the economics discipline. In practice, it may be premature to make any judgements relating to this fourth period; after all, it has been for Australian universities a transitional era. In any event, as the data about the content of the *Economic Record* show, during this time the *Economic Record* has some strong similarities, as well as dissimilarities, to 'core' journals in other nations. It is also important to add that by this fourth period there were other Australian professional journals, notably *Australian Economic Papers*, and further ones covering such sub-fields as agricultural economics, industrial relations, managerial economics, economic history, and economic development.

Analysis of Sub-field Coverage

The Copland Era

If we are to judge by the comparative frequency of article subject classifications by sub-field, it seems that Copland was far more interested, even as an editor, in applied rather than theoretical economics. Yet, within the applied economics area he clearly seems to have focused most strongly on what is now (1977) a leading subtopic, namely economic fluctuations and stabilization. For comparison, the ranking of sub-fields, based on space devoted to title, of all the journals incorporated in the American Economic Association/Yale University Indices, volumes 2 (1925–39) and 3 (1940–9) is given in Table 1.

Of course what stands out is that the *Economic Record* during Copland's incumbency clearly differed in content from the mode, particularly in the eschewal of studies of industrial organization and economic theory. On the other hand, interest in economic fluctuations and stabilization, as mentioned before, was much stronger than the mode. The priority given to articles in agricultural economics, monetary economics (then often called money, credit & banking), fiscal economics and international economics (including commercial policy) was similar to the mode. Copland was clearly not effectively interested in the history of ideas, nor in the historical

TABLE 1

*Rank Ordering of Sub-Fields, The Copland Editorship**
(indicates only those of 5 per cent or more)

	Economic Record	A.E.A./Yale *Index of Economic Articles*	
	1925–46	1925–39	1940–9
1	Economic Stabilization (17)	Industrial Organization (17)	Industrial Organization (12)
2	Public Finance (12)	Agricultural Economics (13)	Theory (11)
3	Agricultural Economics (11)	Theory (12)	Agricultural Economics (11)
4	Money, Credit & Banking (9)	Money, Credit & Banking (9)	War & Defence (9)
5	International Economics (9)	International Economics (8)	International Economics (7)
6	Labour Economics (8)	Labour Economics (6)	Labour Economics (6)
7		Public Finance (5)	Money, Credit & Banking (6)
8			Public Finance (5)

* Figure in parenthesis is the approximate percentage of articles carrying the sub-field classification in the case of the *Economic Record*, and pages in the case of the A.E.A./Yale *Index of Economic Articles*. As an article can carry more than one classification, the percentages will not sum to 100 per cent.

record of economic institutions. But, then again, most editors were not, at the time, interested in those topics either.

One may well ask whether the selection of topics was simply a demand phenomenon, or whether there were important supply aspects as well? The answer is not really obvious. While it is true that editors cannot print what they do not have, it is also clear that their shadow demand tends to create a real supply.

Those who are aware of Copland's final career interest, the establishment of a school to train business managers, should be interested to know that the sub-field of managerial economics received virtually no space during his editorship, a distinction shared with articles on statistical theory and the economics of technological change. Overall Copland organized a journal with a clear and different 'personality' or 'taste'.

The Weller Interregnum

Weller's perception of the contents of the *Economic Record*, as shown in Table 2, reveals three major changes. One is the surge of interest in economic theory, something quite different from what went before, as well as an enthusiasm slightly surpassing the average

TABLE 2

*Rank Ordering of Sub-Fields, The Weller Editorship**
(includes only those of 5 per cent or more)

	Economic Record 1949–54	A.E.A./Yale *Index of Economic Articles* 1950–54
1	Economic Theory (18)	Economic Theory (15)
2	Economic Stabilization (13)	Industrial Organization (11)
3	Economic History (11)	International Economics (11)
4	Agricultural Economics (10)	Agricultural Economics (9)
5	National Economic Accounting (10)	Labour Economics (8)
6	International Economics (8)	Public Finance (6)
7	Public Finance (8)	Money, Credit & Banking (5)
8	Monetary Economics (5)	

* Same as note in Table 1.

standard for all economics journals for that approximate period. Second, the Copland (and perhaps general Australian) fascination with studies of economic fluctuations, although slightly diminished, was still very strong—much stronger than the mode. Third, there was a strong emphasis on economic history articles.

The shift towards economic theory is most easily explained by Weller's editorial 'catching up' with developments in the discipline. As can be seen in Table I, prior to 1940 economic theory was placed third in the world of economics journals; in the 1940s its relative ranking (although not its absolute percentage) rose to second. In the later years of Weller's editorship economic theory ranked first both in the *Economic Record* and in the aforementioned world journals. Weller, in fact, accorded it a higher percentage (18) than the average editor (only 15).

That Weller published few industry studies seems to me to be an area for useful speculation. Why so few? Surely it was a period when Australia was trying to build up both the manufacturing and services sections. Australian statistical data were plentiful and good. An easy answer is not forthcoming, except perhaps that there were very few industrial economists. But by way of contrast, his selection of so many economic history articles seems to be readily explicable. One of his more dynamic Melbourne colleagues, the economic historian Professor J. A. La Nauze, had joined his board of editors and a call had gone out for manuscripts with an historical dimension. (This enthusiasm was supported by Professors Noel and Sydney Butlin). Editorial shadow demand, as noted above, can create a supply; in this instance it clearly did.

Downing's Era

The major changes in the period of Downing's editorship include a resurgence of focus on economic stabilization (possibly reflecting Copland's tutelage), a downgrading of economic theory articles (certainly in absolute percentages), and most of all, a general diffusion of fields with extensive coverage.

The only other things of note are a modified continuation of economic history articles (again reflecting the impact of La Nauze on the *Economic Record's* policy) and an eschewal of industrial organization and managerial economics. The last two areas were, as revealed in Table 3, relatively popular in the world of economics journals. Downing also selected a fair number of articles on national accounting, which the bulk of other contemporary editors did not.

The Recent Collegial Editorship

While it is useful to compare what the latest group of editors have done in terms of what their predecessors did, it is (as before) also interesting to see how they have operated in comparison with the editors of the *JEL* 'core' group, mentioned in note 1 above, as well as

TABLE 3

*Rank Ordering of Sub-Fields, The Downing Editorship**
(including only those with 5 per cent or more†)

	Economic Record	A.E.A./Yale *Index of Economic Articles*		
	1954–68	1955–9	1960–3	1964–5
1	Economic Stabilization (20)	Economic Theory (17)	Economic Theory (17)	Economic Theory (17)
2	Economic Theory (9)	Industrial Organization (13)	Industrial Organization (12)	Industrial Organization (11)
3	National Econ. Accounting (9)	Agricultural Economics (11)	International Economics (10)	International Economics (9)
4	International Economics (9)	International Economics (8)	Agricultural Economics (9)	Agricultural Economics (9)
5	Economic History (7)	Managerial Economics (6)	Labour Economics (8)	Labour Economics (7)
6	Labour Economics (6)	Public Finance (5)	Managerial Economics (6)	{ Money, Credit & Banking (5)
7	Agricultural Economics (6)		Money, Credit & Banking (6)	{ Managerial Economics (5)
8	Econ. Growth & Planning (5)			

* Same as in note in Table 1.
† Bracketed items have the same rank order.

with the editors of two specific journals, the Royal Economic Society's *Economic Journal* and Harvard University's *Quarterly Journal of Economics.* Table 4 shows the field ranking over the whole period.

What can be said? First, although economic theory has returned to top billing, the journal's selection is now more diffused; Weller chose 18 per cent of the articles with an economic theory citation; while the present collegial group have chosen only 13 per cent. Second, international economics is secure in the second ranked place. Third, resource economics is emerging as a leading applied sub-field. Fourth, economic stabilization articles are largely omitted. Fifth, articles on industrial organization are still relatively rare. And finally, economic history articles are absent, reflecting no doubt the establishment of *Business Archives and History* in 1962 and its successor, the *Australian Economic History Review* in 1967.

The diffusion seems to be the deliberate and perhaps expected policy of collegial decision-making. That international economics is so close a second to economic theory may probably most easily be explained by the personal interests of the editors. The interest in resource economics is likely explained by events—Australia has been in and out of mining boom periods since around 1967–8. One cannot seek to explain the relative disappearance of economic stabilization articles.

If the two columns in Table 4 are compared, at least two more

TABLE 4

*Rank Ordering of Sub-Fields, The Recent Period**
(includes only those of 5 per cent or more)

	Economic Record 1969–75 average	The *J.E.L.* 'Core' Journal Sample 1970–4 average
1	Economic Theory (13)	Economic Theory (75)
2	International Economics (12)	Labour Economics (18)
3	Monetary Economics (9.6)	Industrial Organization (15)
4	Resource Economics (8)	Monetary Economics (13)
5	Economic Development Studies (8)	Managerial Economics (12)
6	Economic Growth (8)	International Economics (11)
7	National Accounting (8)	Economic Stabilization (9)
8	Industrial Organization (7)	Econometrics & Statistics (6)
9	Labour Economics (6)	Applied Welfare Economics (6)
		Economic Growth (5)

*Figure in parenthesis is approximate percentage of articles carrying the sub-field classification. As articles usually carry two (and even more) classifications, the percentages will not sum to 100 per cent.

points can be made. Managerial economics is not the *Economic Record's* bag; it never has been. The other is that diffusion of topic may explain why the *Economic Record's* editors have not chosen significantly large numbers of articles on applied welfare economics or, strangely enough, econometrics and statistics.

Table 5 compares the latest two years' selection of the editors of the *Economic Journal* and the *Quarterly Journal of Economics*. Self-perceptions, priorities, taste, and their consequences, subject matter, differ.

The following points arise:
(1) The *Economic Journal* is the most diffused; it has 10–11 sub-fields with more than 5 per cent of the articles in each of the two years. (2) The current *Economic Record* is the least diffused with 7–9 sub-fields. (3) The *Quarterly Journal of Economics* is the most economic theory oriented; the *Economic Record* is the most international economics oriented. (4) The *Economic Record* has now more

TABLE 5

*Rank Ordering of Sub-Fields, 1974 and 1975**
(includes only those of 5 per cent or more†)

1974					
Economic Record		*Economic Journal*		*Quarterly Journal of Economics*	
1	International Economics (16)	1	Economic Theory (32)	1	Economic Theory (51)
2	Economic Theory (16)	2	Economic Stabilization (16)	2	Economic Growth (1)
3	Industrial Organization, etc. (14)	3	Economic Growth (13)	3	Fiscal Economics (8)
4	Economic Growth (12)	4	Labour Economics (11)		Industrial Organization, etc. (8)
	Monetary Economics (12)	5	International Economics (9)		Labour Economics (8)
6	Economic Growth (9)		Industrial Organization, etc. (9)	6	Monetary Economics (6)
	Fiscal Economics (9)		National Accounting (9)		Industrial Economics (6)
8	Agricultural Economics (9)	8	Fiscal Economics (7)		Applied Welfare Economics (6)
9	Labour Economics (7)	9	History of Economic Thought (5)		
			Economic Development (5)		

1975

	Economic Record		*Economic Journal*		*Quarterly Journal of Economics*
1	International Economics (27)	1	Industrial Organization, etc. (22)	1	Economic Theory (51)
2	Economic Theory (23)		Economic Theory (22)	2	Fiscal Economics (12)
3	Monetary Economics (13)	3	Labour Economics (18)	3	International Economics (11)
	Labour Economics (13)	4	Economic Stabilization (17)		Labour Economics (11)
5	Industrial Organization, etc. (7)	5	Fiscal Economics (13)		Monetary Economics (11)
	Economic History (7)	6	History of Economic Thought (10)	4	Economic Growth (7)
	Economic Development (7)	7	National Accounting (7)	5	Industrial Organization, etc. (6)
	National Accounting (7)		Monetary Economics (7)		Economic Systems (6)
	Consumer Economics (7)		Applied Welfare Economics (7)		Resource Economics (6)
		10	Economic Growth (5)		
			Managerial Economics (5)		

* Same as note in Table 4.
† Bracketed items have the same rank order.

studies than previously in the sub-field of industrial organization, and so on. It is now publishing about the same number as the other two journals. (5) What seems most unexpected is that both the *Economic Record* and the *Quarterly Journal of Economics* do relatively little with articles on economic stabilization; the *Economic Journal* seems to feature the topic.

Space does not permit competent speculative analysis of why the editors of the *Economic Journal* and the *Quarterly Journal of Economics* have the mix of sub-fields. My guess is that, like Copland, the editors of both of these two journals have well-defined personal points of focus, a condition which is less likely to be the case in a collegial editorship, particularly where the collegiality is the result of someone not being willing to carry the burden of the editorship for a long period of time. Why no one has done this is uncertain. Perhaps modern Carlyles believe that modern history is the acts of great committees. But if editors are to be as productive for and influential on economic policy as, for example, Copland was, they need to be more than clerks or copy-readers.

References

[1] Naomi Perlman, and Mark Perlman, 'The Changing Modes of Data in Recent Research', in Mark Perlman, (ed.), *The Organization and Retrieval of Economic Knowledge* (Macmillan and Halsted, New York and London, 1977). pp. 197-229.

[2] See *Economic Record*, 22 (1946), p. 133; 36 (1960), pp. 1-4, 124-72; and 47 (1971), pp. 465-9. The 1946 reference is a summary mid-career statement. The 1960 reference relates to the special issue of the *Economic Record* which was brought out in Copland's honour. Finally, the 1971 reference is a personal memoir, written after Copland's death, by Professor R. I. Downing.

[3] This point was rather baldly put when Weller retired in January 1954. See *Economic Record*, 30 (1954), p. 85. (In the early years Copland was listed as editor. Starting in November 1930, he became 'editor-in-chief'. His successors were merely listed as editor.)

KEITH HANCOCK

18 National Superannuation

Introduction

In April 1973 the Australian government, acting on the advice of its minister for social security (Mr W. G. Hayden), established a committee 'to make recommendations to the Government on a suitable national superannuation scheme', and appointed the author as chairman.[1] The National Superannuation Committee of Inquiry has taken longer to perform its task than was originally envisaged. (The reasons for this include the competing demands on the time of part-time committee members, an attempt–largely unsuccessful–to generate public discussion of the issues confronting the committee, and the emergence of serious divisions of opinion within the committee.) Nevertheless, at the time of writing (in early 1977), the committee has almost reached the end of its task and is about to cease existence.[2] This chapter takes a somewhat retrospective view of its work.

The idea of national superannuation was by no means novel in 1973. Indeed, it is the case that most economically advanced nations have chosen to provide retirement incomes for large sections of their aged populations. In Australia, retirement benefits had been included in two abortive Commonwealth proposals for national insurance. The efforts of a Royal Commission on National Insurance, which sat from 1923 until 1927, and an election promise made in 1925 by S. M. Bruce, led in 1928 to the introduction of a National Insurance Bill. It was intended to re-submit this Bill in the new parliament elected at the end of 1928, but this had not occurred by the time of the Bruce government's fall in 1929. The idea was revived by the Lyons government in the mid-1930s and a National Health and Pensions Insurance Act was actually passed in 1938. A National Insurance Commission was appointed, with J. B. Brigden as chairman. However, the scheme embodied in the Act was never implemented. During 1939, the cost of defence preparations served as a 'reason' for delay, and in June 1939 legislation was enacted which postponed indefinitely the scheme's commencement. (As is well known, a dispute about this scheme had precipitated the resignation of R. G. Menzies from the Lyons cabinet.) Both of these pre-World War II initiatives were much influenced by an objective of improving social services without overburdening the general budget. Their failures were due in part to pressure exerted by influential interest groups—in 1929 the friendly societies and in 1939 the medical profession. In the later (but not the earlier) debate, the Labor party vehemently opposed the levying of contributions to finance social services.[3]

Little further discussion of national superannuation occurred for almost twenty years. Proposals for national superannuation might perhaps have been expected to emerge in the debate generated by H. V. Evatt's promise, at the 1954 election, to abolish the means test, but failed to do so. However, Evatt's electoral failure served to emphasize the significance of cost as an impediment to progress in the provision of age pensions and the problem of cost partially explains the interest in contributory national superannuation, dating from the late 1950s, of R. I. Downing.[4] Until his death in 1975, Downing evinced a continuing interest in the subject. He advanced a series of proposals, hoping to obtain effective support, but until the early 1970s there was little response. The first sign that national superannuation might become a significant issue at the political level was the interest shown in it (beginning early in 1971) by Mr Hayden, who was clearly influenced by Downing's proposals. Mr Hayden secured the inclusion of a national superannuation proposal in the Labor party's platform for the 1972 election. Influenced, no doubt, by the Labor party's initiative, the McMahon government, at the time of the 1972 budget, foreshadowed an inquiry into national superannuation. A committee was subsequently appointed (with Sir Leslie Melville as chairman), but had scarcely begun its work before the Labor government established the new committee of inquiry.

Why National Superannuation?

Before suggesting reasons why the idea of national superannuation merits attention as a possible innovation in Australian social welfare, one can dispose of an argument which is essentially semantic but nevertheless threatens to cloud the debate about the committee's proposals. This is the contention that the age pension already constitutes a national superannuation scheme or, if not, will constitute one when the process of abolishing the means test is completed. It is exemplified in the following comment of the president of the Institute of Actuaries of Australia and New Zealand:

> Some people might argue that a national superannuation scheme starts when the Government first begins making payments to

> alleviate poverty in old age. Others might argue that a national superannuation scheme has not started until every old person is paid a pension, irrespective of means. Even on the last approach Australia has a national superannuation scheme now, paid from age 70. So let us rid ourselves of any notion that we do not have a national superannuation scheme yet.[5]

While no one can be denied the liberty of calling a cow a horse, it is fair to remark that national superannuation did not arise as a policy proposal on the basis of a possible renaming of the age pension. Downing certainly intended more than that. The terms of reference for the committee appointed by the McMahon government referred to 'the policy of the Government to abolish the means test within the next three years on age pension elegibility for residentially qualified men and women aged 65 years and over' and directed the committee to report on 'appropriate ways and means of financing the free-of-means test retirement benefits associated with a possible national superannuation scheme'. Likewise, the Whitlam government directed the new committee to 'have regard to the Government's objective to abolish the means test within the life of the present Parliament for those aged 65 years and over and to increase the basic rate of pension to 25 per cent of average weekly earnings' and to report on 'the best way in which free-of-means test benefits could be either replaced by, or integrated into, the national superannuation scheme'. It is clear, therefore, that both the McMahon and the Whitlam governments saw national superannuation as a possible new approach to providing pensions for the aged and hardly contemplated a mere change of nomenclature. This is not of itself a reason for saying there *ought* to be a national superannuation scheme. It is *that* issue and the question of the form that a national superannuation scheme should take which may be the subjects of productive debate.

There are two related objectives which national superannuation might help to achieve. One is the provision of pensions on a less austere basis. The principal improvements would be the removal of the means test and increases in the amounts paid. The means test has been progressively eased over a long period, with the result that by 1974–5 the total cost of providing pensions for persons aged 65 or more was 85 per cent of the estimated cost of paying similar pensions on a free-of-means test basis. Thus the cost of removing the means test for persons aged 65–69—it is already abolished for persons aged 70 or more—would represent a relatively moderate proportion of existing outlays. However, the cost of relaxing the means test has undoubtedly inhibited improvements in pension levels. From the early 1950s to the early 1960s, the age pension was typically about 21 per cent of average weekly earnings, with little sign of any upward or downward trend in the percentage. In 1963–4, a lower rate of pensions was instituted for married pensioners. The stated purpose of this step was to allow more generous provision for single pensioners. In practice, this did not occur. Whereas in 1962–3 the age pension was 21·4 per cent of AWE, in 1973–4 the single-rate age pension was 19·8 per cent and the married rate 17·3 per cent of AWE. It is true that over the next two years the percentages increased to 22·5 and 18·7, respectively. This may signify that the government had accepted the budgetary implications of moving to slightly more generous levels of pensions, but it should be remembered that in 1973 the net cost of pensions was slightly alleviated by making pensions taxable.

The second objective is perhaps implicit in the term 'national superannuation': to extend more generally benefits of superannuation which have hitherto been enjoyed by only a segment of the population. On the most recent evidence[6], 29 per cent of the civilian labour force participate in superannuation schemes. Outside that network are not only the remaining 71 per cent of the labour force, but also those members of the community who are not in the labour force—some 31 per cent of the total population aged from 20 to 64. Of the latter group 82 per cent are described as 'keeping house' and, with few exceptions, are women. The number of persons participating in schemes gives an exaggerated impression of the extent of effective coverage achieved by occupational superannuation, because many participants forfeit potential benefits by leaving the service of particular employers before retirement. For all of these reasons, it is accurate to regard the Australian community as sharply divided into two classes: a minority who have the prospect of getting substantial superannuation benefits and a majority who do not. The enhancement of the expectations of the latter group may seem a reasonable goal for a national superannuation scheme.

It is implicit in the above that national superannuation is a means of overcoming the limitations on provisions for the aged which are inescapable while pensions are simply financed from general revenue. However, the justification for such an innovation is not universally accepted. For example, there is continued support for the means test. Professor R. F. Henderson, as chairman of the Commission of Inquiry into Poverty, wrote as follows:

> Given the limited funds available for social security purposes, it will not be possible to provide an adequate pension without a generally applicable mechanism to limit payments to those who most need them. This mechanism is provided in part by the system of favoured categories, but also at present by the means test. Abolition of the means test releases funds to the wealthy within the favoured disability category. Some of this money can be

> recouped through the income tax, but by no means all of it. We therefore recommend that maintenance and increase of the basic pension rate have priority over the easing of the means test.[7]

Similar views were expressed by the Australian Council of Social Service and the Brotherhood of St Laurence in submissions to the National Superannuation Committee of Inquiry. Another basis of opposition to national superannuation is the belief that the social welfare system should be reformed by moving towards a guaranteed income scheme. The Priorities Review Staff called for public debate of a suggestion that there be 'a reduction in the present plethora of benefits, welfare categories and means tests and, in their place, a modest guaranteed income for all'.[8] One implication of this suggestion, in the judgement of the Priorities Review Staff, was that there would be no place for a national superannuation scheme. Professor Henderson, too, regarded the guaranteed income principle as an attractive alternative to other forms of social security.[9]

Underlying these opinions are a value judgement that the social welfare system should give a near-absolute priority to the alleviation of need and an assumption that need is closely identified with lack of income. These premises find their strongest expression in the use of a 'poverty line' to distinguish those members of the community who should be assisted by social welfare before assistance is given to others. Clearly, the view that the social welfare system should be constructed to accord with such a philosophy is not an 'expert' view; nor (quite obviously) is the contention that other objectives should have some part to play. While the alleviation of need is a most important function of social welfare, there are criteria other than lack of income which it is reasonable to take into account. The principle of repatriation benefits, for example, does not seem offensive although these may be difficult to reconcile with a needs criterion; it does not seem unreasonable for governments, in paying such benefits as child endowment, to prefer to avoid the use of means tests; nor should one oppose, in principle, their having regard to the effects of specific benefits on work incentives. Likewise, it is difficult to accept that social welfare for the aged is justified *merely* because (and to the extent that) the aged are a section of the population in which needy people are to be found. It seems desirable that the social welfare system should provide for people in the latter years of their lives levels of comfort and security, without the necessity of having to take paid work, which are not equally available to younger people. Plainly, this is not to say that the support given to the aged should be unrestrained by the competing claims of needy groups.

Professor Henderson and the Priorities Review Staff did, indeed, make concessions to the judgement that distinctions should be drawn between categories of people on grounds other than lack of income. For example, the Priorities Review Staff, in outlining its guaranteed income scheme, proposed tax credits equal to 100 per cent of the Henderson 'poverty line' for the aged and some other groups, compared with 55 per cent for other income units. However, it is fair to say that both Professor Henderson and the Priorities Review Staff regarded the acceptance of a 'categorical' approach to tax credits as a dilution of their preferred policies, made necessary by the difficulty of gaining acceptance for those policies.

It is appropriate also to comment on the specific contention that the means test for the age pension should be retained so as to concentrate assistance on the most needy members of the aged population. Professor Henderson's recommendation that the achievement of 'an adequate pension' (which, presumably, had not then been achieved) have priority over further relaxation of the means test articulates this contention admirably. However much one might wish that governments had shown more concern about pension levels during the period from the early 1950s to the early 1970s, it is necessary to accept that the process of removing the means test is now far advanced. Given that no one has advocated its removal for women aged 60–64, we are now relying upon the exclusion of a relatively small component of the aged population to contain the aggregate cost of pensions. Admittedly, current economic problems have caused a postponement of the final phases of abolition; but the means test's effectiveness as a distributive instrument is gravely impaired. These comments are not meant to imply unmitigated regret at its passing. In addition to lending an aspect of charity to the age pension, it is a fertile source of anomalies and interpersonal inequities. To take but one example: those retired persons who receive pensions from occupational superannuation schemes cannot avoid having them taken into account for means test purposes; but those who receive benefits in the form of lump sums can arrange their affairs in a variety of ways to preserve their entitlements to the age pension.

The proposal to refashion the social welfare system by implementing a guaranteed income scheme in place of cash benefits raises questions of administrative practicability which are not discussed here.[10] However, it is relevant to consider whether such a scheme, if feasible, represents an attractive *alternative* to national superannuation. Acceptance of the notion of 'categorical' tax credits leaves open the possibility of discriminating in favour of the aged as one category of 'taxpayers'. (For many, of course, the amounts of tax would be negative.) The granting of a special tax credit to the aged is equivalent, as a distributive measure, to paying a universal (i.e. free of means test) flat-rate pension to all aged persons and requiring that the pension be included in the recipient's assessable income. This arrangement has, in fact, existed since 1973 for persons aged 70 or more; and if the special tax credit were granted to persons aged 65 or more it would be equivalent to abolishing the means test for persons aged 65–69. Thus, administrative questions aside, the case for providing for the aged through a categorical tax credit is neither stronger nor weaker than the case for providing for them by a flat-rate age pension paid from general revenue without a means test. The question whether the latter approach was preferable to creating a national superannuation scheme was, of course, the major issue confronting the inquiry and, in the event, the issue which divided its members.

Two of the three members of the committee, including the author, regarded the universal flat-rate pension, paid from general revenue, as an insufficient response to the challenge of providing for the aged. They were influenced by the historical evidence of the 'stickiness' of pension levels. Their doubts about the possibility of achieving a significant advance in the relative economic welfare of the aged without a national superannuation scheme were strengthened by the abundant indications that governments and their advisers see the existing array of taxes as already over-stretched. Further, their concern about the limited coverage of the community by existing superannuation schemes led them to think that a more general mechanism of income deferment was warranted. Related to this view was the judgement that a national superannuation scheme might reasonably provide benefits which were partially income-related, rather than purely flat-rate. It seemed essential that any income-related component of benefits be fairly 'paid for', which in our view precluded complete reliance on general revenue. The primary objective, however, was to achieve a break-through in the general standard of provision for the aged.

This statement of purpose plainly invites the question of what is an appropriate level of provision. On this matter, the majority report contains the following comment:

> Any attempt to prescribe a minimum standard for pensions must, in the final analysis, reflect a subjective judgment of adequacy. We make no pretence that our recommendation of a minimum pension equal to about 30 per cent of AWE can be supported by reference to objective criteria. In our view, there are no such criteria. Moreover, the circumstances of pensioners are varied, and a pension which seemed adequate for some might leave others in conditions of serious hardship. We do not entertain the notion of a 'threshold' pension level such that lower sums can be regarded as inadequate and greater amounts as sufficient. Rather, we assume that every increment to the pension will improve the lot of pensioners and reduce the number who are at risk of suffering severe hardship.[11]

The improvement of living standards for the aged must, of course, be limited by potential conflicts with other objectives and especially by the need to avoid changes in the lifetime pattern of spending which a high proportion of the population would regard as perverse. There can be legitimate disagreement, with no recourse to any test of who is right, about the standard that is chosen. On reflection, it might have been desirable to present the government with alternatives (for example, minimum pensions of 27½ and 30 per cent of AWE, with corresponding differences in financial arrangements). It would be a relatively straightforward task to develop such alternatives. The majority members of the committee were aware that, even with the existing pension levels, some pensioners were able to live comfortably. However, they believed that for many others—with little or no separate income and little or no assistance from their families, and possibly not owning their own houses—the standards of living that could be supported by the age pension were exceedingly austere. At the risk of repetition, it must be stressed that pensions for the aged were *not* viewed merely as a device for alleviating 'poverty'. Rather, the hope was held that the government's and the community's values would favour a level of material well-being which it might not be possible to guarantee for the whole of the population.

The Scheme Proposed

To explain the reasons for proposing a national superannuation scheme is one thing; to suggest a specific scheme is quite another. People who assent to the principle may well disagree strongly with the particular form in which it is expressed. It is impracticable here to give full details of the scheme recommended by the committee or to deal with every objection that has been or might be offered. Instead, it seems useful to outline the main features of the scheme and to refer to some of the choices between alternative strategies which underlie it.

The scheme would provide a minimum pension, for all persons aged 65 or more, equal to 30 per cent of average weekly earnings. It would be financed partially by compulsory personal contributions, and persons with records of past contributions would receive pensions above the minimum. At the inception of the scheme, no one would have any prior contributions, so that initially all persons of 65 or more would receive the minimum amount. By the time that the scheme reached full maturity, virtually everyone would have some record of contributions. Most people would then receive pensions greater than 30 per cent but less than 35 per cent of AWE. Actual pensions would be computed by adding together three separate components: a universal pension equal to 25 per cent of AWE; the purchased pension, 'earned' by past contributions; and supplementation. Supplementation would be payable to persons with purchased pensions of less than 10 per cent of AWE and would be equal to one-half of the shortfall. (Thus a person with no contributions would receive supplementation of five per cent of AWE which, when added to the universal pension, would make up the minimum pension of 30 per cent of AWE.) There would also be modest death benefits and some ancillary payments to certain categories of pensioners. Pensions for females aged 60–64 would be phased out, but the ancillary benefits would include payments for dependent spouses of pensioners.

The contributions required by the scheme would be levied on the personal incomes of taxpayers between ages 19 and 63 at the rate of 5 per cent of income above 30 per cent of AWE. They would be absorbed into the general budget, from which all benefits would be paid. However, records of personal contributions would be kept for the purpose of eventually determining purchased pensions. The method of converting 'accumulated' contributions into pensions implies a real rate of interest on contributions of about one per cent per year, if calculated on a pre-tax basis, and about 2 per cent, if calculated on a post-tax basis. However, it is fair to add that supplementation reduces the pension differences which would otherwise emerge from differences in contributions. This can also be expressed by saying that, for people in the supplementation range, the benefit from contributions consists partly of a *general* upgrading of pensions which is accompanied by a diminution of the personal 'investment' return. Over that range of benefits there is, in effect, a compromise between the flat-rate and the contributory method of determining pensions.

A broad impression of the financial aspects of the scheme can be gained from the accompanying table, which is derived from estimates prepared for the committee by the Australian government actuary.[12] The table is based on a hypothetical commencement of the scheme in 1977 and the data for 2001 and 2021 are intended to illustrate the long-term trends in the scheme's finances. No allowance is made for any effects of the scheme on ordinary tax revenue.[13] It appears from the table that, until the end of the century, contributions would finance all of the benefits other than the universal pension and also a significant proportion of the universal pension itself. After the turn of the century, the scheme would become more dependent upon general revenue finance. The reason for this change is the expected alteration of the age structure of the population due to the recent fall in birth rates. That is, by 2021 there would be relatively more people aged 65 or more and relatively fewer aged between 19 and 63 than at present or in 2001. The

TABLE 1

Financial Structure of National Superannuation Scheme

	1977	*2001*	*2021*
A. Benefits as Percentages of Total			
Universal pension	70·7	71·8	69·3
Purchased pensions	—	6·4	12·7
Supplementation	14·1	11·2	7·8
Other benefits	15·2	10·6	10·2
Total	100·0	100·0	100·0
B. Funds Used as Percentages of Total			
General revenue	58·5	58·2	67·9
Contributions	41·5	41·8	32·1
Total	100·0	100·0	100·0
C. Funds Used as Percentage of GDP	5·1	5·4	7·0

demographic assumptions made by the committee were derived from the Borrie Report. If (as is not unlikely) the Borrie projections have underestimated the fall in fertility, the growth in dependence on general revenue finance would be greater than the Table 1 suggests.

One important question confronting the majority members of the committee, in determining the basic design of the scheme, was the account (if any) to be taken of existing occupational superannuation schemes. A possible approach, for which there were abundant overseas precedents, was to allow members of occupational schemes to be 'contracted out' of national superannuation. An implication of that approach is that occupational schemes must conform to prescribed standards to ensure that their members are not disadvantaged by their exclusion from the national scheme. For a variety of reasons, the majority of the committee preferred the alternative approach of installing a universal national scheme, recognizing that this was likely to require adjustments to occupational schemes so as to avoid excessive benefits and excessive contributions and possibly to restructure the benefits.[14] Among the reasons was, first, that a substantial part of the finance for the national superannuation scheme was to come from general revenue (continuing past practice in relation to the age pension). This would raise difficult problems about the 'right' of contracted-out persons to receive their 'fair share' of benefits in the national scheme. Secondly, the fact that benefits in the scheme were not to be 'funded' (discussed further below) was due in part to a wish to achieve certain purposes with respect to benefits. These included the upgrading of pensions from the inception of the scheme and the distributive effects of supplementation. Contracting out would adversely affect the financial flows underlying these features of the scheme. Finally, the committee's recommendations reflected a preference for avoiding the constraints that would need to be imposed on occupational schemes and the detailed supervision to which they would need to be subjected as conditions for contracting out.

As has been made clear, the contributions required by the scheme would not be paid into and accumulated in a special fund, but would be absorbed into the general budget. The major purpose of requiring contributions–indeed the major reason for having a national superannuation scheme–is to surmount the impediments to improved provision for the aged which are inherent in reliance upon conventional methods of finance. It was the wish of the majority members of the committee to make possible an immediate increase in pensions rather than merely to suggest a device whereby they would rise slowly over several decades. This was one reason for avoiding the constraints of 'funding'. Another was our objective of incorporating a specific set of benefits in the scheme, rather than leaving them to emerge as a by-product of the investment performance of a fund. Moreover, in determining the benefits that can be supported by a non-funded scheme, account can be taken of certain factors affecting the flow of contributions, such as favourable demographic circumstances and a growth rate of real incomes which exceeds the real rate of interest allowed on contributions. It is partly for this reason that a proportion of the revenue from contributions can be used to support 'non-purchased' benefits whose distributive effects are egalitarian. Finally, the reluctance of the majority members to contemplate a funded scheme was reinforced by the fear that the creation of a national superannuation fund, to be invested in income-earning assets, would raise the divisive issue of 'back-door nationalization' which has imperilled national superannuation schemes in other countries.

The decision to recommend a contributory national superannuation scheme plainly gave rise to questions about the nature of the required contributions. Perhaps the most significant of these questions were

(a) what levels of contributions should be required,

(b) whether contributions should be paid by employers, employees or both, and

(c) to which income base the contributions should be related.

Obviously, these questions are interrelated. The answer to question (a) was that contributions should be modest–for most people, below 4 per cent of income, and in no case as high as 5 per cent. This level of contributions appeared adequate for the benefits envisaged and we felt that alternative facilities for retirement saving—especially occupational superannuation—should be left to meet the income-maintenance needs of more affluent members of the community. In response to question (b), the majority members of the committee concluded that employer contributions should not be required. Their reasons included the fact that the scheme was not to be confined to employees; a concern to minimize costs of collection and recording; a conviction that the notion of employer contributions serving to shift the real burden to employers was largely spurious; and a reluctance to complicate the existing arrangement whereby the right to levy payroll taxes has been transferred to the states. Finally, we answered question (c) by recommending that contributions be levied on either net income or taxable income, depending upon government policy with respect to tax concessions or rebates. (The choice between the two income bases is not discussed here.) The use of either base would enable the collection and recording of contributions to be carried out by the Australian Taxation Office in the course of collecting personal income tax and would therefore minimize the administrative cost of the scheme.

It is, of course, an assumption underlying much of what is said in this and the previous section that contributions to the national superannuation scheme are differentiable from a mere addition to taxes. In particular, it is implied that any adverse responses, in terms of incentives and effort, which might result from extra taxes, would be significantly less for contributions. The majority members of the committee, in articulating this assumption, might well have adopted the following comment by Martin Feldstein on the difference between personal taxes and social security taxes:

> Paying a higher social security tax eventually results in higher retirement benefits. The relationship between tax payments and benefits is loose and haphazard, but it is present nevertheless. In contrast, an individual who pays higher personal income taxes does not as a result obtain any more in government services. Because employees perceive that there is a relation between their social security tax payments and their own future benefits, their response to an increase in social security taxes should be quite different from their response to an increase in the personal income tax rates. Indeed, if social security were effectively a compulsory savings program in which each individual, in return for his tax payments, received the same level of benefits that he would have obtained by investing those tax payments, the social security tax would have no effect on work incentives.[15]

Three objections might be raised against a distinction between taxes and contributions. First, it could be asserted that people are irrational and will fail to take account of the direct enhancement of their future well-being due to the payment of contributions. There certainly are elements of irrationality in human behaviour; but to assert that these are so predominant that there would be little or no *perceived* difference between taxes and contributions is to make an extremely strong claim. Feldstein presents cogent evidence (discussed further in the next section) that in the United States people are very much aware of the savings aspect of social security contributions. Secondly, it might be said that the relationship between contributions and benefits is too 'loose and haphazard' for even rational people to be influenced by it. The basis for such a claim would need to be the previously mentioned effect of supplementation in diminishing differences in pensions below a certain level. For many people, this *would* reduce the direct 'pay-off' from contributions, but by no means to zero. Thirdly, it might be contended that the enforced deferment of expenditure required by a scheme of compulsory saving is so inconsistent with people's time preferences that they attach little or no value to the prospective benefits. This cannot be disproved; but the fact is that many people do save for their old age. Those who regard their present provision as adequate could adjust to national superannuation by saving less through other media.

It is a reasonable judgement, in my view, that contributions as required by the scheme would avoid some, but not all, of the effects of increased personal taxes. The assertion that they are no different from taxes and the assertion that they have none of the attributes of taxes are both far too strong. The objective of the majority members of the committee was to find a source of funds that would be significantly different from a mere addition to the tax scales and thus make possible an enhancement of benefits which it would otherwise be difficult to achieve. If the author felt that the scheme as recommended could not achieve this purpose, his response would be, not to abandon the entire scheme, but to consider modifications such as a reduction of supplementation from one-half to one-quarter of the shortfall below 35 per cent of AWE.

Issues for Economists

Believing that economists too frequently propound 'expert recommendations' embodying non-explicit social values, the author approached the task of designing a national superannuation scheme with some intellectual concern. The committee was unequivocally required to tender recommendations. Accordingly, it seemed appropriate that its reports should make as explicit as was practicable the objectives which the recommendations were intended to achieve. At the same time, it was obvious that recommendations founded purely on social values would fail to distinguish what was possible from what was not and that in national superannuation a variety of different types of expertise had to be brought together. The areas of competence relevant to the committee's work included actuarial computation, law, public administration, demography, social welfare and economics. Clearly, a committee comprising an economist and two actuaries was obliged to seek assistance from many other people or to find it in published work. However, having emphasized the diversity of the technical competences required for designing a workable scheme, some questions which are likely to have interest for economists are now mentioned.

The Problem of Incidence

Ideally, in discussing any welfare proposal, one would like to identify fully its distributive implications. To do so, it would be necessary to determine the incidence of both the benefits paid and the measures used to finance them. The problems involved in identifying incidence are, unfortunately, incapable of solution with presently available techniques. The second-best response, typically, is to inquire into first-round effects. Whether this is useful is a question not dwelt on here. But it must be acknowledged that most of the analysis of distributive effects provided in the committee's reports is in terms of first-round effects. Even that analysis has its value diminished by the difficulty of specifying a suitable counter-factual hypothesis: when the range of possible assumptions about pension levels, means tests, tax rates and tax concessions (to mention just a few relevant variables) is recognized, it becomes obvious that the game of describing alternative scenarios is one that many can play. Thus assertions about the distributive effects of superannuation should be regarded with scepticism.

There was one question about incidence, however, which led the committee to look beyond first-round effects. In the previous section, reference was made to the exclusion of employer contributions from the scheme and it was indicated that a reason for this was a disbelief that forcing employers to contribute would make them genuine partners in the scheme. The two directions in which the burden might be shifted by employers were to consumers, by means of higher prices, and to employees, by means of lower wages.[16] Although these effects might perhaps have been explored theoretically, the specification of assumptions would have left room for debate about the value of the results. Instead, the committee referred to two empirical studies of similar problems in other countries. Of these, the more important was *The Payroll Tax for Social Security*, by J. A. Brittain.[17] Brittain used cross-sectional regression analyses to 'explain' differences in wages, the explanatory variables being productivity and the amount of payroll tax paid per worker (with employer contributions to social security identified as a 'payroll tax'). He analysed separately both international data and inter-industry data (within the United States) and his results in both cases led him to conclude that, 'given the level of productivity, the higher the tax, the lower (is) the after-tax wage by about the same amount'. This finding, he added, 'offers empirical support for the plausible a priori proposition that labour bears the entire payroll tax'.[18]

The other study was less directly related to the committee's problem but nevertheless had some bearing on it. In Holland, contributions to finance national retirement benefits are levied wholly upon the employees. An analysis of the effects of these levies, by J. Weitenberg,[19] suggests that about 25 per cent of any increase is initially 'passed on' to employers by successful demands for higher wages. However, this is not the final outcome: about half of the increased burden on employers is redressed by less generous responses to future wage claims, and the remainder flows into higher product prices.

The majority members of the committee may have relied too heavily on these studies. (Regrettably, Australia's experience and data resources do not seem to afford any prospect of undertaking similar investigations.) On the other hand, the judgement that, in the long term, employers will no more absorb contributions than they will absorb other cost increases has an inherent plausibility. Downing's opinion was that the committee, in arguing a case against the notion of employers sharing the real burden of contributions, had laboured the obvious.[20] In his view, the purpose of employer contributions (which he supported) was paternalistic: he favoured a scheme requiring much larger contributions than the committee envisaged and believed that this would require some disguising of the burden actually borne by employees.

Pensions and Saving

The committee's reports contain discussions of the possible impact of national superannuation on capital formation. It is tacitly assumed that the government might prefer to avoid measures which would reduce the long-term rate of economic growth. Brief reference is made to the doubt cast on the importance of physical capital formation in economic growth by E. F. Denison—doubts which are not diminished by Australia's experience of high saving ratios and mediocre growth rates. Nevertheless it seemed desirable to face directly the issue whether improved provision for the aged would curtail saving.

The life-cycle model of saving asserts that household saving is governed by objectives, including retirement-provision, which are age-related. If people perceive publicly provided pensions as meeting (wholly or in part) their retirement needs, their motivation to save is correspondingly reduced. There is now a substantial empirical literature on this hypothesis as applied to the United States. The results of some earlier studies were adverse to it, but Feldstein has largely restored its credibility.[21] His estimates lead him to conclude that there is a complete substitution of 'wealth', in the form of social security entitlements, for other forms of private wealth. In 1971, the estimated value of social security 'wealth' (i.e., the discounted value of expected future benefits) was $U.S. 2 trillion. Feldstein contends that the replacement of other forms of wealth by this form reduced the private capital stock from $5 trillion to $3 trillion. If the social security administration had accumulated wealth of $2 trillion to match its liabilities for future benefits, the aggregate capital stock would not be affected. However, American social security (though contributory) is financed on a pay-as-you-go basis. Thus, in Feldstein's view, the social security programme has been the cause of a major erosion of capital.

The reduction of the capital stock is the outcome of expectations held by people about benefits to be received in the future. The more confident are these expectations, the greater will be the extent to which the anticipated benefits are subjectively capitalized as private wealth. If contributions enhance the confidence with which benefits are anticipated, they will intensify the substitution of social security 'wealth' for other private wealth. This effect aside, however, the 'wealth' created by promises of future benefits does not depend upon the method of financing them. Applied to Australia, the Feldstein hypothesis means that a national superannuation scheme of the kind proposed would reduce household saving as people proceed to restrict their accumulations of private wealth in recognition of the new social security 'wealth' conferred on them by the scheme. As the future benefits promised by the scheme would not be funded, there would be no offsetting increase in publicly held wealth.

Some impression of the order of magnitude of the Feldstein effect may be gained if we assume that the contributions required by the national superannuation scheme are used entirely, as they are received, to provide benefits which would otherwise not be paid. This arrangement may be compared with a requirement that contributions be used only to fund future benefits, the latter becoming available when people reach age 65 or die.[22] The outlays on benefits in any given year are obviously different under the two approaches. The differences are likely to be greatest in the earliest years after the inception of contributions, diminishing as the funded benefits mature. Expressed as percentages of the GDP, they are estimated as follows:

1977	2·1 per cent
1981	2·1 per cent
1991	2·0 per cent
2001	1·8 per cent
2011	1·6 per cent
2021	1·3 per cent

The interpretation of these estimates may perhaps be facilitated by representing them in a different way. If contributions to the scheme were used entirely to build up future benefits, then the amount saved through the scheme in 1977 would be equal to 2·1 per cent of the GDP. On the assumption that social security 'wealth' and private wealth are interchangeable, there would be a matching reduction of private saving. The use of contributions to provide immediate benefits means that the scheme is *not* a saving medium. However, this does not affect the erosion of private saving. Thus in 1977 there would be an overall reduction in saving equal to 2·1 per cent of the GDP. To give the estimates perspective, it may be noted that, in the three years ended 30 June, 1975, gross capital formation amounted to 26·3 per cent of the GDP.

This argument is obviously subject to qualifications. At the theoretical level, it can be pointed out (as Feldstein was well aware) that the additional social security 'wealth' conferred on the household sector will have income effects which are likely to include more ample provision for retirement. As a result, private saving may not fall to the full extent of the accumulation of social security 'wealth'. For example, with benefits assured at age 65 under the national superannuation scheme, many people may become more interested in saving for retirement at an earlier age (possibly using occupational superannuation schemes for the purpose). Moreover, the inception of national superannuation would involve the removal of a 'tax' on saving—in the form of the means test—for which the life-cycle theory does not allow. For these reasons, it might be expected that the diminution of saving, if any, would be less severe than foregoing discussion suggests.

The majority members of the committee were unable to form a firm opinion about the extent of the erosion of capital formation, but did not anticipate so large an effect as to call seriously into question the case for a scheme of the kind recommended. We were conscious that to insist on the additional benefits being fully funded would prevent the early upgrading of pensions which was an important purpose of our proposals.

Real Interest Rates

The purchased benefits provided in the scheme would give rise to differences of pension levels between people. At lower levels, these differences would be compressed by supplementation. However, supplementation would not be available for persons drawing pensions in excess of 35 per cent of AWE. The majority members of the committee were especially concerned that benefits above that level be fairly 'paid for'. This meant, for example, that the difference between a pension of 45 per cent of AWE and one of 35 per cent of AWE should be justifiable in terms of extra contributions paid. To say this, however, is to imply that there is a basis for relating benefits to contributions such that judgements can be formed about the 'price' paid for the benefits.

Because the relation between contributions and benefits has a time dimension, it can most conveniently be expressed in terms of interest rates. The construction of the scheme makes real contributions and benefits substantially independent of the value of money, reflecting the objective (not discussed here) of making the scheme inflation-proof. It follows that the nominal interest rates implicit in the scheme are highly dependent upon future rates of inflation. Accordingly, we found it useful to relate benefits to contributions in terms of real interest rates. For this purpose, future contributions and benefits are expressed in present prices. Next, the prospective real contributions and benefits must be weighted by probabilities of survival to various ages. These probabilities vary between sections of the community, but we took the decision (again, not discussed in this article) to treat the community as homogeneous in this respect. Finally, the interest rate must be identified which, when used to discount future payments, equates the present values of future contributions and future benefits.

The question then arises: what is the real interest rate which will allow us to conclude that benefits are 'paid for'? The majority members of the committee made the normative judgment that this requirement would be met if the rate built into the scheme were close to the rates actually earned on other 'risk-free' assets. This result could be achieved precisely if the *nominal* rate of return on contributions were allowed to vary with interest rates on such other assets. That solution, however, is inconsistent with the objective of inflation-proofing the scheme. It therefore seemed necessary to take a view about future real interest rates. An obvious first step was to consult the historical record. Using data supplied by the Reserve Bank, together with the 'C Series' and Consumer Price Indexes, the secretariat computed real yields on Commonwealth Bonds bought in each year from 1940 to 1973. The predominant pattern was one of negative real yields. For example, a person who invested in ten-year bonds in 1940 and reinvested the sum in new ten-year bonds each time the premiums investment matured, would have experienced a negative real return of 0·92 per cent per annum.[23] The interpretation of this result is complicated, however, by the presence of a systematic time pattern in real yields. Ten-year investments made in the 1940s produced negative real returns (the worst result being a yield of –5·20 per cent on bonds bought in 1947); those made between 1952 and 1963 yielded positive returns (the best rate being 3·17 per cent for bonds bought in 1956); and since 1964 yields have again been negative. This time pattern is clearly related to the rates of inflation occurring after the hypothetical investment. Not only the time pattern, but perhaps also the negative yield experienced over the total period of 34 years, may be due to the capital market's inability to foresee future rates of price increase.

On the other hand, the possibility must be recognized that low real rates of return accord with underlying real forces in the economy. Savers may be prepared to 'pay' for the privilege of deferring spending until times when the marginal utility of expenditure is expected to be higher; and the productivity of investment, *at the margin*, may be extremely low or even negative. The circumstances of the 'euthanasia of the *rentier*' may correspond to the present stage of economic history. Indeed, the *rentier* may already be extinct, the fact being concealed by the existence of investors 'earning' interest rates which fail to compensate them for the falling value of money. Such investors are, of course, living off their capital.

Having weighed these possibilities against each other, the majority members of the committee chose a positive but low real rate of interest. To many, a real interest rate as low as one or two per cent will seem a meagre return. In discussions with groups making submissions to the committee, rates of 3–5 per cent were suggested as fair and realistic. It is doubtful that such rates are consistent with long-term characteristics of the economy. Admittedly, the issue does not lend itself to confident predictions.

Conclusion

The fate of the committee's proposals is as yet unknown, but one cannot be optimistic about their prospects. There is, one suspects, a latent schizophrenia in the community, with a widely held aspiration for better age pensions (paid without means test) coming into conflict with an unwillingness to accept the financial implications of providing them. The negative side in this conflict will be reinforced by the activities of pressure groups anxious to avert any disturbance of existing retirement-provision arrangements and by critics who argue that a national superannuation scheme, though necessary, should take a different form from that proposed. The inherent difficulty of having a specific proposal accepted may be akin to the difficulty of securing an amendment of the Australian Constitution:

there is no necessity for those who coalesce in opposition to have achieved agreement about any positive course of action. These long-term impediments to national superannuation have recently been strengthened by the inception (since the relevant part of the committee's report was completed) of the Medibank levy, which may be seen as partially pre-empting the possibilities of contributory finance.

The practical alternative to national superannuation is the continuation of an austere age pension (with or without the means test), leaving the provision of additional spending power to occupational superannuation and private saving. Many will fare quite well under such an arrangement. Foremost among them will be the members of public service superannuation schemes, enjoying large inflation-proofed pensions and secure in the knowledge that generous reversionary benefits are promised for their surviving dependants, and members of other schemes receiving large lump sum payments which are virtually exempt from tax. There are others (including the great majority of female workers and male manual workers) who will have no such prospect. Having these people in mind, the author would regard the rejection of the proposed scheme as a cause for regret.

References

[1] My colleagues were initially K. J. Hedley (a consulting actuary and company director from Sydney) and J. B. Wright (an adviser in the Reserve Bank of Australia). Mr Wright resigned from the committee after five months and was replaced by R. G. McCrossin (general manager of the Australian Resources Development Bank and also a qualified actuary).

[2] Two reports have been published: *National Superannuation in Australia: Interim Report of the National Superannuation Committee of Inquiry*, June 1974 (Australian Government Publishing Service, Canberra, 1974) and *A National Superannuation Scheme for Australia: Final Report of the National Superannuation Committee of Inquiry, Part One*, April 1976 (A.G.P.S., Canberra, 1976). A third, dealing with occupational superannuation, will be tabled in parliament in the near future.

[3] Fuller discussion of these two attempts to introduce national insurance may be found in: T. H. Kewley, *Social Welfare in Australia* 1900-12 (Sydney University Press, 1973), pp. 143-149 and 159-165.

[4] For an early statement of Downing's views, see 'National Superannuation: Means Test or Contributions' (The Joseph Fisher Lecture, Adelaide, 1958), reprinted in H. W. Arndt and W. M. Corden (eds), *The Australian Economy* (Cheshire, Melbourne, 1965).

[5] R. C. Palmer, 'The National Superannuation Scrap-Heap', a paper presented to the Fifteenth National Conference of the Association of Superannuation Funds of Australia, October 1976.

[6] Australian Bureau of Statistics, *Survey of Superannuation, February 1974*, Reference No. 6.42.

[7] Commission of Inquiry into Poverty, *Poverty in Australia*, vol. I (A.G.P.S., Canberra, 1975), p. 57.

[8] Priorities Review Staff, *Possibilities for Social Welfare in Australia* (A.G.P.S., Canberra, 1975), p. 5.

[9] *Poverty in Australia*, vol. I, op. cit., chapter 6.

[10] A critical view of the proposal to substitute tax credits for social welfare benefits is presented in *A National Superannuation Scheme for Australia: Final Report of the National Superannuation Committee of Inquiry, Part One*, paragraphs 2.15-2.19.

[11] Ibid., paragraph 2.20.

[12] The principal assumptions are stated in paragraphs 6.37 and 6.44 of the report.

[13] Some discussion of these effects may be found in paragraphs 6.41-6.43 of the report.

[14] These adjustments are discussed in the second part of our Final Report which, at the time of writing, is still to be released.

[15] 'Toward a Reform of Social Security', *The Public Interest*, no. 40, 1975, p. 81.

[16] It is not suggested that there would be money wage reductions; but employers might offset some of the cost of contributions by conceding lower increases.

[17] Brookings Institution, Washington, 1972.

[18] Ibid., p. 16.

[19] 'The Incidence of Social Security Taxes', *Public Finance*, vol. 24, 1969.

[20] 'National Superannuation', *Australian Economic Review*, 3rd Quarter, 1974.

[21] The reference in footnote 15 is to a very readable presentation of Feldstein's arguments. A more technical version is 'Social Security, Induced Retirement and Aggregate Capital Formation,' *Journal of Political Economy*, vol. 82, 1974.

[22] The future benefits would depend on the interest 'earned' by the fund. For the purpose of this illustration, we assume a real interest rate of about one per cent per annum before tax. This is the interest rate implicit in the 'purchased' benefits contained in the National Superannuation Scheme.

[23] This is calculated on a free-of-tax basis. The comparable result for a person with a marginal tax rate of 33⅓ per cent is a negative real return of 2·18 per cent per year.

Index

This book is set in 10 point Times on 11 point body.